Sacred
in All Its Forms

Pope John Paul II

Edited with an Introduction
by James V. Schall, S.J.

and
Selected Documents of Offices
of the Holy See and Various Bishops

Indexed by the
Daughters of St. Paul

GLORY TO GOD   PEACE TO MEN

ST. PAUL EDITIONS

Reprinted with permission from *L'Osservatore Romano*, English Edition.

Cover Credit: Cavanaugh—bottom right; DSP—bottom left

Library of Congress Cataloging in Publication Data

John Paul II, Pope, 1920-
    Sacred in all its forms.

    1. Man (Christian theology)—Papal documents.
2. Sociology, Christian (Catholic)—Papal documents.
3. Catholic Church—Doctrines. I. Schall, James V.
II. Title.
BT701.2.J56   1984   233   84-15301

ISBN 0-8198-6845-0 c
        0-8198-6846-9 p

Printed in the U.S.A., by the Daughters of St. Paul
50 St. Paul's Ave., Boston, MA 02130

The Daughters of St. Paul are an international congregation
of Women Religious serving the Church with the
communications media.

CONTENTS

VI. Addresses to Various Specialists Concerned with Life and the Family

VII. Reaffirmations of the Church's Basic Teachings on Scientific Research and the Reasons for Rejecting Contraception, Abortion...

INTRODUCTION

THE FIRST RIGHT OF MAN

Public opinion is not always favorable to marriage and the family. And yet, in our anonymous civilization, they prove to be a place of refuge in the search for a haven and happiness.... The state and society are on the way to their own decline if they do not support marriage and the family more effectively, and do not protect them more, and if they put them on the same level as other non-matrimonial communities of life....

As spouses, you are called to responsible parenthood. This, however, means a family planning that respects ethical norms and criteria.... In this connection, I wish to recall emphatically to your memory today the following: the killing of unborn life is not a legitimate means of family planning. I repeat what I said to workers in the Parisian suburb of Saint-Denis: 'The first right of man is the right to life. We must defend this right and this value. In the contrary case, the whole logic of faith in man, the whole program of really human progress would be shaken and collapse....'*

—Homily at the Mass for Families in Cologne, Germany, November 15, 1980. (II, j, 4 & 6)

On April 29, 1981, doctors at the University of California Medical Center in San Francisco performed a pioneer operation on a young boy two weeks before he

11

was actually born. The surgeon in charge remarked: "This is certainly the first successful surgical intervention 'in utero.' It's a first small step on the way to bigger things" (San Jose, California, *News*, July 27, 1981). Just what these "bigger things" might be and how we ought to evaluate them, of course, need careful consideration. Clearly, it might mean that such corrective operations on a human being "in utero" could come to take place at seven months, or perhaps at five, or even with microsurgery, at three months or less. Should such operations become normal, would a human fetus have a "right" to them? Would they be paid for by medicare insurance? And on what are the doctors operating? Obviously, on something that invariably comes to be born as a human child. Moreover, such doctors, presumably, are not just "experimenting," as on the lower animals which they employed to prepare to operate on a human fetus. Nor were they just trying to obtain information, to write a thesis or research paper. They could only intervene in such a case for the good of a particular, growing human life, already in being, already flourishing, only for its concrete good. Any new knowledge or technique must be obtained as an indirect result of real aid to a real person. Individual human beings are not "means" for some "higher" good. They are already the higher good, to which all else in the physical creation is inferior. However, such is the spiritual and physical unity of all mankind with one another, that knowledge gained from the hurts, problems, sicknesses, or deformities of one can and does aid in the help of others.

Yet, for all this statement of principle and priority, the laws of many nations, including those of the United States and the nations of Europe, permit, sometimes encourage, the destruction of a perfectly normal human fetus at almost any stage in its growth, including even two weeks before birth. Such fetuses are already quite normal, needing no surgical interventions. If allowed to grow and to be born, they would be perfectly healthy babies. On the other hand, the medical profession rejoices that interuterine operations are at hand, while the law does not prevent the destruction of what needs no intervention. All of this happens in a civilization built upon the idea that the weak, the innocent, the tiny ought to receive the greatest care and protection. Does our law, then, now define what we take to be human? Is law its own criterion of what constitutes human life? Or ought the already existing human being, the already begun human life process first oblige the law? In other words, is there only civil law, which we make ourselves, to govern us? The question naturally arises: Does a human being, no matter in what stage of its beginning, growth, maturity, and ending have within itself a basis which would guarantee, simply because of what it is, civil and moral protection for its life, something that would therefore oblige the rest of mankind to observe? The evident satisfaction the doctors had in performing the "first surgical intervention *in utero*," on what was it based? On a show of fine technical skill? On the fact that a dysfunctional human life was successfully repaired? On proving that what was in a human womb was indeed human? What, in other words, is a human life as it appears in this world and what is its value?

John Paul II has often addressed himself to the subject of the meaning, nature, and worth of human life since he has been Pope. In this he continues and deepens his own ref.ections on this subject as a philosopher and a theologian before he reached the See of Peter. In Pope Wojtyla, there is a careful, unique teaching on the subject of human life as it is understood in the Christian tradition, something that sets it apart, that clarifies and ennobles our understanding about this life in all its forms and conditions, all its shapes and fashions. John Paul II's teaching on human life is, first of all, a religious teaching about life's sacredness. This notion of sacredness is intended to include, not exclude, all the other ways of comprehending human life. As the ancient adage went, the higher can understand the lower, but the lower cannot always or necessarily understand the higher. A religious understanding of human life means an understanding that includes man's highest destiny in everything about him. What seems common with the rest of nature in man, with the plants or the animals, is profoundly transformed by the particular destiny given to each human person. This is not an abstraction, but a living, active presence in each human person. This sheds a particular atmosphere around everything human, almost as if man's particular destiny makes him stand transcendent even to himself, which, of course, is the meaning of the Christian doctrine about grace and glory. Thus, while it is true that we can distinguish to understand, that we can weigh a man with scientific accuracy to the millionth of a milligram, without reflecting that he is made in the image of God, nevertheless, a complete understanding of man* includes this likeness.

---

*On the use of the term "man" in general discourse: Because of current usages, usually relating to aspects of the feminist movement, there is a tendency to restrict the use of the word "man" to mean only "male." As the word man or mankind is generally used in English and in translations into that language—the same problem does not always exist in other languages—it can mean either male, that is, it can refer

To say that we know of man's meaning and destiny by religious insight does not mean that this religion-derived knowledge is either opposed to science or irrelevant to it. Rather it means that a form of knowledge exists—faith is addressed to intellect—that must be included if we are to understand with what and with whom we are dealing when we confront a human being.

This is not to forget that part of the religious-philosophical teaching of Christianity includes the doctrine of free will. The nobility of man as such includes at least the possibility of great evil resulting from using this very dignity in a way contrary to God's understanding of man himself. This suggests that the human being called to glory in the life of God, itself a privilege beyond his natural being since only God can live the life of God by His nature, can reject his personal destiny. This rejection will almost always manifest itself in an overemphasis or even elevation of some human project, legitimate, indeed even noble in itself, over against the outlines of the human as revealed in the religious tradition or understood in valid philosophic reflection. This understanding that humans do have a free will wherein to locate the causes of the positive evils that do occur among men prevents us from locating evils in the human body itself or in some class or lesser species of living or inanimate thing. The possibility of using free

to members of the human race who are male, or it can refer to a further *logical abstraction* that *prescinds* from sex altogether to include all members of the human race, male, female, and children, including even the human fetus. Context will usually tell which of these different usages is being employed. The use of "men and women" or "men, women, and children" instead of "men" or "man" or "mankind" each time we wish to refer to the abstraction which includes both male and female is often awkward and reduces the flexibility of the language, which can use the same word to refer to different ideas or realities.

will against human value, paradoxically, is also another way of underscoring the true importance and dignity of man on earth. Man has his own radical autonomy which allows him to accept or reject what he is and can be. Man is distinct from all else that exists by virtue of his combination of matter and spirit, but he exists not just as a sort of museum specimen. He exists to choose God within the choices of his earthly existence. His personal transcendence is discovered and decided amidst the real goods he discovers, the most basic of which are other human persons.

This is why it is characteristic of the Holy Father's teaching to discover a persistent emphasis on the fact that man in creation exists for himself, that the rest of creation is somehow ordained to him and he in turn to God. Man is created for himself, for the end of his personal being and *not* for some collectivity or other abstract entity, including the abstract entity called "mankind." "I do not hesitate to proclaim to you before the world," John Paul II explained in Washington,

> that all human life—from the moment of conception and through all subsequent stages—is sacred, because human life is created in the image and likeness of God. Nothing surpasses the greatness and dignity of the human person.
>
> Human life is not just an idea or an abstraction; human life is the concrete reality of a being that lives, that acts, that grows and develops; human life is the concrete reality of a being capable of love and service to humanity (IV, b, 3).

This is an extremely significant passage both in theology, where it insists that human life in all its forms is sacred from conception, but also in metaphysics, where it grounds the substantial category of the human person over against any collective idea or abstraction which might be considered superior to the human person (cf. John Paul II's two addresses on St. Thomas in Section VI of *The Whole Truth About Man*: John Paul II to University Students and Faculties, Boston, St. Paul Editions, 1981). Human life in all its forms is called to eternity, a call which to be realized requires that it not be positively rejected in the context of a personal life in the world itself. The world, the earth on which human beings live, has a certain incompleteness about it, which leaves it open to human purposes for its own final fashioning. Love and service of humanity — the social context of human life — will, in retrospect, reveal how each person has chosen. Moreover the world itself, in a way, bears the consequences of good or evil resulting from human choice. But this is not the final home for man so there is always a certain distance from the other things in existence in the very context of human life, so one's whole faith cannot be placed in worldly things or in the world itself.

John Paul II, then, constantly rejects any notion that some form of human life is somehow not called to eternity, somehow not a member of this human race, each member of which is sacred in his person and called by and to God. This would include the fetus, children, the deformed, the sick, the aged, with distinction of race or culture making no difference in basic evaluation. There is no radical distinction of value within the human race except on the basis of freedom, which is to be decided by each person in his concrete existence and to be judged finally only by God according to the dignity given to each person. John Paul II almost invariably notes that human life, its sacredness, begins "from conception." The Pope does not intend by this directly to enter into the scientific argument about when conception takes place, though clearly the use of the term "conception" indicates that whenever the initial human cell is formed, this is human life. So once conceived, and in all its subsequent forms, the Pope does hold that all the protection of religion and society are due to this human life now begun. He does not intend, however, to enter the very different legal question of what determines national citizenship, birth by blood or in a given territory. The relation of conception to birth in this area can be safely left to positive law. However, we can presume the Holy Father's agreement with the Italian bishops, who pointed out that even if "conception" has not taken place before a certain short period of time, still what is involved is part of the human, related to human life (VIII, b, 9). Thus, John Paul II remarked to some Argentine bishops: "Do not hesitate either to proclaim a fundamental right of the human being: *that of being born*" (V, e, 4). The right to be born, of course, is merely a graphic way of emphasizing that humans reach sacred, divine destiny from conception, from their radical beginnings as human beings in this world. When this same life, once conceived, reaches real death, when it ends its time in this world, it is not destined to be reduced back to nothing, to be annihilated, but rather to continue to exist as a person to be eventually reunited as a whole in bodily resurrection. Human beings, once begun, do not ever cease to exist. This is the religious fact about each human life that actually begins in this world "from conception." It is the highest truth about man.

Clearly at this point, there is an astonishing convergence between science and religion on the issue over when a particular human life begins, even over when it ends. Christianity does not conceive its revelation to be contrary to reason, but to be addressed to it. What God reveals is intended to make us think, to make us think the truth about ourselves, in fact. This does not mean that suddenly we become equivalent to the divine intelligence, but it does mean that we can know more than we otherwise might. God does not cease to be God in teaching us the highest things about ourselves. This means too that the first task of the Pope and the bishops in Christian teaching is to instruct us consistently and authoritatively what this teaching has handed down. This is its authorization for speaking at all on any topic. On the other hand, philosophical and scientific understandings of man enter into a religious climate the minute, in their own intellectual structures, they make impossible these religious truths. Science and philosophy can, in other words, be wrong in their own spheres. They have often, in fact, been wrong in the area of human life. Revelation, however, is addressed to the human intelligence, so that the doctrine, say, of the Immaculate Conception, or doctrines about the conception of Christ, direct human intelligence to the truth about each person's own origin. The members of the Church, indeed all men and women, have a basic right to know clearly and in words they can understand what the Church teaches about human life, marriage, family, human love, about work, sickness, and death. "One of the greatest rights of the faithful," John Paul II told the United States bishops,

> is to receive the word of God in its purity and integrity as guaranteed by the Magisterium of the universal Church: the authentic Magisterium of the bishops of the Catholic Church teaching in union with the Pope....

The Holy Spirit is active in enlightening the minds of the faithful with His truth, and in inflaming their hearts with His love. But these insights and this *sensus fidelium* are not independent of the Magisterium of the Church, which is an instrument of the same Holy Spirit and is assisted by Him (V, d, 9).

Nowhere more than in the area of human life, marriage, and love has rejection of this fidelity to the Church more led to the erection of theologies and ideologies justifying actions the Church has, in the name of man, consistently refused to approve, no matter how popular or powerful they seemed to be.

In one sense, it can be said that the originality of John Paul II is his capacity to see the dramatic uniqueness and wonder of the classic Christian doctrine about the worth of human life. The Pope speaks of our amazement at what God has given to us. In *Redemptor Hominis*, he wrote:

In reality, the name for that deep amazement at man's worth and dignity is the Gospel, that is to say: the Good News. It is also called Christianity. This amazement determines the Church's mission in the world and, perhaps even more so, 'in the modern world.' This amazement, which is also a conviction and a certitude—at its deepest root it is the certainty of faith, but in a hidden and mysterious way it vivifies every aspect of authentic humanism—is closely connected with Christ. It also fixes Christ's place—so to speak, His particular right of citizenship—in the history of man and mankind (no. 10).

To be sure, very few people by comparison have lived this life in its fullness, in its extraordinary richness. The amazement of it is, however, no less. The modern world, in a way, is in some respects a systematic rejection of Christian teachings or conceptions about abortion, contraception, homosexuality, marriage, life, and death. We now have widespread empirical knowledge about where these rejections lead. Furthermore, the unwillingness to hear or live the Christian view is itself often a product of rejecting it in practice. John Paul II, characteristically, insists that the matter be discussed in terms of precisely "truth." We can know certain basic truths about human life and we can likewise know what happens when we do not live them, for they result in observable human practices and consequences.

In the area of truth and its communicability too, there arises certain ambiguities even about the word "right," which has become, sometimes unfortunately, the main grounds of debate about human life. As the Italian bishops noted, we have also come to speak of "rights" to abortion (VIII, b, 21). We hear of "rights" to active homosexuality, to contraception, to divorce as if conceptually these were parallel to and in the same intellectual and legal categories as "rights" to life or free speech or worship. John Paul II, it would seem, has thus far not fully accounted for this sort of usage, which seems to extend the protection of the rhetoric of human "rights," so often used by the Pope in the social sphere, to activities which the Church defines as inhuman. Indeed, it is quite possible that the Catholic Church and its various organizations will be more and more subjected to civil discrimination in this area wherein civil "law" establishes as enforceable what the Church rejects. It is not inconceivable that the Church will be declared "discriminatory" because it denies the "rights" of women to be ordained, or the "rights" of women to have abortions, or the "rights" of homosexuals to practice their way of life. The whole "rights" usage, for all its admitted advantages in certain respects, will require more careful distinction and application, to prevent it from justifying the very opposite of "rights."

John Paul II, however, insists that all questions at controversy be discussed in civil freedom, according to the manner rational beings proceed, in the area of spirit and respect, but always with the desire to reach and to know "the truth." Christianity is not an intellectual skepticism. Thus, abortion is to be seen in its "truth." That is to say, we are to look at what is aborted. The intellect is always first appealed to, argued with, given evidence, even about dire moral aberrations. There is a moral truth about man. John Paul II is strikingly faithful to this principle that arguments ought to be settled in the way human beings proceed. He holds that truth does oblige us, even to continue an unsettled argument. Thus, the Pope is equally clear about what ideas are and where they lead. Among the Holy Father's most remarkable concerns is for the truth about the human body itself and what Christian teaching about it implies.

> The 'redemption of the body' does not indicate, however, ontological evil as a constituent attribute of the human body, but points out only man's sinfulness, as a result of which he has, among other things, lost the clear sense of the nuptial meaning of the body, in which interior mastery and the freedom of the spirit is expressed....
> A Manichaean attitude would lead to an 'annihilation' of the body—if not real, at least intentional—to negation of the value of human sex, of the masculinity and femininity of the human person, or at least to their mere 'toleration' in the limits of the 'need' delimited by the necessity of procreation (III, a, 2-3).

John Paul II, thus, clearly recognizes that in the moral and intellectual background of the human life question lies something far more sinister and dangerous—the possibility of eliminating sex itself or reducing it to a mere plaything with no consequence or significance. This is why he is deeply concerned to reestablish masculinity and femininity as precisely willed aspects of the person, as gifts. He sees fatherhood and motherhood as distinct and profound realities. The destiny of the distinction of the sexes is not the fusion of one into the other as a kind of asexual neuter, a kind of modern Manichaeanism.

This is what John Paul II, in a lengthy series of General Audiences, has called "the theology of the body." Christianity, in a way, is not a unique religion because it is concerned with man's spiritual life. Rather it is unique because it is not Manichee in finding the body or matter evil, or even nonexistent, as some extreme philosophies might hold. Christianity teaches that the human race is created male and female "from the beginning," so that the mode of life of each sex and the holiness proper to it is complementary to the other. This given difference is itself the basis of a profound sharing and love in which the differences become resolved in the life of marriage and the family, in the abiding respect the dignity of each arouses from the other.

> The constitution of the woman is different, as compared with the man; we know, in fact, today that it is different even in the deepest biological determinants. It is manifested externally only to a certain extent, in the construction and form of her body.... By means of the body, the human person is 'husband' and 'wife'; at the same time, in this particular act of 'knowledge,' mediated by personal femininity and masculinity, also the discovery of the 'pure' subjectivity of the gift: that is, mutual self-fulfillment in the gift, seems to be reached.
>
> Procreation brings it about that 'the man and the woman (his wife)' know each other reciprocally in the

'third,' springing from both. Therefore, this 'knowledge' becomes a discovery, in a way a revelation of the new man, in whom both of them, man and woman, again recognize themselves, their humanity, their living image (III, c, 3-4).

Thus, while John Paul II frequently reaffirms the Christian doctrine about monogamous marriage as the only proper locus of begetting in human love, he does so in a positive fashion, so that the reason for this lies in the worth of masculinity and femininity themselves. The abiding love of marriage is what the human sexes really want, even when it is not actually achieved.

All through John Paul II's social teaching lies the theme, common to earlier papal encyclicals, that the family ought to receive special attention, that the mother ought not to have to "work" outside the family, that fatherhood and labor are bound with caring, providing for wife and children. John Paul II told workers at Terni in Italy, on the Feast of St. Joseph:

> The family rests on the dignity of human fatherhood—on the responsibility of the man, husband and father, as also on his work.... The unity of the family, its stability, is one of the fundamental blessings of man and of society. At the basis of family unity is the indissolubility of marriage. If man, if society seek the ways that deprive marriage of its indissolubility and the family of its unity and stability, then they cut off, as it were, the very root of their health, and deprive themselves of one of the fundamental goods on which human life is built....
>
> Your human fatherhood, dear brothers, is always connected with motherhood. And what is conceived in the womb of the woman-mother unites you spouses, husband and wife, with a particular bond that God the Creator of man blessed right 'from the beginning.' ...Fatherhood is responsibility for life: for the life first conceived in the woman's womb and then born, in order

that a new man, who is blood of your blood and flesh of your flesh, may be revealed....

Men of work, men of hard work know this simple voice of conscience. What they feel most deeply is precisely that bond which unites work and family (II, f, 4-5).

One easily feels in such words that the Pope is close to the heart of an honest working man, close to what he really wants in this world. Fathers are today among the most discriminated against groups in modern society, so it is remarkable to hear such a reaffirmation of their meaning and dignity.

The Holy Father is likewise aware of the pressures on women today, pressures which seem to lessen their worth as wives and mothers, which often seem to understand womanhood mainly as a kind of masculine reflex image. Women, indeed, may be reacting to a loss of confidence by men and fathers in the value of their own being and place in the world. The loss of masculinity, which has been a sign of societies in their decline, may result in a kind of feminism modeled upon this very weakness.

Some (women) suffer and regret being relegated to tasks which they are told are secondary ones. Some are tempted to seek a solution in movements which claim to 'liberate' them, although it would be necessary to ask what liberation it is a question of, and not to mean by this word emancipation from what is their specific vocation as mothers and wives, leading to uniformity, of the way in which the male partner finds fulfillment (II, g, 2).

Again, there is manifest in the Pope's thinking the constant theme in Christian tradition that the model of one sex is not exactly that of the other. Women who follow masculine models or men who follow feminine ones— both male and female are rooted in nature, not merely in culture—end up threatening sex itself, and with it, the way the race reproduces itself and cares for itself. Beyond this, there is a failure to understand the very corporeal mystery in which each man and each woman were created.

" 'Models' of interpretation of the conjugal reality which exclude any reference to the superior values of ethics and religion," John Paul II told the Confederation of Christian Advisory Bureaus,

> are proposed on many sides. The practical behavior which is deduced from them is consequently in contrast not only with the Christian message, but also with a truly human view of that 'intimate partnership of life and love,' which marriage is.
>
> It is the task of the Christian community to proclaim forcefully before present-day society, the joyful announcement of redeemed human love. Christ has 'freed' man and woman for the possibility of loving each other in truth and fullness (VI, c, 1-2).

This passage of Pope Wojtyla is a persistent challenge to the modern world in its own terms, but with the added insights resulting from Christian teaching about love and marriage. Loving in truth and fullness is, of course, something that everyone wants, even when he thinks it impossible or unlikely. But if it is only achieved in its reality within the Christian attitude to the meaning of the human person, to life and the family in human love, then we ought not to neglect to tell this to our contemporaries. Living a Christian marriage in a family is not only a holiness and a blessing for its members, but it is also apostolic by virtue of what it is. Men and women need to know that they are not determined to, bound by the "models" of our times, which cannot yield what human persons really search for.

John Paul II, in his metaphysics, always refuses to place freedom above being and truth. This will sound like an obscure point, at first, but the right intellectual priority remains essential even for the health of the human race. Freedom depends on the reality of what we treat or deal with. A thing's truth follows what it is, what it is created to be. Often today, to acknowledge the truth of something in the face of a theory of freedom that does not restrict itself to reality requires a specific heroism, particularly in the area of the truth of human life and love. To Italian Catholic doctors, Pope Wojtyla said:

> Their (the medical practitioners) courageous and consistent testimony is a very important contribution to the construction of a society which, in order to be fully human, cannot but be based on respect and protection of the basic premise of every other right, that is, the right to live....
>
> The Pope willingly unites his voice to that of all doctors with a sound conscience, and adopts their fundamental requests: the request in the first place, for recognition of the deeper nature of their noble profession which wishes them to be ministers of life and never instruments of death. And then the request for full and complete respect, in legislation and in facts, of freedom of conscience, understood as a fundamental right of the person not to be forced to act contrary to his conscience or prevented from behaving in accordance with it. Finally, as well as the request for an indispensable and firm judicial protection of human life in all its stages, also the request for adequate operational structures, which will encourage the joyful acceptance of life about to be born, its effective promotion during development and maturity, its careful and delicate protection when its decline begins and up to its natural extinction....

> I make no secret of the fact that consistency with
> Christian principles may mean for you the necessity of
> exposing yourselves to the risk of incomprehension,
> misunderstanding and even serious discrimination
> (VI, f).

Consequently, it is not the Holy Father's position that
we should change Catholic "truth" about life to conform
to legal or societal standards which are contrary to it,
but rather that we should expect both law and medicine
to act in accordance with the kind of personal being
found in man's truth.

"For so many men and women of our time new life
is looked on as a threat and something to be feared," the
Pope reflected soberly to a Congress of African and
European thinkers.

> Others, intoxicated with the technical possibilities
> offered by scientific progress, wish to manipulate the
> process of transmission of life and, following only the
> subjective criteria of personal satisfaction, are prepared
> even to destroy newly conceived life.
> The Christian vision and attitude is quite different:
> Inspired by objective moral standards based on an
> authentic and all-embracing vision of the human person,
> the Christian stands in awe of all the laws that God has
> impressed on the body and spirit of man (VI, a, 3).

This means, fundamentally, that the laws of God are
what make men and women freest and most happy, that
man is a certain kind of being whose liberty consists in
discovering what he is created to be in all his aspects.
His life is not one of creating his own laws as if he were
to give them to himself in some kind of Kantian vision,
but rather to use his intelligence and experience to discover laws given to him in his own being and person as
themselves gifts. He is, in effect, to receive a commu-

nication about himself, to recognize that his own happiness, even in his own being, is better "thought of" by his Creator than by himself, even for himself. To receive something as a gift is not to take something away, even from himself. This is why there is no "alienation," no separation of man's being over against God unless man in turn positively wills it so. Rather, there is a communication, a revelation of man about himself that makes him more himself, as he is already created personally in the divine image and likeness.

The Holy Father understands everyone to be bound by and simultaneously to be freed by the truth about persons and families. In particular, he wants bishops, priests, and religious to know and teach this truth of Christian doctrine. He told some Italian Women Superiors, in a touching passage:

> Today, more than ever, many persons are tormented by the problem of existence and of their own identity. They feel the longing to go beyond the limits of history and time, they feverishly look for truth. So the first task and the first duty of the Sister in her relations with the family is to bear witness to *truth*, that is, to help the modern family to discover the real meaning of life and history.
>
> Dear Sisters, bring to families the truth as it was revealed by Christ and as it is taught by the Church: Do not let yourselves be disturbed by the sensation made by the many insistent ideologies which confuse and depress.... Every family wants to know the truth from those who are consecrated to God... (VI, d, 3).

John Paul II knows, no doubt, that this truth is often very difficult to come by and accept in the area of the sacredness of human life and family. This is why he requests and indeed expects loyalty to the doctrine of the Church, to its unity and specificness. He knows that, often, observance is difficult, so that a pastoral compassion ought to guide everyone in meeting the real conflicts spouses and families confront. He remembers St. Thomas' thought on the fact that civil law as such ought not to be more than the generality of men can be expected to observe.

"Innumerable families, especially Christian couples," John Paul II said in Rio de Janeiro,

> desire and ask for secure principles that will help them to put into practice, even if amid unusual difficulties and sometimes with heroic effort, their Christian ideal with regard to faithfulness, fecundity and upbringing of children. No one has the right to betray this expectation or to disappoint this aspiration by concealing the true principles out of timidity, lack of confidence or false respect, or by offering principles that are doubtful even when not openly in conflict with the teaching of Christ transmitted by the Church (IV, d, 7).

In this context, no doubt, the condemnation in principle of contraception has been the most controverted position of the Church. It needs to be said, however, that Pope Wojtyla has reemphasized with all his authority the teaching of Paul VI and previous Popes on this topic, in addition to spelling out more clearly the reasons for it. The Pope in this reaffirmation has wished to place the Church's position in the context of the Church's teaching authority and further to prevent the great amount of confusion that many theologians and critics have caused to Christian people by their denying or questioning the official teaching of the Church, either in its content or in its authority. John Paul II has, in addition to his ecclesiastical authority, also brought to bear his own profound reflections on the subjects of human life and love.

Furthermore, in the context of the faith addressing itself to reason, Pope Wojtyla has argued that the Church's teaching is actually the best guide for the scientific researcher to respect and enhance the meaning and value of human sexuality. The Pope said in the Philippines:

> The Church will never dilute or change her teaching on marriage and the family.... The Church states clearly that marriage should be open to the transmission of life. God willed the loving union of husband and wife to be the source of new life.... God desires that this tremendous power to procreate a new human life should be willingly and lovingly accepted by the couple when they freely choose to marry. Parenthood has a dignity of its own, granted by God Himself. On my part, I owe it to my apostolic office to reaffirm as clearly and as strongly as possible what the Church of Christ teaches in this respect, and to reiterate vigorously her condemnation of artificial contraception and abortion.
>
> Yes, from the moment of conception and through all subsequent stages, all human life is sacred... (IV, g, 5-6).

The Church evidently and clearly treats this as a fundamental issue, because its whole concept of the value of human life and love is at stake on this one, seemingly unimportant issue.

John Paul II, in three very brief, very important Addresses (VII, a, b, and c), has taken up the Church's case in a unique manner. To the Indonesian Bishops, he again reaffirmed the basic position on abortion, declaring that "any willful destruction of human life for any reason whatsoever is not in accord with God's commandment, that it is entirely outside the competence of any individual or group and that it cannot redound to true progress" (VII, a). He agreed that the teaching of Paul VI in *Humanae Vitae* came from "a mandate entrusted to us by Christ." He next pointed out that grace does instruct reason, even in its own terms, that "God's wisdom supersedes human calculation, and grace is powerful in people's lives." The unity of grace and humanity is evident in John Paul II's view. "Christ's grace does not eliminate the need for compassionate understanding and increased pastoral effort on our part, but it does point to the fact that everything depends on Christ."

Perhaps John Paul II's most instructive Address on this topic was given in 1979 to a group of researchers on natural family planning. Here, there was emphasis on the spiritual nature of each human person precisely in his or her sexuality, which is itself a good and a gift to be preserved and developed into its own distinctness. The Pope understood the sorts of problems that often did exist, but a deeper bond of faith and love changed how they were perceived (VIII, c, 4). Marriage existed within the history of salvation itself, an adventure and an event in the meaning of the world (VII, c, 3). The Holy Father again warned against deceiving anyone about the doctrine of the Church in these matters. Moreover, the reasons of faith are in conformity with what science learns and can learn. Yet, people also need "deeply human reasons" to assist them in understanding the Church's position (VII, c, 7). The Pope gently chided the contradictions in the various ideologies of our time on this question:

> At a time when so many ecological movements call for respect for nature, what are we to think of an invasion of artificial procedures and substances in this emi-

nently personal field? To resort to technical measures in place of self-control, self-renunciation for the sake of the other, and the common effort of husband and wife, does not this mark a regression from that which constitutes man's nobility? (VII, c, 7)

John Paul II does not hesitate to find some basic connection between a contraceptive mentality and the rise of abortion's frequency in modern society. "...The generalization of contraception by artificial methods also leads to abortion, for both are, at different levels, certainly, in the same line of fear of the child, rejection of life, lack of respect for the act or the fruit of union such as it is willed between man and woman by the Creator of nature" (VII, c, 8).

Moreover, John Paul II argued that the Church at the local level ought to provide careful and principled instruction to couples on how best to live out the Church's declared teaching. This does not happen automatically and without guidance, so that to expect couples who want to be faithful but to do nothing to teach them leaves them often in some impossible contradiction. Pope Wojtyla saw the great need for scientific research in this area. Perhaps one can legitimately wonder if the vast efforts, also among Catholics, to try to justify contraception or even abortion, would in the past decade have been rather directed to research in natural family planning, whether there would still be a great problem, other than the problem of mutual trust and respect, which exists in any case.

It is necessary to use every possible means to provide practical help for couples to live this responsible parenthood, and here your contribution is irreplaceable. The scientific researches that you carry out and pool in order to acquire more precise knowledge of the female cycle and permit more serene utilization of natural methods of regulating births, deserve to be better known, encouraged and effectively proposed for application....

For what is at stake is the good of families and societies in their legitimate concern to harmonize human fertility with their possibilities, and, provided that an appeal is always made to virtues of love and continence, it is a question of the progress of human self-mastery in conformity with the Creator's plan (VII, c, 7).

John Paul II, thus, follows out the theme of mutual self-mastery in a context of generosity, in a spirit of faith in which sacrifice and gift become possibilities in human lives. It is with this background that he can use the much maligned phrase "responsible parenthood" and tell couples that the number of their children is up to them in this context, always remembering the value of children themselves to each other (IV, f, 6).

The teachings and exhortations of the Pope, of course, do not deal only, or even mainly, with the beginning of life, which latter receives a certain priority, to be sure, because of the practices and philosophies of our era. He deals with men and women and children in every stage of their lives, with particular attention to them in their sickness and death. In two other volumes of St. Paul Editions, in his remarks to university students and faculties and in his teachings on the social order, I have gathered many of the Holy Father's pertinent reflections on youth, intelligence, concern for the public order, for those who are weak or poor, for the political and economic order of the world. In this collection, the concentration is more on the sanctity of the family, on the place of husbands and wives, of children and their coming to be, on what happens to us when we are ill, when we are old, when we die. John Paul II knows and insists on the Christian doctrine, which is taken as an active, operative principle, that it is each individual person who survives death in resurrection. This is the center about whom all reality turns. The family itself, composed of real persons, is likewise a place of sanctity. In a real sense, the family is the most basic and important community, even for the State. It is closer to the roots of our being and ultimate destiny. "I have always thought of visits with families as key moments of my visits to the parish. To meet with the spouses, to pray with them about certain problems which make up the contents of their vocation and the goal of their life," the Pope reflected in a Mass for families in St. Peter's Square (I, 3).

Illness, too, is a part of most human life. It need not be considered to be a curse, he told the lepers in Brazil (II, i, 4). "The cross of illness borne in union with that of Christ becomes a source of salvation, of life, or of resurrection for the sick person himself and for others, for the whole of mankind" (II, i, 4). And to the elderly in the Cologne Cathedral, the Pope said:

> In you it becomes apparent that the meaning of life cannot consist in earning and spending money, that in all our external activities there has to mature something internal, and something eternal in all the temporal....
>
> Without familiarity with God, there is in the last end no consolation in death. For that is exactly what God intends with death, that at least in this one sublime hour of our life, we allow ourselves to fall into His love without any other security than just this love for us (II, j, 7).

Few write about human suffering, about life and death, more beautifully, more theologically, and more correctly, than Pope Wojtyla.

Finally, to conclude, it might be well to ask again whether, for all his own personal charm and intelligence, John Paul II is merely teaching his own private doctrines. When we follow his reflections on the course and meaning of human life, are these intended to be just one man's opinion, however warm or attractive they are? The Holy Father's personal spirit is benign. As he remarked to families at the Synod of 1980:

> From Rome, from this present Synod of Bishops...you draw the conviction, the confidence, and the certainty that it is a right and a duty of the Church to cultivate and carry out her doctrine in pastoral guidance on marriage and the family.
>
> She does not intend to impose this doctrine and guidance on anyone, but is ready to propose them freely and to safeguard them as a reference point that cannot be renounced by those who style themselves Catholics....
>
> The Church considers, therefore, that she can proclaim her convictions on the family, certain that she is rendering a service to all men. She would betray man if she passed over in silence her message on the family (V, a, 7).

This sense that the truth of Christian teaching joins the true well-being of mankind is a consistent and constant theme of John Paul II. Nor does he seek to appeal to this truth except spiritually, on evidence, on argument, on persuasion. Even his own teaching authority binds him only to teach what Christ has handed down in the Church. As a philosopher and as a man, he also finds this noble, reasonable, and worth living. To the objection that these truths of marriage, family, and human life are not clear to non-Christians or to all Christians, the Pope does not simply yield to a principle of civil liberty, whose worth he does not deny, a principle which would seem to leave the "truth" question aside in the area of human life beyond politics. He argues consistently that the Christian position is reasonable, that faith guides us in seeing this, but that the truth of the thing itself can be understood by men's minds, even though many may reject it or not understand it. "It is the divine law proclaimed by Christ that gives rise to the Christian ideal of monogamous marriage, which in turn is the basis of the Christian family" (V, f, 5). The Pope thinks that this ideal, believed in, lived, and reflected upon, is capable of being understood as the proper form of human love among men and women.

These addresses and homilies of John Paul II on human life are given in their entirety. Almost every address given by the Holy Father, to be sure, contains passages that would be pertinent to this important subject. Though there perhaps are other addresses or homilies that might be selected to give a basic appreciation and adequate presentation of Pope Wojtyla's thought on this subject of human life, I have included here what I take to be the most important ones. Many of the other addresses to be found in St. Paul Editions' books on the Holy Father's general audience addresses on human sexuality, on youth, on the social order, and to university students and faculties (cf. Bibliography), certainly, will contain significant references to questions of life, marriage, and family. In addition in this edition, I have included several statements by various organs of the Holy See or individuals on euthanasia, abortion, responsible parenthood, disabled persons, and pluralism, which have appeared in L'Osservatore Romano and which seem to be of special value as commentaries on or declarations elaborating the thought of John Paul II. I believe that a careful, reflective consideration of the work and thought of John Paul II, taken in the spirit in which he himself would obviously have us receive his teaching, is essential to understanding how the Christian teaching on love, marriage, family, on the love and life of the human person, best explains the deepest meaning of our condition and destiny as men and women. The right to life, "from conception," as the Holy Father carefully adds, is the beginning of eternal life for each of us. There is no teaching about man more powerful or more exalting, none more realistic than this. The first right remains the first gift. All Christian teaching is contained in this.

I. Through the Family

"No Other Road to Humanity than Through the Family," Homily in St. Peter's Square, to Representatives of National Catholic Family Movements Gathered for the Synod on the Family, Rome, October 12, 1980.

NO OTHER ROAD TO HUMANITY THAN THROUGH THE FAMILY

On October 12, 1980, the Pope concelebrated with the Fathers of the Synod the "Pro-Familia" Mass, attended by families from the whole world, including representatives sent by the Episcopal Conferences and International and National Catholic Family Movements.

After the Gospel, John Paul II delivered the following homily.

Dear brothers and sisters,

1. Today, a great joy fills our hearts for the opportunity given to us to meet in such an unusual community and such an eloquent one. While the ordinary reunion of the Synod of Bishops is going on, working since September 26 on the theme *"De muneribus familiae Christianae"* ("On the Roles of the Christian Family"), today we have a meeting of families and, above all, the meeting with those couples who with their presence give witness to those roles: *to the duties of the Christian family in the contemporary world.*

This day is truly blessed in the course of the work of the actual Synod! If this were lacking, something essential and important would be missing. It would not suffice, in fact, only to discuss the theme which faces the Synod of Bishops, even if in a competent manner. This theme must become the object of prayer, together with you. It must be given a Eucharistic dimension: it must be brought before the altar and presented to the Eternal Father, including it in the sacrifice of Christ Himself.

THE GREAT CAUSE OF THE CHRISTIAN FAMILY

2. Therefore, I cordially salute you, dearest spouses, united in front of the Basilica of St. Peter.

I greet you, dear Christian spouses, along with the Synod of Bishops who, like me, awaited this day of meeting with great impatience. I salute you and thank you for having come here in such numbers, not only from Rome and the rest of Italy, but also from different countries and various continents from around the entire world.

Dear husbands and wives, I greet you in the love of Christ Jesus and I thank you for coming to Saint Peter's Square, which is a special meeting-place for the Christians of the whole world in the unity of the universal Church. You are here as married couples from many different places in Africa, America, Australia, Asia, and Europe; you have gathered here and are praying for the great cause of the Christian family in the modern world.

Many of you, dear spouses, have come from afar. Because of this, the greater the difficulties confronted and the sacrifices made, so much more esteemed and precious is your presence in this community, which welcomes you with great happiness, with fraternal affection, with deep gratitude.

"This is the day which the Lord has made" (Ps. 117[118]:24). The day of the Lord, particularly chosen for us to be together. I salute you, then, spouses here reunited. I thank you, from the heart, for your presence.

Among the couples united here, I also cordially greet those coming from German-speaking countries. As you know, from its beginning, I have emphasized the need to surround the Synod of Bishops with the prayer of the entire Church for the family.

On this day, this prayer reaches its apex. With your presence, the Church of Rome unites in festive prayer, internal and full of faith, with the community of the entire Church. The Church recommends to the heavenly

Father through the mediation of Christ in the Holy Spirit the duties of the family in the contemporary world.

A UNIVERSAL COMMUNITY

3. It is thanks to all this that the Church today feels itself in a particular way, not only the People of God, but a true divine family. Truly extraordinary is this day. Full of joy and hope. And how necessary this all is among the wrong ways and doubts, the way of the present times. How full in the sureness which derives from the eternal alliance. It is truly a day made by the Lord.

This day reminds me of many other days in my episcopal service, so many encounters with couples in the parishes that I visited. *I have always thought of them as key moments of the visits to the parish. To meet the spouses, to pray with them about certain problems which make up the content of their vocation and the goal of their life.* To unite with them in the communion of the Eucharistic Sacrifice and to bless each couple— spouses and parents (as much as possible with children), to renew in them the grace of the Sacrament of Matrimony.

Today the same thing must be done in our community, not in the dimension of only one parish visited by the bishop, but in a certain way, in the dimension of the universal community of the whole Church, and this thanks to your presence, thanks to your visit, dear brothers and sisters, to the places of the "memories of the Apostles" in Rome. And how I am grateful to you, together with all my brothers in the episcopate united in the present session of the Synod! We hope for a great deal from this day, from this communion of souls, from this prayer, from this Eucharist.

BECAUSE GOD IS LOVE

4. The readings of today's liturgy tell us how God, in His eternal design, has bound the fundamental duty of the family—which is the gift of life offered by parents, a man and woman, to their children, to every new human being—with the vocation of love, in the participation in that love which comes from God, because He is the same as love. Yes, "God is love" (1 Jn. 4:8).

When, in fact, as we read in the book of Genesis, God created man in His image and likeness (cf. 1:2), by calling him into existence by love, He called him at the same time to love. *Since God is love, and man is created "in the image of God," it is necessary to conclude then that the vocation to love is inscribed, so to speak, organically in this image, that is, in the humanity of man, whom God created male and female.*

In light of this fundamental truth about man, who is the image of God, we read again the words spoken in the beginning to the man and the woman: "Be fruitful and multiply, fill the earth and subdue it" (Gn. 1:28).

They are words of blessing. All living creatures have inherited the blessing of the Creator, but in the words pronounced over man, over the male and female, this blessing has confirmed the double gift: the gift of life and the gift of love.

DUTIES TO FULFILL

5. From this double gift of the Creator, the family takes its beginning. The sacrament which is decisive for the family in the history of man and at the same time in

the history of salvation is the Sacrament of Matrimony. To go back to the same foundations of those duties, which the family has had to fulfill in every age—which it has also had to fulfill in the modern world—means to go back to this sacrament, of which St. Paul writes that it is great "in reference to Christ and to the Church" (Eph. 5:22).

During the Synod, we bishops are seeking day after day to do this through reflection and the exchange of ideas, guided by the light of the Holy Spirit and by pastoral solicitude. Today, we desire to do it in a particular way in this community of spouses, those who by their specific vocation express the duties of the Christian family in the Church and in the modern world. We therefore desire to renew together with you, dear brothers and sisters, the consciousness of the sacrament from which is born, and on the basis of which there develops, the Christian family. *We desire to reawaken the divine and at the same time human powers which are in the sacrament.* We desire, in a certain sense, to enter into the eternal design of the Creator and of the Redeemer and to join, as He has joined, the mystery of life with the mystery of love, so that they will work together and be inseparably united one with another.

"What God has joined together, let no man put asunder" (Mt. 19:6).

In this "let no man put asunder" there is contained the essential greatness of marriage and at the same time the moral compactness of the family.

Today we ask such greatness and dignity for all spouses in the world, we ask for such sacramental strength and moral compactness for all families. And we ask this for the good of man! For the good of every man. *Man has no other road to humanity than uniquely through the family.* And this, the family, must be the foundation of every solicitude for the good of man, of every effort to make our human world more human. *Nobody can separate himself from this solicitude: no society, no people, no system; neither the state, nor the Church, and not even the individual.*

6. Love, which unites man and woman as spouses and parents, is, at the same time, a gift and an order. That love is a gift is told to us in the second reading of today's liturgy with the words of St. John's letter: "In this is love, not that we loved God, but that he loved us and sent his Son to be the expiation for our sins" (1 Jn. 4:10).

Thus, therefore, is love a gift: "for love is of God, and he who loves is born of God and knows God" (1 Jn. 4:7). *And at the same time, love is a commandment, is the greatest commandment. God gives it to man, and gives it to him as a duty. He asks it of man.* To the question about the greatest commandment, Christ answers: "You shall love..." (Mt. 22:37).

This commandment is at the base of all the moral order. It is truly "the greatest." It is the key commandment. To do this in the family means to answer the gift of love that the couple receives in the conjugal alliance: "if God so loved us, we also ought to love one another" (1 Jn. 4:11). To accomplish the commandment of love means to realize all the duties of the Christian family. On the whole, all is reduced to this: *faithfulness and conjugal honesty, responsible parenthood and education.* The "little Church"—the domestic Church—

means the family living in the spirit of the commandment of love: its interior truth, its daily work, its spiritual beauty and its strength.

The commandment of love has its internal structure: "You shall love the Lord your God with all your heart, and with all your soul, and with all your mind.... You shall love your neighbor as yourself" (Mt. 22:37).

This structure of the commandment corresponds to the truth of love. *If God is loved above all things, then also man loves and is loved with the fullness of love accessible to him.* If one destroys this inseparable structure, spoken of in Christ's commandment, then man's love will detach itself from the deepest root, will lose the root of fullness and of truth which are essential to him.

We implore for all Christian families, for all the families of the world, this fullness and truth of love, which is shown by Christ's commandment.

RENEWAL
OF THE MARITAL PROMISES

7. Soon, in our large community, there will be a renewal of the marriage promises. These words are marvelous, those pronounced by the couple in the rite of Matrimony as ministers of this sacrament:

"I take you to be my wife (my husband). I promise to be true to you in good times and in bad, in sickness and in health. I will love you and honor you all the days of my life."

This promise, pronounced "in the name of the Father and the Son and the Holy Spirit," is at the same time a prayer addressed to God who is love—and who wishes to unite all at the end in the last alliance of the communion of saints.

At the moment in which you said these words, dear spouses, in different languages, in various places in the world, in different years, months and days, you administered the holy sacrament of your life, of your marriage, of your family: the sacrament in which the love of God for man is reflected in the love of Christ for the Church.

Today you return with the heart and the mind —you return with faith, with hope and with love—to that great moment. And you renew in your souls that which made up the essential content of the Sacrament of Matrimony, its daily reality. You renew the alliance of man and woman! Before the God of alliance you renew this alliance, penetrated by the gift of love and the gift of life.

ETERNAL ALLIANCE
WITH THE GOD OF LOVE

8. Do it in union with the whole Church. In union with all the Christian families in the Church and with all the families of the entire world. Your thought and your prayer will be, at the same time, close to all those difficult situations, that in these days and weeks pass before the eyes of the bishops of the Synod and do not cease to engage their pastoral solicitude. In this humble and profound act, through which you wish to renew the grace of the Sacrament of Matrimony, all the fervent desire of life and of sanctity is felt, which tirelessly beats in the

heart of the Church and is manifested in the witnessing of each Christian family faithful to the eternal alliance with the God of love.

In this manner persevere! That this day will become the new beginning of your testimony and mission. That it will become the light which pervades the darkness of the contemporary world.

In this manner persevere! Trustful that "if we love one another, God abides in us and his love is perfected in us" (1 Jn. 4:12).

Amen.

II. The Sweep of Life

Pastoral Homilies and Addresses on the Stages of Human Life from Conception and Birth, to Childhood, Marriage, Work, Sickness, and Old Age

a) "Love and Respect for Nascent Life," *General Audience, Rome, January 3, 1979.*

b) "Protect Childhood for the Good of Society," *Audience with Committee of European Journalists for the Rights of the Child, January 13, 1979.*

c) "Vocation of Married Couples to the Interior Truth of Love," *to the Congress organized by the "New Families" section of the Focolari Movement, in the Palazzo dello Sport, Rome, May 3, 1981.*

d) "Fundamental Family Values Include Conjugal Love, Life," *Homily at the Church of the Gesú, Rome, December 31, 1978.*

e) "Give Back to the World the Taste for Life," *To the National Pilgrimage of French Families, November 10, 1980.*

f) "Fatherhood and the Family," *Homily on the Feast of St. Joseph, in Liberati Stadium, Terni, Italy, March 19, 1981.*

g) *"Dignity and Rights of Woman,"* To Participants in the Fifth International Congress on the Family, *November 8, 1980.*

h) *"Irreplaceable Role of the Sick in God's Plan of Salvation,"* To a Group of Pilgrims to Rome, *February 11, 1981.*

i) *"The Cross of Suffering,"* Visit to a Leper Colony, in Belém, Brazil, *July 8, 1980.*

j) *"In Your Old Age, Accept the Cross,"* Homily to the Elderly in Cologne Cathedral, Germany, *November 19, 1980.*

LOVE AND RESPECT
FOR NASCENT LIFE

On January 3, 1979, at the general audience in the Paul VI Hall, the Holy Father delivered the following address to the thousands of faithful from Italy and all over the world.

1. Mankind's last night of waiting, which is recalled to us every year by the liturgy of the Church on the eve and the feast of the Nativity of the Lord, is at the same time the night in which the promise was fulfilled. The One who was awaited, who was, and does not cease to be, the end of the advent is born. Christ is born. That happened once, in the night at Bethlehem, but in the liturgy it is repeated every year, in a certain way it "is actualized" every year. And every year, too, it is rich with the same content: divine and human, which is so superabundant that man is not capable of embracing it all with one glance; and it is difficult to find words to express it altogether. Even the liturgical period of Christmas seems to us too short to dwell on this event, which presents more the characteristics of "mysterium fascinosum," than those of "mysterium tremendum." Too short, to "enjoy" fully the coming of Christ, the birth of God in human nature. Too short, to untangle the single threads of this event and of this mystery.

THE HOLY FAMILY,
ALSO HUMAN

2. The liturgy centers our attention on one of those threads, and highlights it particularly. The birth of the Child in the night at Bethlehem started the family. For this reason, the Sunday during the octave of Christmas

is the feast of the Family of Nazareth. This is the Holy Family, because it was molded for the birth of the One whom even his "adversary" will be compelled to proclaim, one day, "the Holy One of God" (Mk. 1:24). The Holy Family—because of the holiness of the One who was born—became the source of an extraordinary sanctification, both of His Virgin Mother, and of her bridegroom, who, as her lawful husband, was considered before men as the father of the Child born during the census in Bethlehem.

This Family is at the same time a human family, and therefore the Church, in the period of Christmas, addresses, through the Holy Family, every human family. Holiness imprints on this Family—in which the Son of God came into the world—a unique, exceptional, unrepeatable, supernatural character. And at the same time *all that we can say of every human family, its nature, its duties, its difficulties, can be said also of this Sacred Family*. In fact, this Sacred Family is really poor; at the moment of the birth of Jesus it is without a roof over its head; then it will be forced to go into exile, and when the danger is over, it remains a Family which lives modestly, in poverty, with the work of its hands.

Its condition is similar to that of so many other families. It is the meeting-place of our solidarity with every family, with every community of a man and a woman in which a new human being is born. It is a Family which does not remain only on the altars, as an object of praise and veneration, but, through so many episodes, well known to us from the Gospel of St. Luke and St. Matthew, approaches, in a certain way every human family. It takes over those deep, beautiful and at the same time difficult problems which married and family life brings with it. When we read attentively what the Evangelists (particularly Matthew) wrote about the events lived by Joseph and Mary before the birth of Jesus, these problems, to which I referred above, become even more evident.

NEW DIGNITY
AND NEW DUTIES

3. The solemnity of Christmas, and, in its context, the feast of the Holy Family, are particularly near and dear to us, just because we meet in them the fundamental dimension of our faith, that is, the mystery of the Incarnation, with the no less fundamental dimension of the affairs of man. *Everyone must recognize that this essential dimension of the affairs of man is precisely the family.* And in the family it is procreation: a new man is conceived and is born, and through this conception and this birth the man and woman, in their capacity as husband and wife, become father and mother, parents, reaching a new dignity and assuming new duties.

The importance of these fundamental duties is very great from many points of view. Not only from the point of view of this concrete community, their family, but also from the point of view of every human community, every society, nation, state, school, profession and environment. *Everything depends, generally speaking, on how the parents and the family carry out their first and fundamental duties, on the way and to the extent to which they teach this creature—who, thanks to them, has become a human being, has obtained "humanity"—to "be a man."* The family cannot be replaced in this. *Everything must be done in order that the family should not be replaced.* That is necessary not only for the "private" good of every person, but also for the common good of every society, nation, and state, of any continent. *The family is placed at the very center of the common good in its various dimensions, precisely because man is conceived and born in it. Everything possible must be done in order that this human being should be desired, awaited and experienced as having a particular, unique and unrepeatable value right from the beginning, from the moment of his conception. He must feel that he is important, useful, dear and of great value, even if infirm or handicapped; even more loved, in fact, for this reason.*

This is what the mystery of the Incarnation teaches us. This is the logic of our faith. This is also the logic of all true humanism. I think, in fact, that it cannot be otherwise. We are not looking here for elements of contrast, but we are looking for meeting points, which are the simple consequence of the full truth about man. Faith does not take believers away from this truth, but brings them right to its heart.

CONCERN
FOR THE MOTHER-TO-BE

4. And another thing. On Christmas night, the Mother who was to give birth (*Virgo paritura*) did not find a roof over her head. She could not find the conditions in which that great, divine, and at the same time human mystery of giving birth to a man normally takes place.

Allow me to use the logic of faith and the logic of a consistent humanism. This fact of which I am speaking is a great cry, it is a permanent challenge to individuals and to all, particularly, perhaps, in our time, in which a great proof of moral consistency is often asked of the expectant mother. *In fact, what is euphemistically defined as "interruption of pregnancy" (abortion) cannot be evaluated with truly human categories other than those of the moral law, that is, of conscience.* Certainly, if not the confidences made in the confessionals, those in the advisory bureaus for responsible motherhood, could tell us a great deal in this connection.

Consequently, the mother who is about to give birth cannot be left alone with her doubts, difficulties and temptations. We must stand by her side, so that she will not put a burden on her conscience, so that the most fundamental bond of man's respect for man will not be destroyed. *Such, in fact, is the bond that begins at the moment of conception, as a result of which we must all, in a certain way, be with every mother who must give birth; and we must offer her all the help possible.*

Let us look to Mary: *Virgo paritura* (the Virgin about to give birth). Let us, the Church, us men, look, and let us try to understand better what responsibility Christmas brings with it towards every man who is to be born on earth. For the present we will stop at this point and interrupt these considerations: we will certainly have to return to them again, and not just once.

PROTECT CHILDHOOD
FOR THE GOOD OF SOCIETY

*On January 13, 1979, the Holy Father John Paul II received in audi-
ence the members of the Committee of European Journalists for the
Rights of the Child and members of the Italian Commission for the
International Year of the Child. John Paul II delivered the following
address.*

Ladies and gentlemen,

I am happy to receive today the "Committee of
European Journalists for the Rights of the Child,"
accompanied by representatives of the Italian National
Commission for the International Year of the Child,
under the patronage of which your first meeting, here,
in Rome, is taking place. I thank you for this visit
and for the trust it shows. In the framework of the International Year of the Child, you have wished to take initiatives in order that you yourselves may study the
situation of certain groups of underprivileged children
and then, I suppose, drive home to your readers the
problems of these children.

The Holy See is not content to regard with interest
and sympathy the good initiatives that will be undertaken this year. It is ready to encourage everything
planned and carried out for the real good of children,
for it is a question of an immense population, a considerable part of mankind, which needs special protection and advancement, in view of the precariousness
of its fate.

The Church, happily, is not the only institution
there is to cope with these needs; but it is true that she
has always considered material, affective, educational
and spiritual assistance for children an important part of

her mission. And if she acted in this way, it was because, without always using the more recent vocabulary of the "rights of the child," *she considered the child, in fact, not as an individual to be utilized, not as an object, but as a subject with inalienable rights, a newborn personality to be developed, having a value in itself, an extraordinary destiny.* There would be no end to enumerating the works that Christianity set up for this purpose. It is only natural, since Christ Himself put the child at the heart of the Kingdom of God: "Let the children come to me...; for to such belongs the kingdom of heaven" (Mt. 19:14). And these words of Christ spoken on behalf of destitute humans, and which will judge us all, "I was hungry and you gave me food...; I was naked and you clothed me, I was sick and you visited me" (Mt. 25:35-36), do they not apply particularly to the helpless child? Hunger for bread, hunger for affection, hunger for education.... Yes, the Church wishes to take an ever greater part in this action in favor of children, and to stimulate it more widely.

But the Church desires just as much to help to form the conscience of men, to make public opinion aware of the child's essential rights which you are trying to uphold. The "Declaration of the Rights of the Child," adopted by the Assembly of the United Nations Organization twenty years ago, already expresses an appreciable consensus on a certain number of very important principles, which are still far from being applied everywhere.

The Holy See thinks that we can also speak of *the rights of the child from the moment of conception, and particularly of the right to life, for experience shows more and more that the child needs special protection,* de facto *and* de jure, *even before his birth.*

Stress could thus be laid on *the right of the child to be born in a real family*, for it is essential that he should benefit from the beginning from the joint contribution of the father and the mother, united in an indissoluble marriage.

The child must also be reared, educated in his family, the parents remaining "primarily and principally responsible" for his education, a role which "is of such importance that it is almost impossible to provide an adequate substitute" (GE 3). That is made necessary by the atmosphere of affection and of moral and material security that the psychology of the child requires. It should be added that procreation founds this natural right, which is also "the greatest obligation" *(ibid.)*. And even the existence of wider family ties, with brothers and sisters, with grandparents, and other close relatives, is an important element—which tends to be neglected today—for the child's harmonious balance.

In education, to which, together with the parents, the school and other organisms of society contribute, the child must find the possibilities "of developing in a healthy, normal way on the physical, intellectual, moral, spiritual and social plane, in conditions of freedom and dignity," as the second principle of the "Declaration of the Rights of the Child" asserts. *In this connection, the child has also the right to the truth, in a teaching which takes into account the fundamental ethical values, and which will make possible a spiritual education, in conformity with the religion to which the child belongs, the orientation legitimately desired by his parents and the exigencies of freedom of conscience,* rightly understood, for which the child must be prepared and formed throughout his childhood and adolescence. On this point, it is natural that the Church should be able to exercise her own responsibilities.

Actually, to speak of the rights of the child is to speak of the duties of parents and educators, who remain in the service of the child, of his higher interests. *But the growing child must take part himself in his own development, with responsibilities that correspond to his capacities; and care must be taken not to neglect to speak to him also of his own duties towards others and towards society.*

Such are the few reflections that you give me the opportunity to express, with regard to the goals that you set yourselves. Such is the ideal towards which it is necessary to strive, for the deepest good of children, for the honor of our civilization. I know that you give prior attention to the children whose elementary rights are not even satisfied, in your own countries as in those of other continents. European journalists, do not hesitate, therefore, to look also to regions of the globe less favored than Europe! I pray to God to enlighten and strengthen your interest in these children.

VOCATION
OF MARRIED COUPLES
TO THE INTERIOR TRUTH
OF LOVE

On May 3, 1981, the Holy Father went to the Palazzo dello Sport in the EUR district to participate in the final phase of the world congress on "The Family and Love," organized by the "New Families" section of the Focolari Movement. About twenty thousand persons from some fifty countries all over the world took part in the event, including also families of Muslims, Buddhists and Hindus, as well as of various Christian confessions.

John Paul II delivered the following address.

Beloved brothers and sisters of the "New Families Movement"!

1. *Veni, Creator Spiritus!*

I greet you with this invocation, which has a special place in this Paschal season, in which, after the resurrection of Christ, we prepare for fifty days for the coming of the Holy Spirit, the fullness of the mystery.

This invocation fits all the more into the present year in which, 1600 years after the First Council of Constantinople, we solemnly commemorate the historic event and wish to revive particularly our faith "in the Holy Spirit, who is the Lord and giver of life," as was recalled in the letter sent to the bishops and to the whole Church, last March 25.

Veni, Creator Spiritus.

I greet you, married couples, with this invocation, which reminds each of you of that great moment in your life when you found yourselves before the altar, to give to each other, in the Holy Spirit, your mutual witness of love, fidelity and matrimonial virtue, swearing to keep them until death: "I take you as my wife—as my husband—and I promise to be faithful to you always, in joy and in sorrow, in health and in sickness, and to love you and honor you all the days of my life."

If the Church invoked the Holy Spirit particularly for this occasion: "Come!" This means that it is really a great moment, *"sacramentum magnum." In fact, marriage bears within it an analogy to the marriage of Christ with the Church* and with the moment in which the Holy Spirit—in the rush of the wind and the glow of the tongues of fire—descended upon the Apostles on the day of Pentecost. Matrimonial consent, that so decisive moment in your lives, brings with it also a certain analogy to the unique episode which took place when the Holy Spirit descended upon the Virgin of Nazareth and "the Word was made flesh" (Jn. 1:14).

I refer to these particular moments and I entrust you, dear brothers and sisters, spouses of the Focolari Movement, to the Holy Spirit, to that Spirit with whom is connected the origin of creation, the origin of redemption and the origin of your own marriage in Christ and in the Church.

UNION OF LOVE

2. Through the work of the Holy Spirit, you have become a unity of two. The power that unites you is love. This human love of yours, which matured in your hearts and decisions, was manifested before the altar, when, to the words of the priest who called upon you to express your generous and definitive consent, you replied with your mutual "I will," and gave each other the blessed ring, the symbol of your perennial fidelity in love.

Love is formed in the human person, embraces body and soul, matures in the heart and in the will; to be "human," love must comprise the person in his physical, psychical and spiritual totality.

Simultaneously, "God's love has been poured into our hearts through the Holy Spirit who has been given to us" (Rom. 5:5).

The reciprocal compenetration of divine love and human love lasts from the day of your marriage. Divine love, in fact, penetrates into human love, giving it a new dimension: it makes it deep, pure and generous; *it develops it towards fullness, ennobles it, spiritualizes it, makes it ready even for sacrifices and self-denial, and at the same time enables it to produce peace and joy as its fruit.*

By means of this love you constitute unity in God: the communio personarum. You constitute the unity of the two gathered in His name and He is in your midst (cf. Mt. 18:20).

This unity in Christ, in a way, spontaneously seeks expression in prayer. Love, in fact, is a gift and it is a commandment: it is a gift from God because He first loved us (cf. 1 Jn. 4:10), and it is also the fundamental commandment of all moral orientation. As I said in the homily at the Mass for Families, on October 12 of last year: *"To carry out the commandment of love means accomplishing all the duties of the Christian family: fidelity and conjugal virtue, responsible parenthood and education.* The 'little Church'—the domestic Church—means the family living in the spirit of the commandment of love, its interior truth, its daily toil, its spiritual beauty and its power." *But to live this poem of love and unity in this way, you absolutely need to pray.* In this sense prayer becomes really essential for love and unity: in fact, prayer strengthens, relieves, purifies, exalts, helps to find light and advice, deepens the respect that spouses in particular must mutually nourish for their hearts, their consciences and their bodies, by means of which they are so close to each other. The Second Vatican Council aptly writes in this connection: *"Outstanding courage is required for the constant fulfillment of the duties of this Christian calling: spouses, therefore, will need grace for leading a holy life; they will eagerly prac-* tice a love that is firm, generous, and prompt to sacrifice, and will ask for it in their prayers" (GS 49).

My wish for you today is that the Emmaus event may constantly be repeated in your lives: that you may know Christ in the breaking of bread and that you may always find Him present in your midst, in your hearts, after this "breaking of bread"!

And I commend you all, every couple, to Christ, who wants to accompany you along your way, just as He accompanied the disciples along the way to Emmaus. I entrust you all to Christ, who knows human hearts!

A NEW DIGNITY
AND A NEW MISSION

3. When Jesus first sent the disciples to proclaim the Good News, He sent them "two by two" (cf. Mk. 6:7). *You too are sent in pairs by the great sacrament,*

which, making you husband and wife, makes you at the same time witnesses to the crucified and risen Christ.

In the sacrament, in fact, you receive as Christians a new dignity—the dignity of husband and wife; and a new mission — that is, participation in the mission which is that of the whole People of God and which, in various ways, takes its place in the triple mission, *tria munera*, of Christ Himself.

You must carry out this mission with your whole life, fulfilling it especially by means of witness. Here again the Second Vatican Council throws light on this matter, with concise and persuasive power: "Authentic conjugal love will be held in high esteem, and healthy public opinion will be quick to recognize it, if Christian spouses give outstanding witness to fidelity and harmony in their love, if they are conspicuous in their concern for the education of their children, and if they play their part in a much needed cultural, psychological, and social renewal in matters of marriage and the family" (GS 49).

How fundamental this witness of yours is! How human it must be and at the same time how profoundly Christian! But precisely to carry out this essential task of witness to faith and love, you married couples have a "charism" of your own, described by the Council as follows: "Authentic conjugal love is caught up into divine love and is directed and enriched by the redemptive power of Christ and the salvific action of the Church, with the result that the spouses are effectively led to God and are helped and strengthened in their lofty role as fathers and mothers. Spouses, therefore, are fortified and, as it were, consecrated for the duties and dignity of their state by a special sacrament; fulfilling their conjugal and family role by virtue of this sacrament, spouses are penetrated with the Spirit of Christ and their whole life is suffused by faith, hope and charity. Thus they increasingly further their own perfection and their mutual sanctification, and together they render glory to God" (ibid., 48).

With your whole life, with your common existence, with your lifestyle, you build up the Church in her smallest and at the same time fundamental dimension: the "Ecclesiola"!

Even the little "domestic Church" is, in fact, expressly willed by God and is founded by Christ and on Christ; it has as its essential mission the proclamation of the Gospel, the transmission of the eternal salvation of its members, and it possesses as its interior power the light and grace of the Holy Spirit.

And today, on the occasion of this meeting of ours, as Bishop and Pastor of the Church, I wish to reconfirm your special "place" in the great community of the People of God; I wish to address to this smaller Church, which you constitute, the expression of a particular love and a special tenderness, which is also manifested in the very term: "Ecclesiola." And I wish to give you again to the Church, understood as the great divine mystery, which is carried out in man's history, and in which man realizes himself and fulfills his destiny and his vocation.

So, be the "Church"!

Build the Church!

Oh, how much this sacred building depends on you!

May your typical spirituality also help you in this commitment. The "Focolarini" Movement, approved by my Predecessors John XXIII and Paul VI, has expanded in these years and has become structured in various branches and diverse activities: from the *"focolarini"* of community life to married *"focolarini"*; from the priestly movement to the connection with men and women religious; from the GEN Movement to the New Families Movement, to whose beginning and development Igino Giordani contributed, he whom you have opportunely wished to recall barely a year after his death, on this day dedicated to the family. Your initiatives are certainly numerous and your many experiences moving; but *your riches lie and must lie in the powerful idea of your spirituality, which is the certainty about God-Love and about His will, the expression of love.* In this sense your spirituality is open, positive, optimistic, serene and conquering: you want to build the Church in hearts, with love and in love, living in Christ and with Christ present in the everyday history of every person, especially in the abandoned, disappointed, frightened, suffering and confused person.

Continue to realize this ideal of yours, in union with the initiatives of the dioceses and other ecclesial movements, in order to help the family institution concretely and effectively in all its spiritual and material needs.

GREAT DIGNITY
AND RESPONSIBILITY

4. In the sacrament of marriage you are called to become, as husband and wife, parents: father and mother.

What a vocation and what a dignity! But also how much responsibility!

I would like to use the most penetrating words to express the beauty of this dignity and the greatness of the vocation which is shared by you through the power of the Holy Spirit, when as "one flesh" you manifest your availability as parents and thus make a place in your lives for the new creature. For new human persons!

That "new" being will be your child: flesh of your flesh and bone of your bones (cf. Gn. 2:23). *You must transmit what is best in your flesh and your soul!* To beget means at the same time to educate; and educating signifies begetting. In the human person what is carnal and what is spiritual interpenetrate, and therefore the two great dimensions of parenthood, procreation and education, also interpenetrate.

To educate means a great deal! You yourselves know how many tasks there are in this great, long and patient process through which you simply teach human behavior to those who are born of you, parents. And since divine sonship has been grafted onto the ground of this humanity, we must teach this person, born of his parents as regards his body and of God as regards his spirit, the fullness of life, that fullness which one has from the Father, in the Son, in Christ, through the Holy Spirit.

In this connection it is opportune to read again the words of Vatican II: "True education is directed towards the formation of the human person in view of his final end and the good of that society to which he belongs and in the duties of which he will, as an adult, have a share.

"Due weight being given to the advances in psychological, pedagogical and intellectual sciences, children and young people should be helped to develop harmoniously their physical, moral and intellectual qualities. They should be trained to acquire gradually a more perfect sense of responsibility in the proper development of their own lives by constant effort and in the pursuit of liberty, overcoming obstacles with unwavering courage and perseverance. As they grow older they should receive a positive and prudent education in matters relating to sex. Moreover, they should be so prepared to take their part in the life of society that, having been duly trained in the necessary and useful skills, they may be able to participate actively in the life of society in its various aspects. They should be open to dialogue with others and should willingly devote themselves to the promotion of the common good" (GE 1; cf. 3).

Oh, how ardently I desire to commend this role of yours as parents, this human parenthood of yours, to the Eternal Father Himself! Be united to Him with Christ! Through the work of the Holy Spirit, utter the word "Abba" often and recite the "Our Father," in order to learn incessantly from God Himself what it means to be a father and a mother; what it means to take the place of the heavenly Father and exercise His authority!

You, who are called to collaborate in the work of the Creator Himself—fathers and mothers—I commend you to the Father!

A SPECIAL LOVE

5. *The dignity of "parents" casts a fundamental light on what you are for yourselves, reciprocally, as spouses; that is, it illuminates your whole love, which is fulfilled through body and soul. You are called, in fact, to a quite special love.*

Also on this so important and delicate subject, the Second Vatican Council gives us guidance. "A love like that," we read in *Gaudium et spes*, "bringing together the human and the divine, leads the partners to a free and mutual giving of self, experienced in tenderness and action, and permeates their whole lives; besides, *this love is actually developed and increased by the exercise of it.* This is a far cry from mere erotic attraction, which is pursued in selfishness and soon fades away in wretchedness" (no. 49).

And it stresses further that "man's sexuality and the faculty of reproduction wondrously surpass the endowments of lower forms of life; therefore the acts proper to conjugal life, ordered according to authentic human dignity, must be honored with the greatest reverence. When it is a question of harmonizing conjugal love with the responsible transmission of life,...all this is possible only if the virtue of conjugal chastity is seriously practiced" (no. 51).

This love must be learned with constancy. Its authentic signs must be discerned. Its interior truth must be protected. You know very well that everything that the Church teaches in, so to speak, her "catechism of conjugal love," has precisely this as its scope: that interior truth of love, to which you are called as spouses.

This love must be learned constantly. It must be learned patiently, on your knees. You must delve little by little into all the profound beauty of the union of the couple. This beauty is of a spiritual nature, not just of sensual nature. And it is at the same time the beauty of conjugal unity, "unity in the body." *Yet what is corporeal in man draws its beauty, its light, its truth, when all is said and done, from the Spirit.*

In these times of ours, in which the true beauty of conjugal love is threatened in so many ways—threatened together with the dignity of fatherhood and motherhood—have courage! Have inflexible courage to look for it, to bear witness to it to each other, and to the world. Be apostles of the dignity of parenthood. Be apostles of beautiful love. So I commend you, dear brothers and sisters, to the Mother of God—to her whom the Church professed as *Theotokos* 1550 years ago at the Council of Ephesus, and whom we recall this year too.

I commend you, spouses of the Focolari Movement, to the Mother of beautiful love! And with great affection I impart the conciliatory apostolic blessing to you all and to the members of your families.

FUNDAMENTAL FAMILY VALUES INCLUDE CONJUGAL LOVE, LIFE

On December 31, 1978, Pope John Paul II presided at the final celebration of 1978, in the church dedicated to the Most Holy Name of Jesus (the "Gesù"). During the ceremony the Holy Father gave the following homily.

Beloved brothers and sisters,

First of all I wish to greet all present here, Romans and visitors, who have come to celebrate the closing of the year 1978—to celebrate it religiously. I address my cordial greeting to the Cardinal Vicar, to my brother bishops, to the representatives of civil authority, to the priests, to the men and women religious, especially those of the Society of Jesus with their Father General.

1. The Sunday within the octave of Christmas, that is, the present Sunday, unites, in the liturgy, the solemn memory of the Holy Family of Jesus, Mary and Joseph. The birth of a child always gives rise to a family. The birth of Jesus in Bethlehem gave rise to this unique and exceptional Family in the history of mankind. In this Family there came into the world, grew and was brought up the Son of God, conceived and born of the Virgin Mother, and at the same time entrusted, from the beginning, to the truly fatherly care of Joseph. The latter, a carpenter of Nazareth, who *vis-à-vis* Jewish law was Mary's husband, and *vis-à-vis* the Holy Spirit was her worthy spouse and the guardian, really in a fatherly way, of the maternal mystery of his bride.

THE FAMILY DIMENSION

The Family of Nazareth, which the Church, especially in today's liturgy, puts before the eyes of all families, really constitutes that culminating point of reference for the holiness of every human family. The history of this Family is described very concisely in the pages of the Gospel. We get to know only a few events in its life. However, what we learn is sufficient to be able to involve the fundamental moments in the life of every family, and to show *that dimension, to which all men who live a family life are called:* fathers, mothers, parents, children. The Gospel shows us, very clearly, the educative aspect of the family. "He went down with them and came to Nazareth, and was obedient to them" (Lk. 2:51).

This submission, obedience, readiness to accept the mature examples of the human conduct of the family, is necessary, on the part of children and of the young generation. Jesus, too, was "obedient" in this way. And parents must measure their whole conduct with this "obedience," this readiness of the child to accept the examples of human behavior. This is the particularly delicate point of their responsibility as parents, of their responsibility with regard to the man, this little and then growing man entrusted to them by God Himself. They must also keep in mind everything that happened in the life of the Family of Nazareth when Jesus was twelve years old; that is, they bring up their Child not just for themselves, but for Him, for the tasks which He will have to assume later. The twelve-year-old Jesus replied to Mary and Joseph: "Did you not know that I must be about my Father's business?" (Lk. 2:40)

NEED TO DEFEND VALUES

The deepest human problems are connected with the family. It constitutes the primary, fundamental and irreplaceable community for man. "The mission of being the primary vital cell of society has been given to the family by God Himself," the Second Vatican Council affirms (AA 11). The Church wishes to bear a particular witness to this also during the octave of Christmas, by means of the feast of the Holy Family. She wishes to recall that the fundamental values which cannot be violated without incalculable harm of a moral nature are bound up with the family. Material perspectives and the "economico-social" point of view often prevail over the principles of Christian and even human morality. It is not enough, then, to express only regret. *It is necessary to defend these fundamental values tenaciously and firmly, because their violation does incalculable harm to society and, in the last analysis, to man.* The experience of the different nations in the history of mankind, as well as our contemporary experience, can serve as an argument to reaffirm this painful truth, that is, *that it is easy, in the fundamental sphere of human existence in which the role of the family is decisive, to destroy essential values, while it is very difficult to reconstruct these values.*

VALUE OF THE PERSON

What are these values? If we had to answer this question adequately, it would be necessary to indicate the whole hierarchy and set of values which define and condition one another. But trying to express ourself concisely, let us say that here it is a question of two fundamental values which fall strictly into the context of what we call "conjugal love." *The first of them is the value of the person which is expressed in absolute mutual faithfulness until death:* the faithfulness of the husband to his wife and of the wife to her husband. The consequence of this affirmation of the value of the person, which is expressed in the mutual relationship between husband and wife, *must also be respect for the personal value of the new life*, that is, of the child, from the first moment of his conception.

GRATITUDE TO GOD

The Church can never dispense herself from the obligation of guarding these two fundamental values, connected with the vocation of the family. Custody of them was entrusted to the Church by Christ, in such a way as leaves no doubt. At the same time, the self-evidence of these values—humanly understood—is such that the Church, defending them, sees herself as the spokesman of true human dignity: of the good of the person, of the family, of the nation. *While maintaining respect for all those who think differently, it is very difficult to recognize, from the objective and impartial point of view, that anyone who betrays conjugal faithfulness, or who permits life conceived in the mother's womb to be wiped out and destroyed, behaves in a way consistent with true human dignity.* Consequently, it cannot be admitted that programs which suggest, which facilitate, which admit such behavior serve the objective well-being of man, the moral well-being, and help to make human life really more human, really more worthy of man, that they serve to construct a better society.

3. This Sunday is also the last day of the year 1978. We have gathered here, in this liturgy, to give thanks to God for all the good He has bestowed on us and has given us the grace to do during the past year, and to ask His forgiveness for all that, being contrary to good, is also contrary to His holy will.

Allow me, in this thanksgiving and in this request for forgiveness, to use also the criterion of the family, this time, however, in the wider sense. As God is the Father, then the criterion of the family has also this dimension: it refers to all human communities, societies, nations and countries; it refers to the Church and to mankind.

THE CHURCH'S OBLIGATION

Concluding this year in this way, let us give thanks to God for everything that—in the various spheres of earthly existence—makes men even more of a "family," that is, more brothers and sisters, who have in common the one Father. At the same time, let us ask for forgiveness for everything that is alien to the common brotherhood of men, that destroys the unity of the human family, that threatens it and impedes it.

Therefore, having always before my eyes my great Predecessor Paul VI, and the most beloved Pope John Paul I, I, their Successor, in the year of the death of both, today say: "Our Father, who art in heaven, accept us on this last day of the year 1978, in Christ Jesus, your Eternal Son, and lead us forward in Him in the future, in the future that You Yourself desire: God of love, God of truth, God of life!"

With this prayer on my lips, I, Successor of the two Pontiffs who died during this year, cross, together with you, the frontier which, in a few hours, will divide the year 1978 from 1979.

GIVE BACK TO THE WORLD
THE TASTE FOR LIFE!

"With our presence we wish to testify to the Holy Father our adherence to his family apostolate, and thank him for the concern he shows with regard to the family. Today we wish to have from him directives for the life and future development of our families, especially in the light of what has emerged from the recent Synod of Bishops, dedicated specially to the family." These are the fundamental reasons that brought over 3,500 French people, taking part in the national pilgrimage of French families organized by the "Confederation des Associations Familiales Catholiques," to the Vatican to participate in the audience granted to them by the Holy Father. The meeting took place on November 10, 1980. The group was led by Alexandre Cardinal Charles Renard, Archbishop of Lyons. In reply to the President's greeting, John Paul II delivered the following address.

Dear Catholic families, mainly from France, but also from overseas,

With the support of the Cardinal Archbishop of Lyons, whom I am happy to greet first of all and very fraternally, you have for a long time prepared this fine pilgrimage. Leaders and participants, you are all entitled to the congratulations of the Pope, who is so happy to welcome you here, just as you yourselves received him so well in France.

1. You have made a point of giving this Rome gathering a complete family character. Well done! I see, in fact, young parents and others who are approaching their silver wedding anniversary, while I notice happy grandparents. I admire the young children, and in particular the seventy who will have the great happiness of receiving First Communion this evening; I shall pray for their faithfulness to Christ. I also see adolescents, who remind me of the unforgettable evening in Parc des Princes. I know, finally, that personalities of the parlia-

mentary world have wished to accompany you, and
that there are also present delegates of Catholic Family
Associations of distant French territories and some
members of refugee families or families working tempo-
rarily in France. To one and all, I express my sentiments
of affection and trust. May Christ and His most holy
Mother — who is also Mother of the Church — assist us
all in the reflection that we are going to carry out
together on some important aspects of the conjugal and
family vocation!

Let us bless the Lord in the first place for the synod
which has just ended! Its fruits are abundant. Through
the hard work of the bishops and lay people, it is the
whole Church, in a way, that has just deepened her
faithfulness to God's plan regarding the family, and cast
her attentive and merciful glance on concrete family situations, so diverse and sometimes very painful. A syn-
thesis will come in due time, bringing enlightenment and
hope.

WE MUST TAKE UP THE CHALLENGE!

2. Today, the very composition of your great
gathering suggests a special reflection. Whereas modern
society is experiencing a phenomenon of demographic
concentration and, paradoxically, of manifold separations according to environments or fields of activity
— the world of labor, of teaching and even of leisure — your family assembly, wide and varied, is in itself
symbolic and, I would say, educative. It seems to me an
apologia of the family in its totality, a community of
persons.

I would like to encourage you all, parents and
children, along this difficult but promising path, all the
more so because modern civilization, badly controlled,

threatens on the one hand to level down and render commonplace the human person, too often uprooted, manipulated by ideological movements, saturated with objects or else gadgets, and on the other hand to develop aggressiveness and violence. Rather than groan, we must take up the challenge!

In this immense work, *Christian families—with humility and tenacity—must be more than ever an inter-personal and personalizing meeting-place, where every-one is himself only for the other and through the other. What a mystery is the human family, which, alone, can cause persons to be born and imprint on them a direc-tion of growth that will mark them for life! What a mys-tery, too, is each person, who is far more than a face, far more than a body!* He is a mind, a freedom, a unique history with a past, a social background, and a future which is sometimes difficult to discern!

RELATIONS BETWEEN PARENTS—
A DECISIVE FACTOR

As you know, the quality of relations between parents is decisive for the harmonious development of the children. A lack in this domain may weigh heavily on the whole life of a human being. The relations of children with their father and mother, of brothers and sisters with one another, will also have repercussions at the level of relations with schoolmates and for their whole life. *Even relations with God are facilitated, or hindered, or alas, rendered non-existent by the style of parental relations.* In this connection, you have prob-ably heard the reflection of St. Therese of Lisieux, when she was a child: "How God must love me, since Daddy loves me so much!"

At a time when studies and diplomas are demanded for everything, it is regrettable to see that such fundamental realities are not considered more, in theory and in practice. *Sexual information, for example, is wide of the mark if it is not completed by a concrete and persevering pedagogy of the harmonious development of the whole person, of the art of being at once the subject and object of love. This love requires*—is it necessary to stress it before you who are so convinced of it?—*the stability and indissolubility of the home.* The present statistical data on unions that are broken, sometimes very early, are a proof of the dilemma in which too many nations find themselves, owing to the destabilization of the family and the terrible consequences that result, the laws having often ratified and encouraged ways of acting instead of laying down their requirements.

3. For you, dear parents, but equally for the young, who love concrete things, I now open the Gospel. Christ's meetings are, in fact, very enlightening. Sometimes the initiative of relationships depends on Him: consider, for instance, the calling of the disciples. Sometimes, He lets Himself be met very simply: this is the case with Zachaeus, the publican. But always, *the meetings of Jesus are interpersonal relations, times of deep communion with the other, when Christ commits Himself entirely with His human aspect, His affectivity, His whole consciousness as a Man and as the Son of God.* Think of the sick people He touches and cures, of the death of Lazarus which moves Him so deeply and makes Him weep, of His long conversation with the Samaritan woman, the way He received the adulterous woman, His dialogue with the rich young man, His accompanying the disciples of Emmaus, etc. *Christ's*

relationships are based on the sense of the person accepted such as he is, with his limits and his riches, his unique character, his interiority and his freedom. He always treats persons as subjects and never as objects.

The personalistic attitude of Jesus, imbued with humility, poverty and trust, enables Him to have a loving knowledge of each one. He draws people to Himself; because He believes in man and desires his complete advancement, He wishes to set him on his way until he discovers or finds again his dignity as a child of God. Christ embodies perfectly the well-known saying of Mounier: "To be is to love." All without exception, we greatly need to contemplate Christ often. *It is He, the Word of God, the image by nature, the perfect witness of the trinitarian mystery, who can reveal to all who were created in the image of God the secret of a personalized and personalizing existence. The apostolate of Christian homes,* while giving a rightful place to human sciences, *must first of all teach married couples, and all the members of the little domestic Church, to see how God loves.*

RESPONSIBLE PARENTHOOD

4. It is against this background panorama that it is possible to meditate on *the family, the source of life, life received indefinitely and transmitted indefinitely.* On last October 12, in the framework of the Sunday specially consecrated to praying for the Synod, very moving testimonies were given by some families of America, the Netherlands, and Italy. These parents spoke of the deep joys that their numerous children bring them. They far outweigh worries and obligations. Yes, if the spouses love each other, they want as many children as

they can rear. *For procreation should not take place except to bring up well.*

That having been said, Christian families can legitimately question themselves about the meaning they give to responsible parenthood. Living in societies which support the planning of births—alas, by every kind of means—are they not contaminated by a concept of responsibility in which the pursuit of a free and comfortable life plays an important, if not predominant, part? Spouses who try to establish person-to-person relations with each other, and who remain in communion with God who called them to this noble vocation of conjugal and procreative love, must consider all that they are and all that they have as so many gifts received from the Lord, and remember the parable of the talents. He who has received five talents owes it to himself to bring back five more. He who has received only one must take care not to bury it but to work with this talent. *In short, if Christian families have to take their place with ease in their times, they must equally, without pharisaism, oppose ideas and morals that lead to decadence and even to the death of man and civilization.* They must contribute to giving back to the present-day world *the zest for life.*

INTERPERSONAL RELATIONS

5. Interpersonal relations within the family sanctuary should also rebound outside, otherwise the Christian home would run the risk of being a refuge, an ivory tower. Deciding to love each other "according to Christ," *all young Christian couples set out to achieve a conjugal and family lifestyle which will consist in a great openness to their future children, their family,*

their friends, their neighbors and their companions at work. They enter the dynamism of a love which wishes to be more and more universal. Parents and children will certainly receive a great deal by bringing to the various sectors of society what they can and must bring it, in appropriate commitments. They furnish and humanize the immense workyard of creation, which is always in the pain of childbirth.

Acting in this way, the domestic Church becomes a visible sign of God among men. *Parents and young people give the world not only the hope but the certainty that with Jesus Christ we have been given everything.* Looking at how Christian couples and their children live, the men of today must be able to catch a glimpse of the universal love of God.

GOD IS WITH YOU

6. In these days in Rome, in the course of masterly lectures, fervent liturgical celebrations, friendly exchanges, personal time for prayer, you have breathed a vivifying air—the air that braces the mountaineer who draws oxygen deep into his lungs as he climbs and discovers marvelous panoramas, without however forgetting anything of the realities of daily life. You feel renewed. Your hearts and minds filled with wonder, you have again discovered how great the sacrament of marriage is! It sets you, frail and sinful as you are and always will be, close to God, nay more, in His trinitarian mystery as in the mystery of the Word Incarnate.

Dear Catholic families of France, continue your mission confidently! God is with you, especially in the Pasch of Jesus Christ, always able to help you to face the daily sacrifices which are this death to yourselves, for a new life with the other and for the other.

NUMEROUS ACTIVITIES

7. As for the methods of your family action, within your family associations and outside, they are numerous, even if it is not possible to carry out all of them immediately and everywhere: the formation of educator-couples, centers of preparation for marriage, talks with parents, spiritual weekends, the elaboration of a statute for the family, political action, etc. Give proof, on your side, of creativeness and boldness, wisdom and solidarity. Appeal to newlyweds to enlarge and renew your numbers. Do not forget, moreover, all the other movements working for the family. Concerted action is more effective than dispersed action. Remain in sincere and trustful dialogue with your bishops and with the family apostolate authorities they have set up. An important aspect of my pontifical ministry is to stimulate the People of God to unity in the diversity of charisms and services.

MARY, OUR MOTHER

8. Before blessing you, I invite you to pray together. We are going to turn to Mary, our Mother. I am sure that the children here present pray to her often. And you parents, you set great store by training them, from the earliest age, to prayer, to religious acts, to the Good News of the Gospel. Even better, you deepen your faith with them and pray with them. Let us ask Mary to lead you to full knowledge of her Son Jesus, to be His disciples and His apostles.

Hail, Mary, full of grace, the Lord is with you; blessed are you among women, and blessed is the fruit of your womb, Jesus. Holy Mary, Mother of God, pray for us sinners, now, and at the hour of our death. Amen!

FATHERHOOD
AND THE FAMILY

On March 19, 1981, the Holy Father spent a very busy day at Terni. After the morning spent with the workers of the Terni steelworks in their factories, the Holy Father dedicated the afternoon to the rest of the population of Terni and the neighboring areas. The central moment of this second phase of the Pope's visit to the Umbrian town was the concelebration of the Eucharist, presided over by the Pope at the "L. Liberati" Stadium. Surrounded by 130 priest concelebrants, seven concelebrating bishops of Umbria, and a multitude of faithful, John Paul II delivered the following homily.

1. "Blessed are those who dwell in your house (Lord), ever singing your praise" (Ps. 83[84]:4).
Dear brothers and sisters!

After this morning's meeting at your place of work, we are now gathered in this large stadium to participate in the Eucharist. Once more I wish to express gratitude to you, because on the day on which the Church venerates St. Joseph, "a just man," who worked in Nazareth at the carpenter's bench, I had the privilege of meeting you in one of the factories where there are the workbenches of so many men residing in Terni and in the neighboring localities. That meeting was centered on the great problem of human work, to which this day particularly directs our thoughts and our hearts.

I greet you here for the second time in a fuller circle: accompanied by your families, your wives and children, relatives, neighbors and acquaintances. Joseph of Nazareth, "a just man," whose solemnity permits us to look with the eyes of faith at the great cause of human work—is simultaneously head of the home and head of the family: of the Holy Family, just as each of you, my brothers and sisters, is a husband and father, a wife and mother, responsible for the family and for the home. *There is a close connection between work and the family: between your work and your family.* St. Joseph is, with a special right, the patron saint of this bond. And so it is a good thing that, after our morning meeting which saw us gathered round your workbenches, we are able to meet here to dedicate the Holy Mass of the Solemnity of St. Joseph to families. To every family and to all families.

I wish to invite more cordially precisely these families to the eucharistic community, which expresses our family unity with God, the Father of Jesus Christ and our Father—and at the same time manifests the reciprocal unity of men, especially those who constitute one family.

ILLUSTRIOUS MARTYRS OF THIS REGION

2. The Eucharist manifests and realizes the family unity of the whole Church. To take part in the sacrifice of Christ, to nourish herself on His body and His blood, the Church gathers as a family at the table of the Divine Word and at the table of the Lord's Bread.

Today, the whole Church of Terni, Narni and Amelia participates in a particular way in this solemn eucharistic assembly.

I wish to greet this Church cordially as the family of the People of God with Bishop Santo Bartolomeo Quadri, who is its pastor, and with the whole presbyterium. I greet the members of the chapters, the educators of the seminary, the parish priests and their collaborators. I also greet the men and women religious of the orders and congregations, who are carrying out their work in the area, making their valuable contribution to the building up of the People of God. I address a respectful thought to the civil authorities, who wished to honor this celebration of ours with their presence.

I wish to reserve a word of greeting for the representatives of the parish of Castelnuovo di Conza, which was hit by the earthquake, and with whom the faithful of this land have commendably established a twinning of solidarity. I also greet with particular cordiality the lay people engaged in the apostolate, especially those who have agreed to take an active part in the various kinds of associations operating both at the diocesan and at the parochial level. And I greet the young, whom I see present in such large numbers: may they always succeed in keeping their hearts open to the values proclaimed in the Gospel, committing themselves to building on them a future more worthy of man. A greeting, finally, to all the faithful of the diocesan communities who, in the daily accomplishment of their family and social tasks, bear witness before their brothers and sisters to the strength of the Christian convictions.

The Churches of Terni, Narni and Amelia can pride themselves on ancient traditions of faith, sealed by the blood of illustrious martyrs: Valentine, Giovenale, and Firmina are names well known to you, which evoke the memory of difficult times, in which adherence to Christ not infrequently involved the sacrifice of one's life. May the example of dauntless fortitude that your holy patrons have left you as a lasting heritage be, for every child of this land, a constant incentive to that courageous consistency of life, without which it is impossible to feel and be truly Christians. Following the example of those ancient Christians who died for their Faith, may you also be able to live your Faith today!

JOSEPH OF NAZARETH

3. The reading of the Gospel according to St. Matthew invites us to meditate on a particular moment in the life of Joseph of Nazareth, a moment full of divine content and at the same time of profound human truth. We read: "Now the birth of Jesus Christ took place in this way. When his mother Mary had been betrothed to Joseph, before they came together she was found to be with child of the Holy Spirit" (Mt. 1:18). When we listen to these words, there come to mind those other well-known words which we recite daily in the morning, noon and evening prayer: "The Angel of the Lord declared unto Mary and she conceived of the Holy Spirit."

Through the Holy Spirit, the Son of God was conceived in order to become a man, the Son of Mary. This was the mystery of the Virgin, who replied to the words of the Annunciation: "Behold, I am the handmaid of the Lord; let it be done to me according to your word" (Lk. 1:38).

And so it happened: "The Word became flesh and dwelt among us" (Jn. 1:14). And above all He came to dwell in the womb of the Virgin who—remaining a virgin—became a mother: "She was found to be with child of the Holy Spirit" (Mt. 1:18).

This was Mary's mystery. Joseph did not know this mystery. He did not know that in her whose bridegroom he was, even though, in obedience to Jewish law, he had not yet received her under his roof, there had been fulfilled that promise of faith made to Abraham, of which St. Paul speaks in the second reading today. That is, that there had been fulfilled in her, in Mary of the family of David, the prophecy which the prophet Nathan had once addressed to David. The prophecy and the promise of faith, whose fulfillment was awaited by the whole people, the Israel of divine election, and the whole of humanity.

This was Mary's mystery. Joseph did not know this mystery. She could not transmit it to him, because it was a mystery beyond the capacity of the human intellect and the possibilities of human language. It was not possible to transmit it by any human means. It was only possible to accept it from God—and believe. Just as Mary believed.

Joseph did not know this mystery and for this reason he suffered a great deal inwardly. We read: "Her husband Joseph, being a just man and unwilling to put her to shame, resolved to divorce her quietly" (Mt. 1:19).

But a certain night came when Joseph too believed. The word of God was addressed to him and the mystery of Mary, his bride and wife, became clear for him. He believed that, lo, the promise of faith made to Abraham and the prophecy that King David had heard, had been fulfilled. (Both Joseph and Mary were of the family of David.)

"Joseph, son of David, do not fear to take Mary your wife, for that which is conceived in her is of the Holy Spirit; she will bear a son, and you shall call his name Jesus, for he will save his people from their sins" (Mt. 1:20-21).

"When Joseph woke from sleep—the Evangelist concludes—he did as the angel of the Lord commanded him" (Mt. 1:24).

4. We, gathered here, hear these words—and we venerate Joseph, a just man. Joseph, of the house of David, who loved Mary most deeply, because he accepted her whole mystery. We venerate Joseph in whom there is reflected more fully than in all earthly fathers the Fatherhood of God Himself. We venerate Joseph who built the family house on earth for the Eternal Word just as Mary gave him a human body. "The Word became flesh and dwelt among us" (Jn. 1:14).

From this great mystery of faith let us direct our thoughts to our homes, to so many couples and families. Joseph of Nazareth is a particular revelation of the dignity of human fatherhood! Joseph of Nazareth, the carpenter, the man of work. Think of that, you, precisely you men of work of Terni, Narni, Amelia and of the whole of Italy, the whole of Europe and of the whole world.

The family rests on the dignity of human fatherhood—on the responsibility of the man, husband and father, as also on his work. Joseph of Nazareth bears witness to this for us.

Are not the words that God speaks to him: "Joseph, son of David, do not fear to take Mary your wife" (Mt. 1:20), addressed to each of you? Dear brothers, husbands and fathers of a family! "Do not fear to take...." Do not give up! It was said at the beginning: "Therefore a man leaves his father and his mother and cleaves to his wife" (Gn. 2:24). And Christ adds: "What therefore God has joined together, let not man put asunder" (Mk. 10:9). *The unity of the family, its stability, is one of the fundamental blessings of man and of society. At the basis of family unity there is the indissolubility of mar-*

riage—if man, if society seek the ways that deprive marriage of its indissolubility and the family of its unity and stability, then they cut off, as it were, the very root of its health, and deprive themselves of one of the fundamental goods on which human life is built.

Dear brothers! May that voice which Joseph of Nazareth heard during that decisive night of his life always reach you, in particular when the danger of the destruction of the family looms up. "Do not fear to persevere!" "Do not give up!" Behave as that just man did.

HUMAN FATHERHOOD FINDS ITS MODEL IN JOSEPH

5. Joseph, son of David, do not fear to take Mary and that which is conceived in her (cf. Mt. 1:20). So God the Father says to the man with whom, in a way, He shares His fatherhood. *God, dear brothers, in a sense, shares His fatherhood with each of you.* Not in the mysterious and supernatural way in which He did with Joseph of Nazareth.... And, yet every fatherhood on earth, every human fatherhood takes its beginning from Him, and finds its model in Him. *Your human fatherhood, dear brothers, is always connected with motherhood. And what is conceived in the womb of the woman-mother unites you spouses, husband and wife, with a particular bond that God the Creator of man blessed right "from the beginning."* This is the bond of fatherhood and motherhood, which is formed from the moment when the man, the husband, finds in the motherhood of the woman the expression and confirmation of his human fatherhood.

Fatherhood is responsibility for life: for the life first conceived in the woman's womb and then born, in order that a new man, who is blood of your blood and flesh of your flesh, may be revealed. God who says: "Do not abandon the woman, your wife," says at the same time: "receive the life conceived in her!" Just as He said to Joseph of Nazareth, although Joseph was not the blood father of Him who was conceived of the Holy Spirit in the Virgin Mary.

God says to every man: "Accept the life conceived of you! Do not allow it to be suppressed!" God says this with the voice of His commandments, with the voice of the Church. But He says so above all with the voice of conscience. The voice of human conscience. This voice is univocal, in spite of everything that is done to prevent people from listening to it, and to stifle it; despite everything that is done, that is, so that man and woman will not listen to this simple and clear voice of conscience.

Men of work, men of hard work, know this simple voice of conscience. What they feel most deeply is precisely that bond which unites work and the family. Work is for the family, since work is for man (and not vice versa)—and precisely the family, first and above all the family, is the specific place of man. It is the environment in which he is conceived, is born and matures; the environment for which he assumes the most serious responsibility, in which he fulfills himself daily; the environment of his earthly happiness and human hope. And so today, on St. Joseph's day, knowing the hearts of the workers, their honesty and responsibility, I express the conviction that precisely they will assure and consolidate these two fundamental goods of man and society: the unity of the family and respect for the life conceived under the mother's heart.

BLESSINGS ON YOUR HOMES
AND FAMILIES

6. "Blessed are those who dwell in your house, Lord" (cf. Ps. 83[84]:4).

I wish you happiness, dear brothers and sisters. I wish you that happiness that springs from a pure conscience. I wish you that happiness that the home offers. From the house of Joseph, Mary and Jesus in Nazareth, from that modest workbench, joined to it, I draw in thought and in the heart a continuous line, as it were, as far as these modern workyards of industrial work in which you toil—and I extend it further: to your homes, to your families. May the happiness that comes from God reign in them. May it be stronger than all the ordeals of life, from which man is never free on earth. And above all may man mature in your homes, in your families, according to the specific extent of his dignity.

Of the dignity given to him by Jesus of Nazareth.... Jesus of whom people spoke as "the carpenter's son" (Mt. 13:55). While He was of the same substance as the Father, the Son of God became incarnate and was born as a Man from the Virgin Mary, of the Holy Spirit.

And He grew in Nazareth at Joseph's side, under his watchful and solicitous eye.

DIGNITY AND RIGHTS
OF WOMAN

1,200 parents taking part in the Fifth International Congress of the Family were received in audience by the Holy Father on November 8, 1980. John Paul II delivered the following address.

Ladies and gentlemen,

1. It is a joy for me to welcome so many families from various countries, immediately after the Synod dedicated to the role of the family. Welcome to this house, which has already received you several times.

You are convinced Christian men and women, resolved to promote and sustain the family as the first and natural place of education. You nourish this conviction in a solid faith and in the light of the teaching of the Church: on this matter, the texts of the Second Vatican Council are calculated to guide your reflection and your action as well as possible. You develop a certain number of far-reaching initiatives to help parents in their role as educators, inviting them to deepen their formation in this matter, by appealing to the best of themselves and to the advice of competent experts. To ensure more effective and universal witness and collaboration, you set up the International Foundation of the Family two years ago.

At that time, I had the opportunity to recall to you everything that could contribute to human and Christian education in the family. The recent Synod of Bishops dealt with this subject at length and the final message of the Fathers echoed it, so that I do not need to return to it in detail this morning.

THEME OF THE CONGRESS

2. For this Fifth Congress, you have studied the subject: "The family and the status of woman." A considerable part was reserved for lectures given by women experts, on subjects about which they can speak from experience.

I am very happy that you have tackled this fundamental and delicate subject, for it deserves to be dealt with in depth, with wisdom, realism, and without fear. Not only is our civilization very sensitive, sometimes hypersensitive, to it, but it corresponds to a real need, for the upheavals in social life and the movement of ideas bring forth many challenges and passions in this field. In fact, God be thanked, many women have fully developed their gifts in their concrete lives and have brought about the development of those around them: we had marvelous testimonies of this at the Synod. But a certain number of women rightly feel the need to be understood better, in their dignity as a person, in their rights, in the value of the tasks which are customarily theirs, in their aspiration to realize fully their feminine vocation within the family, but also in society. Some are weary and almost crushed by so many worries and burdens, without finding sufficient understanding and aid. *Some suffer and regret being relegated to tasks which they are told are secondary ones. Some are tempted to seek a solution in movements which claim to "liberate" them, although it would be necessary to ask what liberation it is a question of, and not to mean by this word emancipation from what is their specific vocation as mothers and wives, or imitation, leading to uniformity, of the way in which the male partner finds fulfillment.* And yet all this evolution and turmoil show clearly that there is a real feminine advancement to be pursued, in many respects. The family of course, but also the whole of society and ecclesial communities, need the specific contributions of women.

FUNDAMENTAL EQUALITY

3. It is essential, therefore, to begin by strengthening woman with a deeper study of a certain number of considerations: *her fundamental equality in dignity with man in God's plan, as the Synod has done* and as I dwell upon every Wednesday; what qualifies her as a human person as compared with man in order to live in a personal communion with him; her vocation as a daughter of God, a wife and mother; her appeal to take part in a free and responsible way in the great tasks of today, contributing the best of herself; and, for this reason, her capacity and her duty of developing her personality fully: apprenticeship in competences, training in the spirit of service, deepening of her faith and her prayer, from which she will make others benefit.

You are right to contemplate the multiple possibilities of the qualified contribution of woman in the various sectors of social and professional life, where her presence would be so beneficial for a more human world and where she herself would find an additional blossoming of her gifts, especially in certain periods of her life. The problem is still open, and, in every country, it offers the opportunity for much discussion on practical ways and means, when it is a question of woman's work outside her home. Many aspects come into play here. They must be contemplated serenely. Without dealing further with this complex matter today, we must take two other considerations into account all the same.

COURAGE, INGENUITY AND HOLINESS

4. *Care must be taken that woman is not, for financial reasons, necessarily tied down to work that is too heavy and hours of work that are too long, in addition to all her responsibilities as homemaker and educator of her children.* Society, as we said at the end of the Synod, should make the effort to organize itself differently.

But above all, and your Congress seems to have emphasized it well, it must be taken into consideration that the commitments of woman at all levels of family life also constitute an unequalled contribution to the future of society and the Church, a contribution which cannot be neglected without great harm to the latter as well as to the woman herself, whether it is a question of the conditions surrounding motherhood, the necessary intimacy with her little ones, the education of children and of the young, the attentive and prolonged dialogue with them, the care to be taken over the many necessities of the home, in order that the latter may be welcoming, cozy, comforting, on the affective plane, and educative on the cultural and religious plane. *Who would dare to deny that in many cases the stability and success of the family, its human and spiritual development, owe a great deal to this presence of the mother in the home.* It is, therefore, a real professional work which deserves to be recognized as such by society; it calls, moreover, for courage, responsibility, ingenuity and holiness.

It is a question, therefore, of helping women to become aware of this responsibility and of all the gifts of femininity that God has put in them, for the greater good of the family and of society. Thought must also be given to women who are suffering from frustrations or precarious conditions, to help them by getting them to help those around them.

"DOMESTIC CHURCH"

5. Finally, dear friends, what you are trying to do within the foundation that you have set up, many other associations or family movements are also trying to carry out, in a complementary way. Moreover, the family, the cell of society and the "domestic Church," is not an aim in itself; it must make it possible to introduce the young little by little into wider educational communities. This means that all initiatives in this field must not remain in ignorance of one another, far less withdraw into themselves, but they must work in the same direction, in trustful union with the pastors of the Church, so that families may play their role fully and integrate the dynamism of their riches into pastoral life and the apostolate of Christian communities and in the prophetic witness to be given to the world.

May your families, in joy as well as in hardship, be a reflection of God's love! May the Virgin Mother, contemplated and prayed to within each Christian family, lead you along the way to her Son and open you up to the light and power of the Holy Spirit, in peace! I willingly bless all the members of your families, husbands and wives, children and young people, grandparents. And I also bless the couples who are dear to you and who are relying on your witness.

IRREPLACEABLE ROLE
OF THE SICK IN GOD'S
PLAN OF SALVATION

On February 11, 1981, the Holy Father concelebrated in the Vatican Basilica Holy Mass for the sick and pilgrims of UNITALSI and of the Roman Work of Pilgrimages on the occasion of the liturgical commemoration of the first apparition of the Virgin to Bernadette Soubirous. John Paul II delivered the following homily.

1. "Blessed are you among women, and blessed is the fruit of your womb!" (Lk. 1:42) The words addressed by Elizabeth to the Blessed Virgin on the day of the visitation rise spontaneously to our lips while, gathered in communion of faith and love round the altar of Christ, we bear witness to our gratitude to the heavenly Mother for what she has done and continues to do in that "spiritual crossroads" of the modern world, which is the city of Lourdes.

I wish, in the first place, to address my cordial greeting to all those present at this Eucharistic Celebration, promoted by the Roman Work of Pilgrimages and by UNITALSI. In particular my greeting is addressed to you, Your Eminence, to the bishops, to the priests who, with the help of willing lay people, promote this highly meritorious form of pastoral work; and then to those who have been to Lourdes on pilgrimage and who have wished to meet again in this basilica this afternoon, to relive, as it were, the unforgettable emotions felt in that place of grace. I greet the sick, who are the privileged guests of this prayer meeting. With them I greet all those who have generously offered themselves to ensure the necessary assistance; and then all those who are participating in this Eucharist to express their devotion to the Virgin and also to manifest their solidarity with so many suffering brothers and sisters.

MARY'S GREETING BRINGS JOY

2. Mary is spiritually present among us: we heard her voice reecho in the Gospel page just proclaimed. We look at her with the same eyes with which Elizabeth looked at her, when she saw her arrive hurriedly and heard her greeting: "When the voice of your greeting came to my ears, the babe in my womb leaped for joy" (Lk. 1:44).

How could we fail to accept this first call to reflection? Elizabeth's start of joy emphasizes the gift that can be contained in a mere greeting, when it comes from a heart full of God. How often can the darkness of loneliness, oppressing a soul, be dispelled by the shining ray of a smile and a kind word!

A good word is soon said; yet sometimes we find it difficult to utter. We are restrained by fatigue, we are distracted by worries, we are checked by a feeling of coldness or selfish indifference. *Thus it happens that we may pass by persons, although we know them, without looking at their faces and without realizing how often they are suffering from that subtle, wearing sorrow which comes from feeling ignored.* A cordial word, an affectionate gesture would be enough, and something would at once awaken in them: a sign of attention and courtesy can be a breath of fresh air in the stuffiness of an existence oppressed by sadness and dejection. Mary's greeting filled with joy the heart of her elderly cousin Elizabeth.

VIRTUE OF FAITH

3. "Blessed is she who believed that there would be a fulfillment of what was spoken to her from the Lord" (Lk. 1:45). So said Elizabeth, answering our Lady's greeting. They are words dictated by the Holy Spirit (cf. Lk. 1:41). They highlight Mary's main virtue: faith. The Fathers of the Church stopped to reflect on the meaning of this virtue in the spiritual life of the Virgin and they did not hesitate to express evaluations which may seem surprising to us. Let it suffice to quote St. Augustine for them all: "Her relationship as mother would not have benefited Mary in any way, if she had not borne Christ more richly in her heart than in her body" (De Sancta Virgine, 3:3).

Faith permitted Mary to approach fearlessly the unexplored abyss of God's plan of salvation: it was not easy to believe that God could "become flesh" and come to "dwell among us" (cf. Jn. 1:14), that is, that *He wished to conceal Himself in the insignificance of our daily life, donning our human frailty, subject to so many and such humiliating conditions.* Mary dared to believe in this "impossible" plan; she trusted the Almighty and became the main collaborator of that admirable divine initiative which reopened our history to hope.

The Christian too is called to such an attitude of faith, which leads him to look courageously "beyond" the possibilities and limits of the purely human event. He knows he can rely on God, who, to affirm His own sovereign freedom with regard to human conditions, not infrequently chooses what is weak and despised in the world to shame the wise and the strong, "so that no human being might boast in the presence of God" (1 Cor. 1:29).

In the bimillenary history of the Church, sensational confirmation can be cited of this extraordinary way of acting that God has, *which continues to leave puzzled those who seek merely human explanations of the designs of Providence.* Let it suffice to mention only the name of St. Bernadette. *But incomparably more numerous are the happenings whose social importance remains hidden for the present: it is the immense host of souls who have spent their lives working in the anonymity of the home, the factory, the office; who have been consumed in the praying solitude of the cloister; who have been sacrificed in the daily martyrdom of illness.* The revelation of the Parousia will come and then it will be seen what a decisive role they played in the developments of world history, in spite of appearances to the contrary. And this, too, will be a cause of joy for the blessed who will draw from it reason for perennial praise to God, three times holy.

GRANTED TO "LITTLE ONES"

4. A foretaste of this joy is granted even here below to "little ones," to whom the Father reveals His plans (cf. Mt. 11:25). Mary leads the host of these "little ones," who have God's wisdom in their hearts. For this reason she could utter to Elizabeth the song of the *Magnificat,* which remains through the centuries the purest expression of the joy that gushes forth in every faithful soul.

It is joy that springs from amazement at the almighty power of God, who can permit Himself to carry out "great things," in spite of the inadequacy of human instruments (cf. Lk. 1:47-49). It is joy at the superior justice of God, who "has put down the mighty from their thrones, and exalted those of low degree; he has filled the hungry with good things, and the rich he has sent away" (Lk. 1:52f.). It is, finally, joy at the mercy of God who, faithful to His promises, gathers under the wing of His love the children of Abraham, "from generation to generation," assisting them in all their necessities (cf. Lk. 1:50, 54-55).

This is Mary's song. It must become the song of every day of our life: there is no human situation, in fact, that cannot find in it an adequate interpretation. The Virgin utters it while over her spirit there thicken questions about the reactions of her betrothed, who still knows nothing about the divine intervention, and above all questions about the future of this Son, over whom there hang disquieting prophetic words (cf. Is. 53).

MARY'S SENTIMENTS

5. We will be able to sing the *Magnificat* with interior exultation of spirit, if we seek to have within us Mary's sentiments: her faith, her humility, her purity. There is a beautiful expression of Ambrose, with which the holy bishop of Milan specifically exhorts us to this: "Let Mary's soul," he says, "magnify the Lord in each one; let Mary's spirit exalt God in each one; if, according to the flesh, the Mother of Christ is one only, according to the faith all souls beget Christ; for each one receives the Word of God in it, provided that it pre-

serves chastity with unblemished modesty, keeping itself spotless and free from sin" *(Expos. Ev. sec. Lucam,* II, 26).

This, beloved brothers and sisters, is what our Lady wished to say to us this afternoon. If we are able to listen to her voice, she will repeat for us, gathered round her Son's altar, the words we listened to in the first reading: "As one whom his mother comforts, so I will comfort you; you shall be comforted in Jerusalem" (Is. 66:13).

We know to what Jerusalem this refers: it is the Jerusalem "above" (Gal. 4:26), which John saw "coming down out of heaven from God, prepared as a bride adorned for her husband" (Rv. 21:2). We raise our eyes to this Jerusalem, towards which our hope strains, because in it there will finally be fulfilled the prophetic promise that we have listened to once more: "Your bones shall flourish like the grass; and it shall be known that the hand of the Lord is with his servants" (Is. 66:14).

While waiting for this supreme manifestation of the "hand of the Lord," we meanwhile continue our way along the path that divine Providence opens for us, day by day. We have with us the "Bread of Pilgrims," the sacrament of the body and blood of Christ, which is offered to us like an inexhaustible spring, from which to draw power, serenity, and confidence in every moment of our existence. *Tu qui cuncta scis et vales*—we repeat with delight—*qui nos pascis hic mortales; tuos ibi commensales, coheredes et sodales fac sanctorum civium. Amen.* (You who know and weigh all things, who feed us mortals here; make us yours there, equals, coheirs, and companions of the holy citizens. Amen.)

THE CROSS OF SUFFERING

On July 8, 1980, the Holy Father paid a visit to the Marituba leper colony, in Belém. The Pope delivered the following address.

Dear sons,

1. Since I announced my journey to Brazil and during the preparation of this journey, I received from various leper colonies of this country a large number of letters inviting me to visit them. God knows how much I would have liked to have done so. Coming here to Marituba, meeting you and greeting you with fatherly affection, it is as if I were visiting at this moment all the leper colonies of Brazil. May my word reach them to tell them how much I esteem them, how much I think of them and pray for them.

Blessed be God, therefore, for granting us the grace of this meeting. It is, indeed, a grace for me to be able, like the Lord Jesus whose minister and representative I am, to go to meet the poor and the sick, for whom He had a real preference. I cannot, it is true, cure bodily ills as He did, but He in His kindness will give me that ability to relieve souls and hearts in some way. In this sense *I wish this meeting to be a grace for you also*. It is in the name of Jesus that we are gathered here: may He be in our midst as He promised (cf. Mt. 18:20).

2. When persons meet for the first time and want to make friends, they usually introduce themselves. Is it necessary to do so? You already know my name and possess some facts about my person. But since I intend to make friends with you, *I will introduce myself: I come to you as a missionary sent by the Father and by Jesus to continue to proclaim the kingdom of God which begins in this world but is realized only in eternity, in*

order to consolidate the faith of my brothers, to create a deep communion among all sons of the same Church. I come as minister and unworthy Vicar of Christ to watch over His Church; as the humble Successor of the Apostle Peter, the Bishop of Rome and Pastor of the universal Church.

In a solemn moment, the Lord Jesus had declared to Simon Peter, despite the fact that, like every human creature he was weak and sinful, that He would build the Church on him, as on a firm rock (Mt. 16:18). He also promised him the keys of the kingdom with the guarantee that whatever he bound or loosed on earth would be bound or loosed in heaven (cf. Mt. 16:19). When he was about to return to the Father, it was again to Peter that He said: "Feed my lambs, feed my sheep" (cf. Jn. 21:15ff.). *I come as Peter's Successor: the heir to the mysterious and indescribable spiritual authority which had been conferred on him, but also to the tremendous responsibility entrusted to him. Like Peter, I accepted to be the universal Pastor of the Church, eager to know, love, and serve all the members of the flock entrusted to me. I am here to know you. I must say that my affection for one and all is great.* I am sure that I can help you, at least in some way.

FEEL DEEPLY INVOLVED IN THE COMMUNITY

3. And you, who are you? *For me you are first and foremost human persons, rich in the immense dignity which the state of person gives you; rich, each one, in the personal, unique, and unrepeatable character with which God made him.* You are persons redeemed by the blood of Him whom I like to call, as I did in my first let-

ter written to the whole Church and to the world, the "Redeemer of man." You are sons of God, known and loved by Him. You are now, and henceforth you will always be, my friends, very dear friends. As to friends, I would like to leave you a message on the occasion of this meeting which divine Providence enables me to have with you.

4. My first word cannot but be one of comfort and hope. *I know very well that, under the weight of illness, we are all exposed to the temptation of losing heart. One often wonders sadly: why have I fallen ill? What wrong have I done to deserve it? A look at Jesus Christ in His earthly life and a look of faith, in the light of Jesus Christ, at our own situation, change our way of thinking.* Christ, the innocent Son of God, knew suffering in His own flesh. The passion, the cross, death on the cross, were terrible ordeals: as the prophet Isaiah had announced, He was disfigured, no longer having a human appearance (Is. 53:2). He did not veil or conceal His suffering; in fact, when it was most atrocious, He asked the Father to remove the cup from Him (cf. Mt. 26:39). But the depths of His heart were revealed by the words: "Not my will, but thine be done" (Lk. 22:42). *The Gospel and the whole of the New Testament tell us that, accepted and lived in this way, the cross became redemptive.*

Your life is no different. *Illness is truly a cross, sometimes a heavy cross, an ordeal that God permits in a person's life, within the unfathomable mystery of a plan that escapes our ability to understand.* But it must not be regarded as a blind fatality. Nor is it necessarily and in itself a punishment. It is not something that destroys without leaving anything positive. On the contrary, even when it weighs on the body, *the cross of ill-*

ness borne in union with that of Christ becomes a source of salvation, of life, or of resurrection for the sick person himself and for others, for the whole of mankind. Like the Apostle Paul, you too can affirm that you complete in your bodies what is lacking in Christ's afflictions, for the sake of the Church (cf. Col. 1:24).

I am sure that, seen in this light, illness, even if it is painfully and humanly mortifying, brings with it seeds of hope and new comfort.

5. My second word is a request, but even more an invitation and an incentive: do not isolate yourselves because of your sickness. All those who with dedication, love, and competence look after you, even perhaps dedicating all their talent, time, and energies to you, insist on saying that nothing is better than feeling deeply involved in the community of other brothers and not isolated from it. We say in a loud voice to these brothers, with the strength of all our conviction: *make an effort to get to know your brother lepers, be close to them, welcome them, cooperate with them, accept and bring forth their cooperation.* But to you, too, we must say: do not refuse for any reason to take your place in the environment that surrounds you and that opens up to you. Feel that you are members, to the highest possible extent, of the human community, which is becoming more and more aware that it needs you, as it needs each of its members.

You can offer this community, on the human level, the contribution of the gifts you have received from God. The field of this possible cooperation is, within natural limits, quite wide and varied. On the supernatural level, which is that of grace, I wished to remind you a moment ago that, in union with the mystery of

Christ's cross, the cross of your suffering too becomes a source of grace, life, and salvation. It would be a great pity to waste, for any reason, this source of God's grace. May it serve for many people, especially for the Church. Being in Amazonia, where missionary work is intense and fruitful, and whose fruits you too receive, I venture to ask you: make your condition as sick people a missionary act of immense significance, changing it into a source from which missionaries can draw spiritual energies for their work.

VALUABLE HELP OF YOUR SUFFERING

6. My third word is of trust: *the Pope, together with the whole Church, esteems you and loves you.* He assumes before you and with you the commitment to do everything in his power for you and on your behalf. Even if the Pope has to go off to new tasks, according to the program of this visit and of his exacting mission, he remains with you spiritually: may my dear brother Mons. Aristide Pirovano, your great friend, may the doctors, the nurses, the assistants who do everything they can for you here, be the Pope's representatives among you, doing everything that he would do and as he would do it if he could always remain here. *I, for my part, also rely on you: just as I ask for the help of the prayers of monks and sisters and so many holy persons so that the Holy Spirit may inspire and give strength to my pontifical ministry, in the same way I ask for the valuable help that can come from the offering of your sufferings and your illness.* Let this offering unite with your prayers, or better let it be changed into prayer for me, for my direct collaborators, for all those who entrust to me their afflictions and their sorrows, their needs and their intentions.

But, why not begin this prayer at once?

Lord, with the faith You have given us, we acknowledge You as God almighty, our Creator and provident Father, the God of hope in Jesus Christ our Savior, the God of love in the Holy Spirit our Comforter!

Lord, trusting in Your promises which do not pass away, we want to come to You always, and find in You relief in our suffering. However, disciples of Jesus as we are, let not our will, but Yours be done throughout our whole life!

Lord, grateful for Christ's preference for the lepers who had the good fortune to come into contact with Him, seeing ourselves in them...we also thank You for the favors we receive in everything that helps us, gives us relief, and consoles us. We thank You for the medicine and for the doctors, for the care and for the nurses, for the circumstances of life, for those who console us and who are consoled by us, for those who understand us and accept us, and for others.

Lord, grant us patience, serenity, and courage; grant that we may live a joyful charity, for love of you, toward those who are suffering more than we and toward those who though not suffering, have not grasped the meaning of life.

Lord, we want our life to be useful, we want to serve: to praise, give thanks, atone and implore with Christ, for those who worship You and for those who do not worship You in the world, and for the Church, scattered all over the earth.

Lord, through the infinite merits of Christ on the cross, a "suffering servant" and our Brother with whom we unite, we pray to You for our families, friends, and benefactors, for the successful outcome of the Pope's visit, and for Brazil. Amen.

IN YOUR OLD AGE, ACCEPT THE CROSS

On November 19, 1980, in the Cathedral in Munich, the Holy Father met with representatives of a notable part of the German populace, the elderly. The Pope offered them the following message.

My dear brothers and sisters who are advanced in age!

It fills me with special joy that during my visit to Germany I am allowed to meet with you in a special hour of prayer. I come as to familiar friends, for I know that in my service I am supported in a special way by your concern, prayer, and sacrifice. So I greet you here in the Cathedral of Our Lady in Munich with heartfelt gratitude. Especially I thank you for the profound words of welcome and for your prayer by which you accompanied me during these days. Together with you I greet all the people of your age group in your country, especially those who through radio and television are united with us in this moment. *Grüss Gott* to all of you who, longer than I, have "endured the work and heat of the day" (Mt. 20:12), who, longer than I, have exerted yourselves to meet the Lord and to serve Him in all fidelity, in the great things and in the small ones, in joy and in suffering!

1. The Pope bows with devotion before old age, and he invites all people to do the same with him. *Old age is the crown of the steps of life.* It gathers in the harvest, the harvest from what you have learned and experienced, the harvest from what you have done and achieved, the harvest from what you have suffered and undergone. As in the finale of a great symphony, all the great themes of life combine to a mighty harmony. And this harmony bestows wisdom—the wisdom which

112

young King Solomon is praying for (cf. 1 Kgs. 3:9-11) and which means more to him than power and riches, more than beauty and health (cf. Wis. 7:7, 8, 10)—the wisdom about which we read in the rules of life of the Old Testament: "How attractive is wisdom in the aged, and understanding and counsel in honorable men! Rich experience is the crown of the aged, and their boast is the fear of the Lord" (Sir. 25:5f.).

To today's older generation, that is to you, my dear brothers and sisters, this crown of wisdom is due in a very special way: some of you in two world wars had to see and to endure immense pain; many of you have thereby lost your relatives, your health, your profession, your house and your home country; you have come to know the abyss of the human heart, *but also its ability for heroic willingness to help, and for loyalty to the Faith, as well as its power to dare a new beginning.*

Wisdom confers distance, but not a distance which stands aloof from the world; it allows people to be above things, without despising them; it allows us to see the world with the eyes—and with the heart!—of God. It allows us with God to say "yes" even to our limitations, even to our past—with its disappointments, omissions and sins. For "we know that in everything God works for good with those who love him" (Rom. 8:28). From the conciliative power of this wisdom spring up kindness, patience, understanding, and—that precious ornament of age—the sense of humor.

You yourselves know best, my dear sisters and brothers, that this precious harvest of life which the Creator has apportioned to you is not an uncontested possession. It requires vigilance, carefulness, self-control, and sometimes even a resolute battle. Otherwise it is endangered, easily to be eaten away or to be corroded by idleness, by moods, by superficiality, by arrogance, or even by bitterness. Do not lose heart; with the grace of our Lord start over and over again, and use the sources of power which He offers you: in the sacraments of the bread and of forgiveness; in the Word which comes to you in sermons and in reading and in spiritual conversation! In this place I am sure that I am allowed also in your name most cordially to thank the priests who reserve a decisive place in their work and in their hearts for the pastoral work among the aged. In this way they at the same time render the best service to their whole community; for thereby they win for it, in a sense, a legion of faithful intercessors.

Next to the priests who serve you with their pastoral work I should like to address myself to the priests of your age group. My dear confreres! The Church thanks you for your lifelong work in the vineyard of the Lord. To the younger priests Jesus says in the Gospel of John (4:38): "Others have labored, and you have entered into their labor." Most venerable priests, keep on bringing the needs of the Church before God through your priestly service of prayer—*ad Deum, qui laetificat iuventutem vestram!"* (Ps. 43:4)

A TREASURE TO THE CHURCH

2. Brothers and sisters of the older generation, you are a treasure for the Church, you are a blessing for the world! *How often you have to relieve the young parents, how well you know how to introduce the youngsters to the history of your family and of your home country, to the tales of your people and to the world of faith!* The young adults with their problems often find an easier way to you than to their parents' generation.

To your sons and daughters you are the most precious support in their hours of difficulty. With your advice and your engagement you cooperate in many committees, associations and initiatives of ecclesiastical and public life.

You are a necessary complement in a world which shows enthusiasm for the vitality of youth and for the power of the so-called "best years," in a world where what can be counted counts so much. You remind it that it continues building upon the diligence of those who have been young and strong earlier, and that one day it, too, will place its work in younger hands. *In you it becomes apparent that the meaning of life cannot consist in earning and spending money, that in all our external activities there has to mature something internal, and something eternal in all the temporal*—according to the words of St. Paul: "Though our outer nature is wasting away, our inner nature is being renewed every day" (2 Cor. 4:16).

Indeed, old age deserves our devotion, a devotion which also shines forth from Holy Scripture when it places before our eyes Abraham and Sara, when it calls Simeon and Anna to the Holy Family in the temple, when it calls the priests "elders" (Acts 14:23; 15:2; 1 Tm. 4:14; 5:17, 19; Ti. 1:5; 1 Pt. 5:1), when it sums up the worship of the whole of creation in the adoration of the twenty-four elders, and when finally God calls Himself: "the Ancient of Days" (Dn. 7:9, 22).

ACCEPT THE BURDEN OF OLD AGE

3. Is it possible to intone a higher song in honor of the dignity of old age? But, my dear elder listeners, I am sure you would be disappointed if the Pope would not also mention another aspect of becoming old; if he

would have brought you only—maybe unexpected—the honors, but would have failed to bring you consolation. Just as there belongs to the beautiful season in which we are, not only the harvest and the solemn splendor of color, but also the branches being stripped of their leaves, the leaves falling and decaying; not only the soft and full light, but also the wet and dreary fog; in the same way old age is not only the strong final accord or the conciliative sum of life, but also the time of fading, a time when the world becomes strange and life can turn into a burden, and the body into pain. And so I add to my call, *"Be aware of your dignity,"* the other one, *"Accept your burden."*

For most people the burden of old age means in the first place a certain frailty of the body; the senses are no longer as acute, the limbs no longer as pliable as they used to be, the organs become more sensitive (cf. Sir. 12:3f.). The things one may experience in younger years in days of sickness, often become one's daily—and nightly!—companions in old age. One is forced to give up many activities which used to be familiar and dear.

Also the memory may refuse its service: new facts are no longer received easily, and old ones fade away. *And so the world ceases to be familiar; the world of one's own family with the living and working conditions of the adults utterly changed, with the interests and forms of expression of young people so completely different, with the new learning goals and methods of the children.* The home-country becomes strange with its growing cities, the increasing density of population, and the landscape many times remodeled. The world of politics and economics turns strange, the world of social and medical care becomes anonymous and unintelligible. And even that domain where we should feel at home most of all—the Church in her life and doctrine—has become strange to many of you through her effort to meet the demands of the time and the expectations and needs of the younger generation.

By this world which is hard to understand, you feel misunderstood and often enough rejected. Your opinion, your cooperation, your presence is not asked for —that is how you feel and how, unfortunately, sometimes it actually is.

A REDEEMING SUFFERING

4. What can the Pope say to this? How shall I console you? I do not want to take it too easily. I do not want to belittle the anxieties of old age, your weaknesses and illnesses, your helplessness and loneliness. But I would like to see them in a conciliatory light—in the light of our Savior "who for us did sweat blood, who for us was scourged at the pillar, who for us was crowned with thorns." In the trials of old age He is the companion of your pain, and you are His companions on His way to the cross. *There is no tear you have to shed alone,* and none you shed in vain (cf. Ps. 5:9). By His suffering He has redeemed suffering, and through your suffering you cooperate in His salvation (cf. Col. 1:24). Accept your suffering as His embrace and turn it into a blessing by accepting it from the hand of the Father who in His inscrutable, yet unquestionable wisdom and love is using just this to bring about your perfection. It is in the furnace that metal turns into gold (cf. 1 Pt. 1:7); it is in the press that the grape becomes wine.

In this spirit—which God alone can give us—it becomes also easier to be understanding with those who through negligence, carelessness, heedlessness, contribute to cause our need, and it becomes possible for us to forgive also those who knowingly and even intentionally make us suffer without, however, completely conceiving how much pain they cause us. "Father, forgive them, for they do not know what they are doing!" (Lk. 23:34) Also with regard to us has this word been spoken which alone brings salvation.

MODEL IN ST. ELIZABETH

5. In this Spirit—whom we want to implore together and for each other in this hour—we are also going to be awake and grateful for all loving thoughts, words, and deeds which we receive each day, which we so easily get used to and which therefore we easily take for granted and which we overlook. We are celebrating today the feast of St. Elizabeth, a saint your nation has given to the whole world as a symbol of self-sacrificing charity. She is the sublime example and great patroness of all who serve their fellow creatures in need—be it through their profession or on a volunteer basis; be it in the circle of their friends and relatives—and who meet Christ in them, whether they know it or not. That, my dear elderly people, is the reward which you give to those for whom you dislike being a burden. *You are the occasion for them to meet the Lord, the opportunity to outgrow themselves, and by your turning to them you let them share in the already mentioned fruits of life which God allowed to mature in you!* Therefore do not bury your requests in a timid, disappointed or reproachful heart, but express them in all naturalness—being convinced of your own dignity and of the good in the hearts of the others. And be happy over

each opportunity to practice that royal word of "thank you" which rises from all altars and which is going to fill our eternal beatitude.

And so I am sure that I will be allowed together with you to thank all those people who work for the well-being of the older generation, for their well-being in body and mind, in order to help them find a fulfilled life and a permanent home in society, all those who work in the many ecclesiastic, civil and public organizations, associations, and initiatives, on a communal or on a higher level, in legislature and administration, or just on a private basis. I commend especially the fact that working for the elderly people is becoming more and more working with the elderly people.

SOMEONE STILL POORER

6. With this I turn again to you, my elderly brothers and sisters, and to the consolation you expect from me. There is a saying: "When you are lonely, go and visit somebody who is still lonelier than you!" This wisdom I would like to recommend to you. *Open your mind for those companions on your road who in whatever respect are in a still poorer condition than you, whom you can help in one way or another—through a conversation, through giving a hand, some favor, or at least your expressed sympathy!* I promise to you in the name of Jesus: in this you are going to find strength and consolation (cf. Acts 20:35).

In this way you simultaneously practice in small matters what we all are as a whole. *We are one body in many members: those who bring help and those who receive help;* those who are more healthy and those who are more sick; those who are younger and those who are older; those who have stood the test of life, those who are still standing it, and those who just are growing into it; those who are young and those who once have been young; those who are old and those who are going to be old tomorrow. We all together represent the fullness of the Body of Christ, and we all together mature into this fullness—"into the perfect Man, fully mature with the fullness of Christ" (Eph. 4:13).

CONSCIOUS OF DEATH

7. The last consolation we are seeking together, my dear fellow pilgrims "in this vale of tears" *(Hail, Holy Queen)*, is the consolation in the face of death. Since our birth we have been going to meet it, but in our old age we become more conscious of its approaching from year to year—if only we do not forcefully suppress it from our thoughts and feelings. *The Creator has arranged it so that in old age accepting and standing the test of death is being prepared for, made easier and learned in an almost natural manner*, because becoming old, as we have seen, means a slow taking leave of the unbroken fullness of life, of the unimpeded contact with the world.

The great school of living and dying then brings us to many an open grave; it makes us stand at many a deathbed before it will be us around whom other people will be standing in prayer—so may God grant it. An old person has experienced such lessons of life in a greater number than young ones do, and he is seeing them with increasing frequency. That is his great advantage on the way to that great threshold which we often in a biased way conceive of as being an abyss and night.

The view across the threshold is dark from our side; but in His love God will allow those who have gone before us to accompany our lives and to surround us with care more often than perhaps we think. It has been the conviction of deep and living faith which has given to a church in this city the name of "All Souls Church." And the two German churches in Rome are called: Santa Maria in Campo Santo and Santa Maria dell'Anima. *The more the fellow beings of our visible world reach the limits of their ability to help, the more we should see the messengers of the love of God in those who already have passed the test of death and who are now waiting for us over there:* the saints, especially our personal patrons, and our deceased relatives and friends whom we hope are at home in God's mercy.

Many of you, my dear sisters and brothers, have lost the visible presence of your partner. To you I direct my pastoral admonition. Allow God ever more to be the partner of your lives; then you will also be united to the one whom He gave you as a companion once upon a time and who himself now has found in God his center.

Without familiarity with God there is in the last end no consolation in death. For that is exactly what God intends with death—that at least in this one sublime hour of our life we allow ourselves to fall into His love without any other security than just this love of His. How could we show Him our faith, our hope, our love in a more lucid manner!

One last consideration in this context. I am sure it echoes the conviction of many a heart. Death itself is a consolation! Life on this earth, even if it were no "vale of tears" could not offer a home to us forever. It would turn more and more into a prison, an "exile" (*Hail, Holy Queen*). "For all that passes is just a parable!" (Goethe, *Faust II*, final chorus) And so the words of Saint Augustine which never lose their color come to our lips:

"You have created us for Yourself, Lord; and our heart is restless until it finds its rest in You!" (*Confessiones I*, 1, 1)

And so there are not those who are destined to die and those who stand in the so-called life. What is awaiting all of us is a birth, a transformation whose pains we fear with Jesus on the Mount of Olives, but whose radiant exit we already carry within ourselves since at our Baptism we have been submerged into the death and victory of Jesus (cf. Rom. 6:3-6; Col 2:12).

Together with all of you, together with you here in Our Lady's Cathedral, with you before radio and television, with all those whom I was allowed to meet in these blessed days, with all the citizens and guests of this beautiful country, with all those who believe, and for all those who are seeking, with the children and young people, with the adults and the old people, I would like in this hour of farewell to turn our meditation into prayer!

"Upon thee I have leaned from my birth; forsake me not when my strength is spent!" (Ps. 71:6, 9)

"Come to our aid with your mercy and keep us safe from temptation and sin, so that we may be full of confidence as we await the coming of our Savior Jesus Christ!" (Order of the Mass)

And here in Our Lady's Cathedral I would like to combine our prayer, which always is spoken in the Spirit of Jesus and only through Jesus arrives at the Father, with the prayer of the one who, being the first to have been saved, is our Mother and our Sister (Paul VI at the conclusion of the third session of the Council, *Insegnamenti* II, pp. 675 and 664):

"Holy Mary, Mother of God, pray for us sinners, now and at the hour of our death! Amen."

Amen. Praised be Jesus Christ!

III. The Theology of the Body

Four Brief Addresses to General
Audiences in Rome

*a) "Realization of the Value of the Body
According to the Plan of Creation,"* October 22,
1980.

*b) "St. Paul's Teaching on the Sanctity and
Respect of the Human Body,"* January 28, 1981.

*c) "The Mystery of Woman Revealed in
Motherhood,"* March 12, 1980.

*d)"The Power of Redeeming Completes the
Power of Creating,"* October 29, 1980.

REALIZATION OF THE VALUE OF THE BODY ACCORDING TO THE PLAN OF CREATION

On October 22, 1980, Pope John Paul delivered the following message to the faithful gathered in St. Peter's Square for the weekly audience.

1. At the center of our reflections, at the Wednesday meetings, there has been for a long time now the following enunciation of Christ in the Sermon on the Mount: "You have heard that it was said, 'You shall not commit adultery.' But I say to you that everyone who looks at a woman lustfully has already committed adultery with her (towards her) in his heart" (Mt. 5:27-28). These words have an essential meaning for the whole theology of the body contained in Christ's teaching. Therefore, we rightly attribute great importance to their correct understanding and interpretation. Already in our preceding reflection, we noted that the Manichaean doctrine, both in its primitive and in its later expressions, contradicts these words.

It is not possible, in fact, to see in the sentence of the Sermon on the Mount analyzed here a "condemnation" or an accusation of the body. If anything, one could catch a glimpse of a condemnation of the human heart. However, the reflections we have made so far show that, if the words of Matthew 5:27-28 contain an accusation, it is directed above all at the man of lust. With those words the heart is not so much accused as subjected to a judgment, or, better, called to a critical, in fact a self-critical, examination: whether or not it succumbs to the lust of the flesh. Penetrating into the deep meaning of the enunciation of Matthew 5:27-28, we must note, however, that the judgment contained in it about "desire," as an act of lust of the flesh, brings with it not the negation, but rather the affirmation, of the body as an element which, together with the spirit, determines man's ontological subjectivity and shares in his dignity as a person. In this way, therefore, the judgment on the lust of the flesh has a meaning essentially different from the one which the Manichaean ontology presupposes and which necessarily springs from it.

THE BODY MANIFESTS THE SPIRIT

2. *The body, in its masculinity and femininity, is called "from the beginning" to become the manifestation of the spirit.* It does so also *by means of the conjugal union of man and woman, when they unite in such a way as to form "one flesh."* Elsewhere (cf. Mt. 19:5-6) Christ defends the inviolable rights of this unity, by means of which the body, in its masculinity and femininity, assumes the value of a sign—in a way a sacramental sign. Furthermore, by warning against the lust of the flesh, *He expresses the same truth about the ontological dimension of the body and confirms its ethical meaning, consistent with His teaching as a whole.* This ethical meaning has nothing in common with the Manichaean condemnation, and is, on the contrary, deeply penetrated by the mystery of the "redemption of the body," of which St. Paul will write in the letter to the Romans (cf. Rom. 8:23). *The "redemption of the body" does not indicate, however, ontological evil as a constituent attribute of the human body, but points out only man's sinfulness, as a result of which he has, among other things, lost the clear sense of the nuptial meaning of the body, in which interior mastery and*

the freedom of the spirit is expressed. It is a question here—as we have already pointed out previously—of a "partial," potential loss, where the sense of the nuptial meaning of the body is confused, in a way, with lust, and easily lets itself be absorbed by it.

TRANSFORMATION OF CONSCIENCE AND ATTITUDES

3. The appropriate interpretation of Christ's words according to Matthew 5:27-28, as well as the "praxis" in which the authentic ethos of the Sermon on the Mount will be subsequently expressed, must be absolutely free of Manichaean elements in thought and in attitude. *A Manichaean attitude would lead to an "annihilation" of the body—if not real, at least intentional—to negation of the value of human sex, of the masculinity and femininity of the human person, or at least to their mere "toleration" in the limits of the "need" delimited by the necessity of procreation.* On the basis of Christ's words in the Sermon on the Mount, on the other hand, Christian ethos is characterized by a transformation of the conscience and attitudes of the human person, both man and woman, such as to express and realize the value of the body and of sex, according to the Creator's original plan, placed as they are in *the service of the "communion of persons," which is the deepest substratum of human ethics and culture.* Whereas, for the Manichaean mentality, the body and sexuality constitute, so to speak, an "anti-value"; for Christianity, on the contrary, they always remain a "value not sufficiently appreciated," as I will explain better further on. The

second attitude indicates what must be the form of ethos in which the mystery of the "redemption of the body" takes root, so to speak, in the "historical" soil of man's sinfulness. That is expressed by the theological formula which defines the "state" of "historical" man as *status naturae lapsae simul ac redemptae*. (The state of fallen, but at the same time redeemed, nature.)

QUESTION OF DETACHMENT

4. Christ's words in the Sermon on the Mount (Mt. 5:27-28) must be interpreted in the light of this complex truth about man. If they contain a certain "accusation" leveled at the human heart, *all the more so they address an appeal to it*. The accusation of the moral evil which "desire," born of intemperate lust of the flesh, conceals within it, is at the same time a call to overcome this evil. *And if victory over evil must consist in detachment from it* (hence the severe words in the context of Matthew 5:27-28), *it is, however, only a question of detaching oneself from the evil of the act* (in the case in question, the interior act of "lust"), *and never of transferring the negative character of this act to its object.* Such a transfer would mean a certain acceptance—perhaps not fully conscious—of the Manichaean "anti-value." *It would not constitute a real and deep victory over the evil of the act, which is evil by its moral essence, and so evil of a spiritual nature;* on the contrary, *there would be concealed in it the great danger of justifying the act to the detriment of the object* (the essential error of Manichaean ethos consists, in fact, just in this). It is clear that in Matthew 5:27-28 Christ demands detachment from the evil of "lust" (or of the

look of disorderly desire), but *His enunciation does not let it be supposed in any way that the object of that desire, that is, the woman who is "looked at lustfully," is an evil.* (This clarification seems to be lacking sometimes in some "wisdom" texts.)

KNOWING THE DIFFERENCE

5. We must, therefore, specify the difference between the "accusation" and the "appeal." Since the accusation leveled at the evil of lust is at the same time an appeal to overcome it, this victory, consequently, must be united with an effort to discover the true values of the object, in order that the Manichaean "anti-value" may not take root in man, in his conscience, and in his will. In fact, as a result of the evil of "lust," that is, of the act of which Christ speaks in Matthew 5:27-28, the object to which it is addressed constitutes for the human subject a "value not sufficiently appreciated." If, in the words of the Sermon on the Mount (Mt. 5:27-28) which have been analyzed, the human heart is "accused" of lust (or is warned against that lust), at the same time, by means of the words themselves, it is called to discover the full sense of what, in the act of lust, constitutes for him a "value that is not sufficiently appreciated." As we know, Christ said: "Everyone who looks at a woman lustfully has already committed adultery with her in his heart." "Adultery committed in the heart" can and must be understood as "devaluation," or as the impoverishment of an authentic value, as an intentional deprivation of that dignity to which the complete value of her femininity corresponds in the person in question. *The words of Matthew 5:27-28 contain a call to discover this value and this dignity, and to reassert them.* It

seems that only when the words of Matthew are understood in this way, is their semantic significance respected.

To conclude these concise considerations, it is necessary to note once more that the Manichaean way of understanding and evaluating man's body and sexuality is essentially alien to the Gospel, not in conformity with the exact meaning of the words of the Sermon on the Mount spoken by Christ. *The appeal to master the lust of the flesh springs precisely from the affirmation of the personal dignity of the body and of sex, and serves only this dignity.* Anyone who wanted to see in these words a Manichaean perspective would be committing an essential error....

TO THE YOUNG

I greet all the dear young people present here and assure them of my special affection. I call upon you always to be strong and joyful witnesses to your faith in Christ, whom the world of today needs so much. Always be proud of your Christian identity, which you must discover more and more, and the whole Church will be proud of you; she relies a great deal, in fact, both on your enthusiasm and on your sense of responsibility for the building of a more radiant future. Therefore, I bless you willingly.

TO THE SICK

A very special greeting goes to the sick people gathered here. Beloved in Christ, I thank you for your presence, always so significant. It says that you are fully part of the Church, and, in fact, are members in quite a special way. For what the suffering have in common with Christ reminds everyone that, precisely through His sufferings, He redeemed us from the alienation of sin and reestablished our communion with God. To you, therefore, goes my wish, as well as the assurance of my prayer, in order that you may be able to penetrate more and more the consoling mystery of redemption, which does not elude, but on the contrary necessarily includes, human suffering. And let my fatherly blessing accompany you.

ST. PAUL'S TEACHING
ON THE SANCTITY AND RESPECT
OF THE HUMAN BODY

After dedicating the previous week's audience to the theme of Christian unity, the Pope resumed his catechesis on the Christian concept of man at the general audience of January 28, 1981, in the Paul VI Hall.

1. St. Paul writes in the First Letter to the Thessalonians: "...this is the will of God, your sanctification: that you abstain from unchastity, that each one of you know how to control his own body in holiness and honor, not in the passion of lust like heathens who do not know God" (1 Thes. 4:3-5). And after some verses, he continues: "God has not called us for uncleanness, but in holiness. Therefore whoever disregards this, disregards not man but God, who gives His Holy Spirit to you" *(ibid.,* 4:7-8). We referred to these sentences of the Apostle during our meeting on last January 14. We take them up again today, however, because they are particularly important for the subject of our meditations.

PURITY, A CAPACITY

2. The purity of which Paul speaks in the First Letter to the Thessalonians (4:3-5, 7-8) is manifested in the fact that man "knows how to control his own body in holiness and honor, not in the passion of lust." In this formulation every word has a particular meaning and therefore deserves an adequate comment.

In the first place, purity is a "capacity," that is, in the traditional language of anthropology and ethics, an aptitude. And in this sense it is a virtue. If this ability, that is, virtue, leads to abstaining "from unchastity," that happens because the man who possesses it "knows how to control his own body in holiness and honor, not in the passion of lust." *It is a question here of a practical capacity which makes man capable of acting in a given way, and at the same time of not acting in the opposite way.* For purity to be such a capacity or aptitude, it must obviously be rooted in the will, in the very foundations of man's willing and conscious acting. Thomas Aquinas, in his teaching on virtues, sees in an even more direct way the object of purity in the faculty of sensitive desire, which he calls *appetitus concupiscibilis.* Precisely this faculty must be particularly "mastered," subordinated and made capable of acting in a way that is in conformity with virtue, in order that "purity" may be attributed to man. According to this concept, purity consists in the first place in containing the impulse of sensitive desire, which has as its object what is corporeal and sexual in man. Purity is a different form of the virtue of temperance.

MASTERY REQUIRED

3. The text of the First Letter to the Thessalonians (4:3-5) shows that the virtue of purity, in Paul's concept, consists also in mastery and overcoming of "the passion of lust"; that means that the capacity of controlling the impulses of sensitive desire, that is, the virtue of temperance, belongs necessarily to its nature. At the same time, however, the same Pauline text turns our attention to another role of the virtue of purity, to another of its dimensions which is, it could be said, more positive than negative. That is, the task of purity, which the author of the letter seems to stress above all, is not only (and not so much) abstention from "unchastity" and from what leads to it, and so abstention from

"the passion of lust," but, at the same time, the control of one's own body and, indirectly, also that of others, in "holiness and honor."

These two functions, "abstention" and "control," are closely connected and dependent on each other. Since, in fact, it is not possible to "control one's body in holiness and honor" if that abstention "from unchastity" and from what leads to it is lacking, it can consequently be admitted that control of one's body (and indirectly that of others) "in holiness and honor" confers adequate meaning and value on that abstention. This in itself calls for the overcoming of something that is in man and that arises spontaneously in him as an inclination, attraction, and also as a value that acts above all in the sphere of the senses, but very often not without repercussions on the other dimensions of human subjectivity, and particularly on the affective-emotional dimension.

MANIFESTATION OF LIFE

4. Considering all this, it seems that the Pauline image of the virtue of purity—an image that emerges from the very eloquent comparison of the function of "abstention" (that is, of temperance) with that of "control of one's body in holiness and honor"—is deeply right, complete and adequate. Perhaps we owe this completeness to nothing else but the fact that Paul considers purity not only as a capacity (that is, an aptitude) of man's subjective faculties, but, at the same time, as a concrete manifestation of life "according to the Spirit," in which human capacity is interiorly made fruitful and enriched by what Paul calls, in the letter to the Galatians 5:22, the "fruit of the Spirit." *The honor that arises*

*in man for everything that is corporeal and sexual, both
in himself and in any other person, male and female, is
seen to be the most essential power to control the body
"in holiness."* To understand the Pauline teaching on
purity, it is necessary to penetrate fully the meaning of
the term "honor," which is obviously understood here
as a power of the spiritual order. It is precisely this interior power that confers its full dimension on purity as a
virtue, that is, as the capacity of acting in that whole
field in which man discovers, within himself, the multiple impulses of "the passion of lust," and sometimes,
for various reasons, surrenders to them.

ABOUT THE HUMAN BODY

5. To grasp better the thought of the author of the
first letter to the Thessalonians, it will be a good thing to
keep in mind also another text, which we find in the first
letter to the Corinthians. Paul sets forth in it his great
ecclesiological doctrine, according to which the Church
is the Body of Christ; he takes the opportunity to formulate the following argumentation about the human
body: "...God arranged the organs in the body, each
one of them, as he chose" (1 Cor. 12:18); and further on:
"On the contrary, the parts of the body which seem to
be weaker are indispensable, and those parts of the
body which we think less honorable we invest with the
greater honor, and our unpresentable parts are treated
with greater modesty, which our more presentable parts
do not require. But God has so composed the body, giving the greater honor to the inferior part, that there may
be no discord in the body, but that the members may
have the same care for one another" *(ibid.,* 12:22-25).

WORTHY OF HONOR

6. Although the specific subject of the text in question is the theology of the Church as the Body of Christ, it can be said, however, in connection with this passage, that Paul, by means of his great ecclesiological analogy (which recurs in other letters, and which we will take up again in due time), contributes, at the same time, to deepening the theology of the body. While in the first letter to the Thessalonians he writes about control of the body "in holiness and honor," in the passage now quoted from the first letter to the Corinthians he wishes to show this human body as, precisely, worthy of honor; it could also be said that he wishes to teach the receivers of his letter the correct concept of the human body.

Therefore this Pauline description of the human body in the first letter to the Corinthians seems to be closely connected with the recommendations of the first letter to the Thessalonians: "that each one of you know how to control his own body in holiness and honor" (1 Thes. 4:4). This is an important thread, perhaps the essential one, of the Pauline doctrine on purity.

THE MYSTERY OF WOMAN REVEALED IN MOTHERHOOD

During the general audience in the Paul VI Hall on March 12, 1980, the Holy Father delivered the following address.

1. In the preceding meditation, we analyzed the sentence of Genesis 4:1 and, in particular, the term "knew," used in the original text to define conjugal union. We also pointed out that this biblical "knowledge" establishes a kind of personal archetype[1] of corporality and human sexuality. *That seems absolutely fundamental in order to understand man, who, from the "beginning," is in search of the meaning of his own body. This meaning is at the basis of the theology of the body itself.* The term "knew" (Gn. 4:1-2) synthesizes the whole density of the biblical text analyzed so far.

The "man" who, according to Genesis 4:1, "knows" the woman, his wife, for the first time, in the act of conjugal union, is, in fact, that same man who, by imposing names, that is also by "knowing," "differentiated himself" from the whole world of living beings or *animalia*, affirming himself as a person and subject. The "knowledge," of which Genesis 4:1 speaks, does not and cannot take him away from the level of that original and fundamental self-awareness. So—whatever a one-sidedly "naturalistic" mentality might say about it—in Genesis 4:1 it cannot be a question of passive acceptance of one's own determination by the body and by sex, precisely because it is a question of "knowledge"!

It is, on the contrary, a further discovery of the meaning of one's own body, a common and reciprocal discovery, just as the existence of man, whom "God created male and female" is common and reciprocal from the beginning. Knowledge, which was at the basis of man's original solitude, is now at the basis of this unity of the man and the woman, the clear perspective of which was enclosed by the Creator in the very mystery of creation (Gn. 1:27; 2:23). In this "knowledge," man confirms the meaning of the name "Eve," given to his wife, "because she was the mother of all the living" (Gn. 3:20).

MYSTERY OF FEMININITY REVEALED

2. According to Genesis 4:1, *the one who knows is the man and the one who is known is the woman-wife, as if the specific determination of the woman, through her own body and sex, hid what constitutes the very depth of her femininity.* The man, on the other hand, is the one who—after the sin—was the first to feel the shame of his nakedness, and was the first to say: "I was afraid because I was naked; and I hid myself" (Gn. 3:10). It will be necessary further to return separately to the state of mind of them both after the loss of original innocence.

Straightway, however, it should be noted that in the "knowledge," of which Genesis 4:1 speaks, the mystery of femininity is manifested and revealed completely by means of motherhood, as the text says: "she conceived and bore...." *The woman stands before the man as a mother, the subject of the new human life that is conceived and develops in her, and from her is born into the world.* Likewise, the mystery of man's masculinity, that is, the generative and "fatherly" meaning of his body, is also thoroughly revealed.[2]

BY MEANS OF THE BODY

3. The *theology of the body*, contained in the book of Genesis, is concise and sparing of words. At the same time, fundamental contents, in a certain sense primary and definitive, find expression in it. Everyone finds himself again in his own way, in that biblical "knowledge." *The constitution of the woman is different, as compared with the man; we know, in fact, today that it is different even in the deepest biophysiological determinants. It is manifested externally only to a certain extent, in the construction and form of her body.* Maternity manifests this constitution internally, as the particular potentiality of the female organism, which with creative peculiarity serves for the conception and begetting of the human being, with the help of man. "Knowledge" conditions begetting.

Begetting is a perspective, which man and woman insert in their mutual "knowledge." The latter, therefore, goes beyond the limits of subject-object, such as man and woman seem to be mutually, since "knowledge" indicates on the one side him who "knows," and on the other side her who "is known" (or vice versa). In this "knowledge" is enclosed also the consummation of marriage, the specific *consummatum*; in this way the reaching of the "objectivity" of the body, hidden in the somatic potentialities of the man and of the woman, is obtained, and at the same time the reaching of the objectivity of the man who "is" this body. *By means of the body, the human person is "husband" and "wife." At the same time, in this particular act of "knowledge,"*

*mediated by personal femininity and masculinity, also
the discovery of the "pure" subjectivity of the gift:
that is, mutual self-fulfillment in the gift, seems to be
reached.*

THEIR LIVING IMAGE

4. Procreation brings it about that "the man and
the woman (his wife)" know each other reciprocally in
the "third," sprung from them both. *Therefore, this
"knowledge" becomes a discovery, in a way a revelation
of the new man, in whom both of them, man and
woman, again recognize themselves, their humanity,
their living image.* In everything that is determined by
both of them through the body and sex, "knowledge"
inscribes a living and real content. *So "knowledge" in
the biblical sense means that the "biological" determination of man, by his body and sex, stops being something passive, and reaches the specific level and content
of self-conscious and self-determinant persons.* Therefore it involves a particular consciousness of the meaning of the human body, bound up with fatherhood and
motherhood.

EULOGY OF MOTHERHOOD

5. The whole exterior constitution of woman's
body, its particular aspect, the qualities which, with the
power of perennial attractiveness, are at the beginning
of the "knowledge," of which Genesis 4:1-2 speaks
("Adam knew Eve his wife"), are in close union with
motherhood. The Bible (and subsequently the liturgy),
with its characteristic simplicity, honors and praises
throughout the centuries "the womb that bore you and

the breasts that you sucked" (Lk. 11:27). These words constitute a eulogy of motherhood, of femininity, of the female body in its typical expression of creative love. And they are words referred in the Gospel to the Mother of Christ, Mary, the second Eve. The first woman, on the other hand, at the moment when the maternal maturity of body was revealed for the first time, when "she conceived and bore," said: "I have gotten a man with the help of the Lord" (Gn. 4:1).

WOMAN FULLY AWARE

6. These words express the whole theological depth of the function of begetting-procreating. *The woman's body becomes the place of the conception of the new man.*[3] In her womb, the conceived man assumes his specific human aspect before being born. The somatic homogeneousness of man and woman, which found its first expression in the words: "This is bone of my bones and flesh of my flesh" (Gn. 2:23), is confirmed in turn by the words of the first woman-mother: "I have gotten a man!" *The first woman, giving birth, is fully aware of the mystery of creation, which is renewed in human generation.* She is also fully aware to the creative participation that God has in human generation, His work and that of her husband, since she says: "I have gotten a man with the help of the Lord."

There cannot be any confusion between the spheres of action of the causes. *The first parents transmit to all human parents*—even after sin, together with the fruit of the tree of knowledge of good and evil and almost at the threshold of all "historical" experiences—*the fundamental truth about the birth of man in the image of God, according to natural laws.* In this new man—born of the woman-parent thanks to the man-parent—there is reproduced every time the very "image of God," of that God who constituted the humanity of the first man: "God created man in his own image; male and female he created them" (Gn. 1:27).

WITH THE LORD'S HELP

7. Although there are deep differences between man's state of original innocence and his state of hereditary sinfulness, that "image of God" constitutes a basis of continuity and unity. The "knowledge," of which Genesis 4:1 speaks, is the act which originates being, or rather, which in union with the Creator, establishes a new man in his existence. The first man, in his transcendental solitude, took possession of the visible world, created for him, knowing and imposing names of living beings *(animalia)*. The same "man," as male and female, knowing each other in this specific community-communion of persons, in which the man and woman are united so closely with each other as to become "one flesh," constitutes humanity, that is, confirms and renews the existence of man as the image of God. Every time both of them, man and woman, take up again, so to speak, this image from the mystery of creation they transmit it "with the help of the Lord God."

The words of the book of Genesis, which are a testimony of the first birth of man on earth, enclose within them at the same time everything that can and must be said of the dignity of human generation.

FOOTNOTES

1. As for archetypes, C. G. Jung describes them as "a priori" forms of various functions of the soul: perception of relations, creative fantasy. The forms fill up with content, with materials of

experience. They are not inert, but are charged with sentiment and tendency (see particularly: "Die psychologischen Aspekte des Mutterarchetypus," Eranos 6, 1938, pp. 405-409).

According to this conception, an archetype can be met with in the mutual man-woman relationship, a relationship which is based on the dual and complementary realization of the human being in two sexes. The archetype will fill up with content by means of individual and collective experience, and can trigger off fantasy, the creator of images. It would be necessary to specify that the archetype: a) is not limited to, or exalted in, physical intercourse, but includes the relationship of "knowing"; b) it is charged with tendency: desire-fear, gift-possession; c) the archetype, as proto-image ("Urbild") is a generator of images ("Bilder").

The third aspect enables us to pass to hermeneutics, in the concrete, that of texts of Scripture and of Tradition. Primary religious language is symbolic (cf. W. Stählin, *Symbolon*, 1958; I. Macquarrie, *God Talk*, 1968; T. Fawcett, *The Symbolic Language of Religion*, 1970). Among the symbols, he prefers some radical or exemplary ones, which we can call archetypal. Well, among them the Bible uses the symbol of the conjugal relationship, concretely at the level of the "knowing" described.

One of the first poems of the Bible, which applies the conjugal archetype to God's relations with His people, culminates in the verb commented on: "You shall know the Lord" (Hos. 2:22: *we yadacta 'et Yhwh*; weakened to "You will know that I am the Lord" = *wydct ky 'ny Yhwh*: Is. 49:23; 60:16; Ez. 16:62, which are the three "conjugal" poems). A literary tradition starts from here, which will culminate in the Pauline application of Eph. 5 to Christ and to the Church; then it will pass to patristic tradition and to that of the great mystics (for example "Llama de amor viva" of St. John of the Cross).

In the treatise "Grundzüge der Literatur—und Sprachwissenschaft," vol. I, München 1976, 4 ed., p. 462, archetypes are defined as follows: "Archaic images and motifs which, according to Jung, form the content of the collective unconscious common to all men; they present symbols, which, in all times and among all peoples, bring to life in a figurative way what is decisive for humanity as regards ideas, representations and instincts."

Freud, it seems, does not use the concept of archetype. He establishes a symbolism or code of fixed correspondences between present-patent images and latent thoughts. The meaning of the symbols is fixed, even if not just one; they may be reducible to an ultimate thought that is irreducible, which is usually some experience of childhood. These are primary and of sexual character (but he does not call them archetypes). See T. Todorov, *Théories du symbole*, Paris,

1977, pp. 317f; also: J. Jacoby, *Komplex, Archetyp, Symbol in der Psychologie C. G. Jungs*, Zurich 1957.

2. Fatherhood is one of the most important aspects of humanity in Holy Scripture.

The text of Genesis 5:3: "Adam...became the father of a son in his own likeness, after his image," is explicitly linked up with the narrative of the creation of man (Gn. 1:27; 5:1) and seems to attribute to the earthly father participation in the divine work of transmitting life, and perhaps also in that joy present in the affirmation: (God) "saw everything that he had made, and behold, it was very good" (Gn. 1:31).

3. According to the text of Genesis 1:26, the "call" to existence is at the same time the transmission of the divine image and likeness. Man must proceed to transmit this image, thus continuing God's work. The narrative of the generation of Seth stresses this aspect: "When Adam had lived a hundred and thirty years, he became the father of a son in his own likeness, after his image" (Gn. 5:3). Since Adam and Eve were the image of God, Seth inherits this likeness from his parents to transmit it to others.

In Holy Scripture, however, every vocation is united with a mission; so the call to existence is already predestination to God's work: "Before I formed you in the womb I knew you, and before you were born I consecrated you" (Jer. 1:5; cf. also Is. 44:1; 9:1-5).

God is the one who not only calls to existence, but sustains and develops life from the first moment of conception: "Yet thou art he who took me from the womb; thou didst keep me safe upon my mother's breasts. Upon thee was I cast from my birth, and since my mother bore me thou hast been my God" (Ps. 22:10, 11; cf. Ps. 139:13-15).

The attention of the biblical author is focused on the very fact of the gift of life. Interest in the way in which this takes place is rather secondary and appears only in the later books (cf. Jb. 10:8, 11; 2 Mc. 7:22-23; Wis. 7:1-3).

THE POWER OF REDEEMING COMPLETES THE POWER OF CREATING

On October 29, 1980, the Holy Father delivered the following address to the faithful gathered in St. Peter's Square for the weekly general audience.

1. For a long time, now, our Wednesday reflections have been centered on the following enunciation of Jesus Christ in the Sermon on the Mount: "You have heard that it was said, 'You shall not commit adultery.' But I say to you that everyone who looks at a woman lustfully has already committed adultery with her (with regard to her) in his heart" (Mt. 5:27-28). We have recently explained that the above-mentioned words cannot be understood or interpreted in a Manichaean key. They do not contain, in any way, a condemnation of the body and of sexuality. They merely contain a call to overcome the three forms of lust, and in particular the lust of the flesh. *This call springs precisely from the affirmation of the personal dignity of the body and of sexuality, and merely confirms this affirmation.*

To clarify this formulation, that is, to determine the specific meaning of the words of the Sermon on the Mount, in which Christ appeals to the human heart (cf. Mt. 5:27-28), is important not only because of "inveterate habits," springing from Manichaeanism, in the way of thinking and evaluating things, but also because of some contemporary positions which interpret the meaning of man and of morality. Ricoeur described Freud, Marx and Nietzsche as "masters of suspicion"[1] (*"Maîtres du soupçon"*), having in mind the set of systems that each of them represents, and above all, per-

144

haps, the hidden basis and the orientation of each of them in understanding and interpreting the *humanum* itself.

It seems necessary to refer, at least briefly, to this basis and to this orientation. It must be done to discover on the one hand a significant convergence, and on the other hand also a fundamental divergence, which has its source in the Bible, to which we are trying to give expression in our analyses. What does the convergence consist of? It consists of the fact that the above-mentioned thinkers, who have exercised, and still do, a great influence on the way of thinking and evaluating of the men of our time, seem substantially also to judge and accuse man's "heart." Even more, they seem to judge it and accuse it because of what, in biblical language, especially Johannine, is called lust, the three forms of lust.

THE PRIDE OF LIFE

2. Here a certain distribution of the parts could be made. In the Nietzschean interpretation, the judgment and accusation of the human heart correspond, in a way, to what is called in biblical language "the pride of life"; in the Marxist interpretation, to what was called "the lust of the eyes"; in the Freudian interpretation, on the other hand, to what is called "the lust of the flesh." The convergence of these conceptions with the interpretation of man founded on the Bible lies in the fact that, discovering the three forms of lust in the human heart, we, too, could have limited ourselves to putting that heart in a state of continual suspicion. However, the Bible does not allow us to stop here. The words of Christ according to Matthew 5:27-28 are such that, while manifesting the whole reality of desire and lust,

they do not permit us to make this lust the absolute criterion of anthropology and ethics, that is, the very core of the hermeneutics of man. In the Bible, lust in its three forms does not constitute the fundamental and perhaps even unique and absolute criterion of anthropology and ethics, although it is certainly an important coefficient to understand man, his actions, and their moral value. Also the analysis we have carried out so far shows this.

TO THE "MAN OF LUST"

3. Though wishing to arrive at a complete interpretation of Christ's words on man who "looks lustfully" (cf. Mt. 5:27-28), we cannot be content with any conception of "lust," even if the fullness of the "psychological" truth accessible to us were to be reached; we must, on the contrary, draw upon the first letter of John 2:15-16 and the "theology of lust" that is contained in it. The man who "looks lustfully" is, in fact, the man of the three forms of lust; he is the man of the lust of the flesh. Therefore he "can" look in this way and he must even be conscious that, leaving this interior act at the mercy of the forces of nature, he cannot avoid the influence of the lust of the flesh. In Matthew 5:27-28 Christ also deals with this and draws attention to it. His words refer not only to the concrete act of "lust," but, indirectly, also to the "man of lust."

ETHOS OF REDEMPTION

4. Why cannot these words of the Sermon on the Mount, in spite of the convergence of what they say about the human heart[2] with what has been expressed in

the interpretation of the "masters of suspicion," why cannot they be considered as the foundation of the aforesaid interpretation or a similar one? And why do they constitute an expression, a configuration, of a completely different ethos?—different not only from the Manichaean one, but also from the Freudian one? I think that the set of analyses and reflections made so far gives an answer to this question. Summing up, it can be said briefly that *Christ's words* according to Matthew 5:27-28 *do not allow us to stop at the accusation of the human heart and to regard it continually with suspicion, but must be understood and interpreted above all as an appeal to the heart. This derives from the very nature of the ethos of redemption.* On the basis of this mystery, which St. Paul (Rom. 8:23) defines *"the redemption of the body,"* on the basis of the reality called "redemption" and, consequently, on the basis of the ethos of the redemption of the body, we cannot stop only at the accusation of the human heart on the basis of desire and lust of the flesh. Man cannot stop at putting the "heart" in a state of continual and irreversible suspicion due to the manifestations of the lust of the flesh and libido, which, among other things, a psychoanalyst perceives by means of analyses of the unconscious.[3] *Redemption is a truth, a reality, in the name of which man must feel called, and "called with efficacy."* He must realize this call also through Christ's words according to Matthew 5:27-28, reread in the full context of the revelation of the body. Man must feel called to rediscover, nay more, to realize the nuptial meaning of the body and to express in this way the interior freedom of the gift, that is, of that spiritual state and that spiritual power which are derived from mastery of the lust of the flesh.

THAT GOOD BEGINNING

5. *Man is called to this by the word of the Gospel, therefore from "outside," but at the same time he is also called from "inside."* The words of Christ, who in the Sermon on the Mount appeals to the "heart," induce the listener, in a way, to this interior call. If he lets them act in him, he will be able to hear within him at the same time almost the echo of that "beginning," that good "beginning" to which Christ refers on another occasion, *to remind His listeners who man is, who woman is, and who we are for each other in the work of creation.* The words of Christ uttered in the Sermon on the Mount are not a call hurled into emptiness. They are not addressed to the man who is completely absorbed in the lust of the flesh, unable to seek another form of mutual relations in the sphere of the perennial attraction, which accompanies the history of man and woman precisely "from the beginning." Christ's words bear witness that the original power (therefore also the grace) of the mystery of creation becomes for each of them the power (that is grace) of the mystery of redemption. That concerns the very "nature," the very substratum of the humanity of the person, the deepest impulses of the "heart." *Does not man feel, at the same time as lust, a deep need to preserve the dignity of the mutual relations, which find their expression in the body, thanks to masculinity and femininity?* Does he not feel the need to impregnate them with everything that is noble and beautiful? Does he not feel the need to confer on them the supreme value which is love?

REAL MEANING OF LIFE

6. Rereading it, this appeal contained in Christ's words in the Sermon on the Mount cannot be an act

detached from the context of concrete existence. *It always means*—though only in the dimension of the act to which it refers—*the rediscovery of the meaning of the whole of existence, the meaning of life, in which there is contained also that meaning of the body which here we call "nuptial."* The meaning of the body is, in a sense, the antithesis of Freudian libido; the meaning of life, the antithesis of the interpretation "of suspicion." This interpretation is very different, it is radically different from what we rediscover in Christ's words in the Sermon on the Mount. *These words reveal not only another ethos, but also another vision of man's possibilities.* It is important that he, precisely in his "heart," should not feel irrevocably accused and given as a prey to the lust of the flesh, but that he should feel forcefully called in this same heart. Called precisely to that supreme value that is love. *Called as a person in the truth of his humanity, therefore also in the truth of his masculinity and femininity, in the truth of his body.* Called in that truth which has been his heritage "from the beginning," the heritage of his heart, which is deeper than the sinfulness inherited, deeper than lust in its three forms. The words of Christ, set in the whole reality of creation and redemption, reactivate that deeper heritage and give it real power in man's life.

NOTES

1. Cf. Paul Ricoeur, *Le conflit des interprétations*, Paris, 1969 (Seuil, pp. 149-150).

2. Cf. also Mt. 5:19-20.

3. Cf., for example, the characteristic affirmation of Freud's last work (S. Freud, *Abriss der Psychoanalyse, Das Unbehagen der Kultur*, Frankfurt-M. Hamburg 1955, (Fisher), pp. 74-75).

Then that "core" or "heart" of man would be dominated by the union between the erotic instinct and the destructive one, and life would consist in satisfying them.

IV. Love, Life, and Families

Homilies to Families While on Journeys

a) *"The Place of the Family,"* Homily at Mass for Families in Puebla, Mexico, January 28, 1979.

b) *"Let Us Celebrate Life!"* Homily at Mass on Capitol Mall, Washington, D.C., October 7, 1979.

c) *"Christian Marriage, the Leaven of Moral Progress,"* Homily at Mass for the Family in Kinshasa, Zaire, May 3, 1980.

d) *"Courageous Family Apostolate,"* Homily in Rio de Janeiro, Brazil, July 1, 1980.

e) *"Safeguard the Family, Where Love Begets Life,"* Homily in the Cathedral in Velletri, Italy, September 7, 1980.

f) *"The Kingdom of God and the Christian Family,"* Homily at Mass for Families at the Butzweiler Hof Stadium, in Cologne, Germany, November 15, 1980.

g) *"The Church's Teaching on Marriage,"* Homily at Mass for Families, in Cebu City, Philippine Islands, February 19, 1981.

h) *"Pope John XXIII, a Man Sent by God!"* Homily at Sotto il Monte on Pope John XXIII's Teachings on the Family, April 26, 1981.

THE PLACE OF THE FAMILY

On January 28, 1979, Pope John Paul II celebrated Holy Mass for the people of Puebla de Los Angeles in the courtyard of the Palafox Major Seminary. After the Gospel the Holy Father delivered the following homily.

Beloved sons and daughters,

Puebla de Los Angeles: today the sonorous and expressive name of your city is on millions of lips throughout Latin America and all over the world. Your city becomes a symbol and sign for the Church in Latin America. It is here, in fact, that from today the bishops of the whole continent, convened by the Successor of Peter, gather to reflect on the mission of pastors in this part of the world, in this extraordinary hour of history.

The Pope has desired to come up to this high place from where the whole of Latin America seems to open up. And it is with the impression of contemplating the picture of each one of the nations that the Pope has wished to celebrate the Eucharistic Sacrifice on this altar erected on the mountains, to invoke on this conference, on its participants and on its work, the light, the warmth and all the gifts of the Spirit of God, the Spirit of Jesus Christ.

There is nothing more natural and necessary than to invoke Him on this occasion. The great assembly which is opening is, in fact, an ecclesial meeting in its deepest essence: ecclesial because of those who meet here, the pastors of the Church of God in Latin America; ecclesial because of the subject it studies, the mission of the Church in the continent; ecclesial because of its aims: to make more living and effective the original contribution that the Church has the duty of making to the welfare, the harmony, the justice and peace of these peoples. Well, there is no ecclesial assembly if the Spirit of God is not there in the fullness of His mysterious action.

The Pope invokes Him with all the fervor of his heart. May the place where the bishops meet be a new Upper Room, much larger than the one in Jerusalem, where the Apostles were only eleven in number that morning, but, like that in Jerusalem, open to the call of the Paraclete and to the strength of a renewed Pentecost. May the Spirit accomplish in you bishops, gathered here, the multiform mission that the Lord Jesus entrusted to him: as interpreter of God to make understood His plan and His word, *which are inaccessible to mere human reason* (cf. Jn. 14:26), may He open the understanding of these pastors and introduce them to the Truth (cf. Jn. 16:13); as witness of Jesus Christ, may He give witness in their conscience and heart and transform them in turn into consistent, credible, and efficacious witnesses during their work (cf. Jn. 15:26); as Counselor or Comforter, may He instill courage against the sin of the world (cf. Jn. 16:8) and put on their lips what they must say, particularly at the moment when testimony costs suffering and fatigue.

So I ask you, beloved sons and daughters, to unite with me in this Eucharist, in this invocation to the Spirit. It is not for their own sake or out of personal interest that the bishops, from all parts of the continent, are meeting here; it is for you, People of God in these lands, and for your good. So take part in this third conference also in this way: by asking every day for the abundance of the Holy Spirit for one and all of them.

It has been said, in a beautiful and profound way, that our God in His deepest mystery is not a solitude,

but a family, since He has in Himself Fatherhood, Son-
ship and the essense of the family, which is Love. This
subject of the family is not, therefore, extraneous to the
subject of the Holy Spirit. Allow the Pope to say some
words to you on this subject of the family—which will
certainly occupy the bishops during these days.

You know that the Conference of Medellín spoke of
the family in pithy and urgent terms. In that year, 1968,
the bishops saw, in your profound sentiment for the
family, a fundamental feature of your Latin American
culture. They showed that, for the good of your countries, Latin American families should always have three
dimensions: education in the faith, formation of persons, promotion of development. They also emphasized
the serious obstacles that families meet with in carrying
out this threefold task. "For this reason" they recommended pastoral attention for families, as one of the
prior considerations of the Church in the continent.

Ten years later, the Church in Latin America feels
happy at everything it has been able to do in favor of
the family. But it humbly recognizes how much still
remains to be done, while it perceives that the family
apostolate, far from having lost its character of priority,
is more urgent than ever today, as a very important element in evangelization.

The Church is aware, in fact, that the family is up
against serious problems in Latin America in these
times. Recently some countries have introduced divorce
into their legislation, which brings a new threat to the
integrity of the family. In most of your countries it is a
lamentable fact that an alarming number of children,
the future of these nations and the hope for the future,

are born into homes without any stability or, as they are called, into "incomplete families." Moreover, in certain places of the "Continent of Hope," this same hope runs the risk of vanishing, since it grows within families many of which cannot live normally owing to the particular impact upon them of the most negative effects of development: truly depressing indices of unhealthiness, poverty and even want, ignorance and illiteracy, inhuman housing conditions, chronic malnutrition and so many other realities that are no less sad.

In defense of the family against these evils, the Church undertakes to give her help, and calls upon governments to take as the key point of their action an intelligent policy with regard to society and the family, a bold and persevering one, recognizing that the future —the hope—of the continent certainly lies here. It should be added that this family policy must not be understood as an indiscriminate effort to reduce the birth rate at all costs—which my Predecessor Paul VI called "reducing the number of guests at the banquet of life"—*when it is well known that a balanced birthrate is indispensable even for development.* It is a question of uniting efforts to create conditions favorable to the existence of healthy and balanced families: "to increase the food on the table," to use again an expression of Paul VI.

As well as the defense of the family, we must also speak of advancement of the family. Many organisms have to contribute to this promotion: governments and governmental organisms, the school, the trade unions, the media of social communication, groups in poor districts, the various voluntary or spontaneous associations which flourish everywhere today.

The Church must also offer her contribution in the line of her spiritual mission of proclaiming the Gospel and leading men to salvation, which also has an enormous repercussion on the welfare of the family. And what can the Church do, uniting her efforts with those of others? I am certain that your bishops will endeavor to give this question adequate, just and efficacious answers. I point out to you how valuable what the Church is already doing in Latin America for the family; for example: to prepare fiances for marriage; to help families when, in the course of their existence, they go through normal crises which, if wisely guided, may even be fruitful and enriching; to make each Christian family a real "domestic church," with all the rich content of this expression; to prepare many families for the mission of evangelizing other families; to emphasize all values of family life; to help incomplete families; to stimulate the rulers to bring forth in their countries that family social policy of which we were just speaking. The Puebla Conference will certainly support these initiatives and perhaps suggest others. We are happy to think that the history of Latin America will thus have reasons to thank the Church for all that it has done, is doing, and will do for the family in this vast continent.

Beloved sons and daughters: now, beside this altar, the Successor of Peter feels particularly close to all Latin American families. It is as if every home were to open and the Pope were able to enter into each of them: houses where there is no lack of bread or prosperity but where, perhaps, harmony and joy are lacking; houses where families live far more modestly and uncertain of the morrow, helping one another to lead a hard but dignified existence; poor houses in the suburbs of your cities, where there is much hidden suffering although there exists in the midst of them the simple joy of the poor; humble huts of peasants, natives, emigrants, etc. *For each family in particular the Pope would like to be able to say a word of encouragement and hope.* You families that can enjoy prosperity, do not shut yourselves up in your happiness; open up to others to distribute what is superfluous for you and what others lack. Families oppressed by poverty, do not lose heart, and, without taking luxury as your ideal, or riches as the principle of happiness, seek with the help of all to overcome difficult moments while waiting for better days. Families visited and tormented by physical or moral pain, sorely tried by sickness or want, do not add to these sufferings bitterness or despair, but temper sorrow with hope. All families of Latin America, be sure that the Pope knows you and wishes to know you even better because he loves you with a father's tenderness.

This is, in the framework of the Pope's visit to Mexico, the Day of the Family. Receive then, Latin American families—with your presence here, round the altar, by means of radio or television—receive the visit that the Pope wishes to make to each one. And give the Pope the joy of seeing you grow in the Christian values that are yours, in order that Latin America may find in its millions of families reasons to trust, to hope, to struggle and to build.

LET US CELEBRATE LIFE!

About a million persons were present for the Holy Father's con-celebrated Mass held on Capitol Mall. It was the last religious function before the Pope's departure from the United States. After the Gospel the Pope delivered the following homily.

Dear brothers and sisters in Jesus Christ,

1. In His dialogue with His listeners, Jesus was faced one day with an attempt by some Pharisees to get Him to endorse their current views regarding the nature of marriage. Jesus answered by reaffirming the teaching of Scripture: "At the beginning of creation God made them male and female; for this reason a man shall leave his father and mother and the two shall become one. They are no longer two but one flesh. Therefore let no man separate what God has joined" (Mk. 10:6-9).

The Gospel according to Mark immediately adds the description of a scene with which we are all familiar. This scene shows Jesus becoming indignant when He noticed how His own disciples tried to prevent the people from bringing their children closer to Him. And so He said: "'Let the children come to me and do not hinder them. It is to just such as these that the kingdom of God belongs....' Then he embraced them and blessed them, placing his hands on them" (Mk. 10:14-16). In proposing these readings, today's liturgy invites all of us to reflect on the *nature of marriage, on the family, and on the value of life*—three themes that are so closely interconnected.

INVIOLABILITY OF HUMAN LIFE

2. I shall all the more gladly lead you in reflecting on the Word of God as proposed by the Church today, because all over the world the bishops are discussing

marriage and family life as they are lived in all dioceses and nations. The bishops are doing this in preparation for the next World Synod of Bishops, which has as its theme: "The Role of the Christian Family in the Contemporary World." Your own bishops have designated next year as a year of study, planning and pastoral renewal with regard to the family. For a variety of reasons there is a renewed interest throughout the world in marriage, in family life, and in the value of all human life.

This very Sunday marks the beginning of the annual Respect Life Program, through which the Church in the United States intends to reiterate its conviction regarding *the inviolability of human life in all stages*. Let us then, all together, renew our esteem for the value of human life, remembering also that, *through Christ, all human life has been redeemed.*

HUMAN LIFE IS SACRED

3. I do not hesitate to proclaim before you and before the world that *all human life—from the moment of conception and through all subsequent stages—is sacred, because human life is created in the image and likeness of God. Nothing surpasses the greatness or dignity of a human person. Human life is not just an idea or an abstraction; human life is the concrete reality of a being that lives, that acts, that grows and develops; human life is the concrete reality of a being that is capable of love, and of service to humanity.*

Let me repeat what I told the people during my recent pilgrimage to my homeland: "If a person's right to life is violated at the moment in which he is first conceived in his mother's womb, an indirect blow is struck also at the whole of the moral order, which serves to ensure the inviolable goods of man. Among those goods, life occupies the first place. *The Church defends the right to life, not only in regard to the majesty of the Creator, who is the first Giver of this life, but also in respect to the essential good of the human person"* (June 8, 1979).

LIFE IS FOREVER

4. *Human life is precious because it is the gift of a God whose love is infinite, and when God gives life, it is forever.* Life is also precious because it is the expression and the fruit of love. This is why life should spring up within the setting of marriage, and why marriage and the parents' love for one another should be marked by generosity in self-giving. The great danger for family life in the midst of any society whose idols are pleasure, comfort and independence, lies in the fact that people close their hearts and become selfish. *The fear of making permanent commitments can change the mutual love of husband and wife into two loves of self*—two loves existing side by side until they end in separation.

In the sacrament of marriage, a man and a woman—who at Baptism became members of Christ and hence have the duty of manifesting Christ's attitudes in their lives—are assured of the help they need to develop their love in a faithful and indissoluble union, and to respond with generosity to the gift of parenthood. As the Second Vatican Council declared: Through this sacrament, Christ Himself becomes present in the life of the married couple and accompanies them, so that they may love each other and their children, just as Christ loved His Church by giving Himself up for her (cf. GS 48; Eph. 5:25).

FAMILY
RESPONSIBILITY

5. *In order that Christian marriage may favor the total good and development of the married couple, it must be inspired by the Gospel, and thus be open to new life—new life to be given and accepted generously.* The couple is also called to create a family atmosphere in which children can be happy, and lead full and worthy human and Christian lives.

To maintain a joyful family requires much from both the parents and the children. Each member of the family has to become, in a special way, the servant of the others and share their burdens (cf. Gal. 6:2; Phil. 2:2). Each one must show concern, not only for his or her own life, but also for the lives of the other members of the family: their needs, their hopes, their ideals. Decisions about the number of children and the sacrifices to be made for them must not be taken only with a view to adding to comfort and preserving a peaceful existence. Reflecting upon this matter before God, with the graces drawn from the sacrament, and guided by the teaching of the Church, parents will remind themselves that *it is certainly less serious to deny their children certain comforts or material advantages than to deprive them of the presence of brothers and sisters, who could help them to grow in humanity and to realize the beauty of life at all its ages and in all its variety.*

If parents fully realized the demands and the opportunities that this great sacrament brings, they could not fail to join in Mary's hymn to the Author of life—to God who has made them His chosen fellow workers.

EVERY PERSON IS UNIQUE

6. *All human beings ought to value every person for his or her uniqueness as a creature of God, called to be a brother or sister of Christ by reason of the Incarnation and the universal redemption.* For us, the sacredness of human life is based on these premises. And it is on these same premises that there is based our celebration of life—all human life. This explains our efforts to defend human life against every influence or action that threatens or weakens it, as well as our endeavors to make every life more human in all its aspects.

And so, we will stand up every time that human life is threatened. *When the sacredness of life before birth is attacked, we will stand up and proclaim that no one ever has the authority to destroy unborn life.* When a child is described as a burden or is looked upon only as a means to satisfy an emotional need, we will stand up and insist that *every child is a unique and unrepeatable gift of God, with the right to a loving and united family.* When the institution of marriage is abandoned to human selfishness or reduced to a temporary, conditional arrangement that can easily be terminated, we will stand up and affirm the indissolubility of the marriage bond. When the value of the family is threatened because of social and economic pressures, we will stand up and reaffirm that the family is "necessary not only for the private good of every person, but also for the common good of every society, nation and state" (General Audience, January 3, 1979). When freedom is used to dominate the weak, to squander natural resources and energy, and to deny basic necessities to people, we will stand up and reaffirm the demands of justice and social love. When the sick, the aged or the dying are abandoned in loneliness, we will stand up and proclaim that they are worthy of love, care and respect.

UPHOLD VALUES

7. I make my own the words which Paul VI spoke last year to the American bishops: "We are convinced, moreover, that *all efforts made to safeguard human rights actually benefit life itself.* Everything aimed at banishing discrimination—in law or in fact—which is based on race, origin, color, culture, sex or religion (cf. OA 16) is *a service to life.* When the rights of minorities are fostered, when the mentally or physically handicapped are assisted, when those on the margin of society are given a voice—in all these instances the dignity of life and the sacredness of human life are furthered.... In particular, every contribution made to better the moral climate of society, to oppose permissiveness and hedonism, and all assistance to the family, which is the source of new life, effectively uphold the values of life" (May 26, 1978).

NEED FOR COURAGE

8. Much remains to be done to support those whose lives are wounded and to restore hope to those who are afraid of life. Courage is needed to resist pressures and false slogans, to proclaim the supreme dignity of all life, and to demand that society itself give it its protection. A distinguished American, Thomas Jefferson, once stated: *"The care of human life and happiness and not their destruction is the just and only legitimate object of good government"* (March 31, 1809). I wish therefore to praise all the members of the Catholic

Church and other Christian Churches, all men and women of the Judaeo-Christian heritage, as well as all people of good will who unite in common dedication for the defense of *life in its fullness* and for the promotion of all human rights.

Our celebration of life forms part of the celebration of the Eucharist. Our Lord and Savior, through His death and resurrection, has become for us "the bread of life" and the pledge of eternal life. In Him we find the courage, perseverance and inventiveness which we need in order to promote and defend life within our families and throughout the world.

Dear brothers and sisters: we are confident that Mary, the Mother of God and the Mother of life, will give us her help so that our way of living will always reflect our admiration and gratitude for God's gift of love that is life. We know that she will help us to use every day that is given to us as an opportunity to defend the life of the unborn and to render more human the lives of all our fellow human beings, wherever they may be.

And through the intercession of Our Lady of the Rosary, whose feast we celebrate today, may we come one day to the fullness of eternal life in Christ Jesus our Lord. Amen.

CHRISTIAN MARRIAGE— LEAVEN OF MORAL PROGRESS

On May 3, 1980, the Holy Father's second day in Zaire, his first engagement was a Mass for the family in the church of St. Pierre, the oldest church in the city of Kinshasa. The following is the text of the Pope's homily.

Dear Christian spouses, fathers and mothers of families,

1. Emotion and joy fill my heart as the universal Pastor of the Church, because I have been granted the grace of meditating for the first time with African married couples—and for them—on their particular vocation: Christian marriage. May God—who revealed Himself as being "One in Three Persons"—assist us throughout this meditation! The subject is a marvelous one, but the reality is difficult! If Christian marriage is comparable to a very high mountain which places spouses in the immediate vicinity of God, it must be recognized that its ascent calls for a great deal of time and effort. But is that a reason for suppressing or lowering this summit? *Is it not through moral and spiritual ascents that the human person realizes himself fully and dominates the universe, even more than through technical and even space records, however admirable they may be?*

Together, we will make a pilgrimage to the sources of marriage, then we will try to gauge better its dynamism in the service of spouses, the children, society and the Church. Finally, we will gather our energies to promote a more and more effective family apostolate.

SPLENDOR OF HUMAN LOVE

2. Everyone knows the famous narrative of creation with which the Bible begins. It is said there that

God made man in His likeness, creating him man and woman. This is surprising at first sight. Mankind, to resemble God, must be a couple, two persons moving one towards the other, two persons whom perfect love will gather into unity. This movement and this love make them resemble God, who is love itself, the absolute unity of the three Persons. The splendor of human love has never been sung so beautifully as in the first pages of the Bible: "This at last," Adam says contemplating his wife, "is bone of my bones and flesh of my flesh. Therefore a man leaves his father and his mother and cleaves to his wife, and they become one flesh" (Gn. 2:23-24). Paraphrasing Pope St. Leo, I cannot help saying to you: "O Christian spouses, recognize your eminent dignity!"

This pilgrimage to the sources also reveals to us that the initial couple, in God's plan, is monogamous. This is again surprising, for civilization—at the time when the Bible narratives take shape—was generally far from this cultural model. *This monogamy, which is not of Western but Semitic origin, appears as the expression of the interpersonal relationship, the one in which each of the partners is recognized by the other in an equal value and in the totality of his person. This monogamous and personalistic conception of the human couple is an absolutely original revelation,* which bears the mark of God, and which deserves to be studied more and more deeply.

CHRISTIAN MARRIAGE

3. But this story, which began so well in the luminous dawn of mankind, experiences the drama of the rupture between this new couple and the Creator. *It*

is original sin. This rupture, however, will be the occasion of another manifestation of God's love. Compared very often to an infinitely faithful husband, for example, in the texts of the psalmists and prophets, God constantly renews His covenant with this capricious and sinful humanity. These repeated covenants will culminate in the definitive covenant that God sealed in His own Son, sacrificing Himself freely for the Church and for the world. St. Paul is not afraid to present this covenant of Christ with the Church as the symbol and model of every covenant between man and woman (cf. Eph. 5:25), united as spouses indissolubly.

Such are the letters patent of nobility of Christian marriage. They produce light and strength for the everyday fulfillment of the conjugal and family vocation, for the benefit of the spouses themselves, their children, the society in which they live, and the Church of Christ. African traditions, judiciously utilized, may have their place in the construction of Christian homes in Africa. *I am thinking in particular of all the positive values of the family feeling, so deeply rooted in the African soul and which take on multiple aspects, which can certainly give so-called advanced civilizations food for thought: the seriousness of the matrimonial commitment at the end of a long process; priority given to the transmission of life and therefore the importance attached to the mother and children; the law of solidarity among families related by marriage, which is exercised especially in favor of old persons, widows and orphans; a kind of co-responsibility in taking charge and bringing up the children, which is capable of relieving many psychological tensions; the cult of ancestors and of the dead which promotes faithfulness to traditions.*

Certainly, the delicate problem is to assume all this family dynamism, inherited from ancestral customs, while transforming it and purifying it in the perspectives of the society which is springing up in Africa. But in any case, the conjugal life of Christians is lived—through different ages and situations—in the footsteps of Christ, the liberator and redeemer of all men and of all the realities that make up men's lives. "Do everything in the name of the Lord Jesus," as St. Paul said to us (Col. 3:17).

UNION OF HEARTS

4. It is, therefore, by conforming to Christ who gave Himself up for love of His Church that spouses have access, day after day, to the love of which the Gospel speaks to us: "Love one another, as I loved you," and more precisely to the perfection of indissoluble union on all planes. Christian spouses have promised to share with each other all they are and all they have. It is the most audacious contract that exists, the most marvelous one, too!

The union of their bodies, willed by God Himself as the expression of the even deeper communion of their minds and their hearts, carried out with equal respect and tenderness, renews the dynamism and the youth of their solemn commitment, of their first "yes."

The union of their characters! *To love a being is to love him such as he is, it is to love him to the extent of cultivating in oneself the antidote of his weaknesses or his faults, for example, calmness and patience, if the other manifestly lacks them.*

The union of hearts! *There are innumerable fine shades of difference between the love of man and that of*

*woman. Neither of the partners can demand to be loved
in the same way as he or she loves.* It is important—on
both sides—to renounce the secret reproaches that separate hearts and to free oneself of this sorrow at the
most favorable moment. *To share the joys and, even
more so, the sufferings of the heart, is a strong bond of
unity. But it is just as much in common love of the children that the union of hearts is strengthened.*

The union of intelligences and wills! Spouses are
also two forces different but united for their mutual
service, for the service of their home, their social
environment, and the service of God. Essential agreement must be manifested in the determination and pursuit of common aims. The more energetic partner must
support the will of the other, replace it sometimes, and
act on it skillfully—in an instructive way—as a lever.

Finally the union of souls, themselves united with
God! *Each of the spouses must reserve moments of solitude with God, for "heart-to-heart" communication in
which the partner is not the first concern. This indispensable personal life of the soul with God is far from
excluding the sharing of all conjugal and family life.* On
the contrary it stimulates the Christian couple to look
for God together, to discover His will together and to
carry it out in practice with the light and the energies
drawn from God Himself.

LOVE FOR CHILDREN

5. This view and this realization of the covenant
between man and woman go far beyond the spontaneous desire that unites them. Marriage is really for
them a way of advancement and sanctification. And a

source of life! Do not Africans have an admirable respect for life about to be born? They love children deeply. They welcome them with great joy. Christian parents will be able to put their children on the way of an existence related to human and Christian values. By showing them through a whole lifestyle—courageously revised and perfected—the meaning of respect for every person, disinterested service of others, renunciation of caprice, forgiveness often repeated, loyalty in everything, conscientious work, the meeting of faith with the Lord, Christian spouses introduce their own children into the secret of a successful existence which goes far beyond the discovery of a "good position."

MORAL PROGRESS

6. Christian marriage is also called to be a leaven of moral progress for society. Realism makes us recognize the threats that weigh on the family as a natural and Christian institution, in Africa as elsewhere, as a result of certain customs, and also of generalized cultural changes. Does it never happen to you to compare the modern family to a canoe on the river, pursuing its course in the midst of rough waters and obstacles? You know as well as I do how much the concepts of faithfulness and indissolubility are attacked by opinion. You know too that the frailty and break-up of homes lead to a series of miseries, even if African family solidarity tries to put things right as regards the taking over of the children. Christian couples—thoroughly prepared and duly accompanied—have to work without losing heart at the restoration of the family which is the first cell of society and must remain a school of social virtues. The state must not fear such homes but protect them.

MANIFESTING GOD

7. A leaven of society, *the Christian family is also a presence, a manifestation of God in the world.* The Pastoral Constitution *Gaudium et spes* (no. 48) contains luminous pages on the influence of this "intimate partnership of life and love" which is at the same time the very first grass-roots ecclesial community. "The Christian family springs from marriage, which is an image and a sharing in the partnership of love between Christ and the Church; it will show forth to all men Christ's living presence in the world and the authentic nature of the Church by the love and generous fruitfulness of the spouses, by their unity and fidelity, and by the loving way in which all members of the family cooperate with each other." What dignity and what responsibility!

Yes, this sacrament is a great one! And let spouses have confidence: their faith assures them that they receive, with this sacrament, the strength of God, a grace that will accompany them throughout their life. May they never neglect to draw upon this gushing source which is in them!

FAMILY APOSTOLATE

8. I would not like to end this meditation without warmly encouraging African bishops to continue—despite the well-known difficulties—their efforts of "apostolate of Christian homes," with renewed dynamism and unfailing hope. I know that this is already the constant concern of many and I admire them. I likewise congratulate the many African families who already realize the Christian ideal of which I have

spoken, with specifically African qualities, and who are an example and an attraction for so many others. But I take the liberty of insisting.

Without abandoning any of their concerns for the human and religious formation of children and adolescents, and taking into account African sensibility and customs, *dioceses must gradually set up an apostolate aimed at the two spouses together and not just at one of the partners.* Let preparation of the young for marriage be intensified, encouraging them to follow a real preparation for married life, which will reveal to them the meaning of the Christian identity of the couple, and make them mature for interpersonal relations and for their family and social responsibilities. These centers of preparation for marriage need the united support of dioceses and the generous and competent help of chaplains, experts and married couples able to bear witness to high quality. I stress above all the mutual help that each Christian couple can give to another.

DAYS OF RETREAT

9. This family apostolate must also accompany young married couples, as they set up their home. Days of spiritual renewal, retreats, meetings of married couples will support young couples in their human and Christian progress. Let care be taken on all these occasions that *there be a good balance between doctrinal formation and spiritual animation. The part of meditation, conversation with God who is faithful, is of essential importance.* It is near Him that spouses draw the grace of faithfulness, understand and accept the necessity of asceticism, which generates true freedom, resume or decide their family and social commitments

which will make their homes centers of influence. It would certainly be very useful for married couples of a parish and a diocese to form groups in order to create a vast family movement, not only to help Christian couples to live according to the Gospel, but to contribute to the restoration of the family by defending its values against attacks of all kinds, and in the name of the rights of man and the citizen. On this vital plane of the family apostolate, more and more adapted to the needs of our time and your regions, I have full confidence in your bishops, my beloved brothers in the episcopate.

10. May you find in this talk the sign of the great interest that the Pope takes in the serious problems of the family, the testimony of his trust and his hope in your Christian homes, and the courage to work, you yourselves, more than ever, in this African land, for the greater good of your nations and for the honor of the Church of Christ, at the solid construction of family communities "of life and love" according to the Gospel! I promise you that this great intention will always have a place in my heart and my prayer. May God, who revealed Himself as a family in the unity of the Father, the Son and the Spirit, bless you, and may His blessing remain upon you for ever!

COURAGEOUS
FAMILY APOSTOLATE

On July 1, 1980, John Paul II left Belo Horizonte for Rio de Janeiro. After having been welcomed by the local ecclesiastical and civil authorities, he drove in an open car to the Flamengo Waterfront Park where he celebrated Mass in the presence of more than a million people.

Beloved brother, Archbishop of St. Sebastian
in Rio de Janeiro, and his auxiliary bishops;
Dear sons living in this marvelous city;
Dear sons who have come from other parts of Brazil for this meeting:

1. Many of those who are now taking part in this Eucharist will be recalling in memory the other Masses celebrated in this same place in July 1955. It was on the occasion of the Thirty-fifth International Eucharistic Congress; and on a strip of land snatched from the sea, artists' hands had raised the monumental altar on which the Pontifical Legate had opened and closed the great event. The voice of my immortal Predecessor, Pius XII, resounded here with a fatherly message addressed to a million persons gathered in this place.

I cannot fail to recall, I too, this twenty-fifth anniversary, happy to do so with you and in your midst, while you prepare the imminent Tenth National Eucharistic Congress of Fortaleza. God grant that these events recalled, lived, awaited, will renew your thanks to the Lord and that you will express them in what is thanksgiving by definition and par excellence, namely, the Eucharist, in devotion to which may He make you grow.

2. A priest—be he the Pope, a bishop or a country parish priest—in celebrating the Eucharist, a Christian in participating in the Mass and receiving the body and blood of Christ, cannot but be rapt in the marvels of this sacrament. There are so many dimensions in which It can be considered. It is Christ's Sacrifice which is mysteriously renewed; It is the bread and wine transformed, transubstantiated into the body and blood of the Lord; it is grace that is communicated by means of this spiritual food to the soul of the Christian.... On this occasion I wish to dwell on a no less significant aspect: *the Eucharist is a family meeting, a meeting of the large family of Christians.*

The Lord Jesus willed to institute this great sacrament on the occasion of an important family meeting: the Paschal Supper, and on that occasion His family was the Twelve who had been living with Him for three years. For a long time, at the beginning of the Church, it was in the houses of families that other families met for the "breaking of bread." Every altar will always be a table, around which there gathers a family of brothers, more or less numerous. The Eucharist gathers this family, manifests it in the eyes of everyone and draws closer the ties that unite its members, all at the same time. St. Augustine was thinking of all this when he called the Eucharist: "a sacrament of piety, a sign of unity, a bond of charity" (*In Joannis Evang.* Tract. XXVI, cap. 6, no. 13; PL 35, 1613).

Celebrating this Eucharist, I turn my eyes in spirit to all the areas of this immense country. I try to embrace in one glance the 120 million Brazilians and I pray for the immense family constituted by all the sons of this country and by those who have found a new home here.

3. May I confide something to you? The first time someone spoke to me of Brazil, when I knew very little about this country, it was not to extol its natural beauties, which are marvelous, or to exalt the riches of its soil and its subsoil, which are inexhaustible, or to highlight the feats of this or that famous Brazilian. The person who was speaking to me—he was a great authority on Brazil—just said to me that Brazil was a great nation, in spite of all the problems it might have, because all races can be found here, people who have come from all horizons of the world, gathered in one people, without preconceptions, without discriminations or segregations, in a clear fusion of minds and hearts. "It is a family," my interlocutor said, enchanted.

I pray that this family spirit will never be weakened or disappear; that it will prevail over any germ of discord or division, over any threat of rupture or separation. I pray that, while there may be fewer and fewer differences among Brazilians as regards progress and prosperity, opportunities of access to the goods of culture and civilization, possibilities of finding work worthy of man, of having health and education and of bringing up one's children, the "large family" of Brazilians, of which my first "teacher of Brazil" spoke, will become more and more a reality. I also pray that, to a world often dominated by conflicts between peoples and races, Brazil may be able to give—without ostentation—in fact, with the spontaneity and naturalness that characterize its people, an essential lesson, that of real integration: of how persons who have come from the most distant corners of the world can live like one family, in a country of continental dimensions. I pray, finally, for the members of this "large family" who rest under this war memorial, whose sacrifice is a permanent appeal for union among peoples.

4. This Eucharist, a family gathering, now leads my thought to Brazilian families.

The most authoritative testimonies about Latin America—I am thinking of the documents of Medellin and Puebla, of the reports that reach me from the bishops and episcopal conferences of this subcontinent, but I am thinking also of the more serious sociological studies—have taught me that *for you Latin Americans the family is an extraordinarily important reality.* The place that the family occupied in the peoples that are at the root of your nations and the Latin American influence that the family had in the formation of your culture, justify this importance abundantly. Brazil, far from being an exception, confirms this fact to an outstanding extent. It is not surprising that the family spirit is manifested here with special vigor, as well as the essential dimensions of the family reality: respect imbued with love and tenderness, generosity and the spirit of solidarity, appreciation of a certain privacy in the home tempered by a desire for openness.

I do not wish to fail to stress, among other things, two fundamental dimensions of the family that are particularly significant for you: it has been in the course of the centuries the great means of transmitting cultural, ethical and spiritual values from one generation to the other. *On the religious and Christian level, very often, when other channels were lacking or were extremely precarious, it was the only, or at least the principal, channel through which faith was communicated from parents to children for many generations.*

5. Having said this, how can we close our eyes to the serious situations in which large numbers of your families find themselves in actual fact, and to the grave threats that weigh on families in general?

Some of these threats are of a social character and are connected with the subhuman conditions of housing, hygiene, health and education in which millions of families find themselves, in the interior of the country and in the outskirts of large cities, owing to unemployment or low wages. Others are of a moral character and refer to the widespread disintegration of the family, owing to ignorance and lack of esteem or respect for human and Christian norms concerning the family, in the various strata of the population. Others again are of a civil character, bound up with family law. *In the whole world the laws concerning the family are more and more permissive and therefore less and less encouraging for those who are endeavoring to follow the principles of a higher ethics as regards the family.*

God grant that it will not be so in your country and that, in accordance with the Christian principles that inspire your culture, those who are responsible for drawing up and promulgating laws will do so in respect for the irreplaceable values of Christian ethics, *first among which are the value of human life and the indefeasible right of parents to transmit life.* Other threats, finally, are of a religious character and derive from an inadequate knowledge of the sacramental dimensions of marriage in God's plan.

6. These considerations are enough to show the importance and the necessity of an intelligent, courageous and persevering family apostolate. Speaking to

the people of the city of Puebla, *in the homily of the unforgettable Mass celebrated there, I recalled that many Latin American bishops do not hesitate to recognize that the Church has still a lot to do in this field.* Precisely for this reason, on opening the Puebla Conference, I recommended the family apostolate as an important priority in all your countries. The Puebla Document dedicated an important chapter to the family. God grant that attention to other themes and statements of this document, which are certainly important but not exclusive, will not mean less attention to the family apostolate; this would be an error that we would have cause to regret in the future.

This family apostolate involves many fields and complex requirements. Your pastors know this. Many lay people engaged in various effective and meritorious family movements are attentive to these fields and these requirements. You certainly do not expect the Pope to speak of them here: it is not the moment to do so. However, how could I fail to recall, at least by mentioning them, some of the most significant aspects of this apostolate?

I am thinking of all that must be done in the field of preparation for marriage, of course, in the period that precedes its celebration, but also from the years of adolescence, in the family, in the Church, in the school; namely, a serious, broad and deep education to true love; and that is a far more demanding thing than to provide sexual education. I am thinking of the generous and courageous effort that must be made to create in society an environment favorable to the realization of a Christian family ideal, based on the values of unity, faithfulness, indissolubility and responsible fecundity. I am thinking of the care to be given to couples who, as a result of various reasons and circumstances, are going through moments of crisis, which they will be able to overcome if they are helped, whereas they may flounder if this help is not forthcoming. I am thinking of the contribution that Christians, especially the laity, can make to stimulate a social policy sensitive to the requirements and values of the family and to avoid a legislation harmful to its stability and balance. I am thinking, finally, of the incalculable value of a family spirituality, to be perfected constantly, to be promoted and to be spread. Nor can I fail to add, once more, a word of stimulus and encouragement to the family movements which dedicate themselves to this particularly important work.

7. There are not lacking in the experience and in the Magisterium of the Church very efficacious elements for a pastoral attention to families that is clear-sighted, vast and courageous. My Predecessors have left us important documents. Many pastors and theologians have offered us the fruit of their experience and their reflections. In the near future the Synod of Bishops, studying "the role of the Christian family in the modern world," will certainly give us guidelines in this delicate sphere. A real family apostolate should draw on this source—not on its fringes or far from it, much less in conflict with it.

Innumerable families, especially Christian couples, desire and ask for secure principles that will help them to put into practice, even if amid unusual difficulties and sometimes with a heroic effort, their Christian ideal with regard to faithfulness, fecundity and the upbringing of children. *No one has the right to betray this*

*expectation or to disappoint this aspiration by conceal-
ing the true principles out of timidity, lack of confidence
or false respect, or by offering principles that are doubtful even when not openly in conflict with the teaching of
Christ transmitted by the Church.*

8. Beloved brothers and sons, at the end of this
reflection, let us turn our attention to the New Testament texts which we had the joy of listening to in this liturgy.

One of them, that of the Gospel of John, takes
up again Jesus' teaching on the Bread of Life in the
synagogue of Capernaum. *This bread,* as the Savior
assures us, *is His own flesh which, having become
the nourishment of His disciples, gives them a life that
begins here on earth and leads to eternity.* The promise made at Capernaum is fully fulfilled in the Last
Supper and in the mystery of the Eucharist. This is
the bread that becomes the body of Christ to give life
to men.

The deepest and most heartfelt desire of the Pope at
this time would be to be able to enter miraculously the
home of every Brazilian family, to be the guest of every
Brazilian family. To share the happiness of happy families and thank the Lord with them. To be close to families that are weeping because of some hidden or visible
suffering, in order to give, if possible, some comfort. To
speak to families in which nothing is lacking, in order to
invite them to distribute what is superfluous to the
have-nots. To sit at the table of poor families, where
bread is scarce, to help them, not to become rich in
the sense in which the Gospel condemns riches, but to
obtain what is necessary for a worthy life.

If this is an impossible desire, I want at least, when I shortly take in my hands the body of Jesus and His precious blood, to express a wish and a prayer: that this Eucharist celebrated in this temple without frontiers under the dome of this sky of Rio de Janeiro, far vaster and more grandiose than Michelangelo's, may become a source of real life for the Brazilian people so that it may be a real family, and for every Brazilian family in order that it may be a cell forming this people.

SAFEGUARD THE FAMILY, WHERE LOVE BEGETS LIFE

On September 7, 1980, the Holy Father made a pastoral visit to the diocese of Velletri, bringing to the people of that region the joy of once again receiving a Pope in their midst.

It was back in 1863 that the inhabitants last welcomed a reigning Pontiff, Pope Pius IX.

During the concelebrated Mass in front of the cathedral, Pope John Paul delivered the following homily.

My dearest brothers and sisters!

1. I wish first of all to tell you of my great joy in being able to be among you today, in your very beautiful Velletri. I greet you with particular warmth and thank you heartily for your cordial welcome. My greetings go in a special way to Cardinal Sebastiano Baggio, Prefect of the Sacred Congregation for Bishops, Titular Bishop of this glorious suburbicarian Church; the worthy Bishop Dante Bernini, the members of the diocesan presbyterate, all the representatives of the religious orders, male and female, to the future priests, to those who are preparing for the permanent diaconate, to those enrolled in the School of Theology for the Laity and to all those who belong to the various lay associations. This meeting of ours, ennobled by the context of the Mass that we are celebrating, is an excellent occasion to confess together our mutual faith in Christ Jesus our Lord, and to express our mutual communion.

I know I am in a city with an ancient and illustrious history, both in the civil as well as the ecclesiastical spheres; as for the former, suffice it to think about its origins in the Emperor Octavian Augustus; in the latter field the figures of not a few bishops of Velletri have been elevated either to the See of Peter or even to the honors of the altars. But I also know very well that the vitality of the Velletrians is not at all limited to the past, but constitutes a fertile patrimony in the present, for which reason your city is distinguished for its dynamism on various levels. I recognize this and as I rejoice in it, I paternally encourage you to continue with equal commitment, seeking above all always to keep high the Christian name that sets you apart.

"GIVE US, O LORD, WISDOM OF HEART"

2. The biblical readings, proposed to us by this Sunday's liturgy, center around the concept of Christian wisdom which each of us is invited to acquire and deepen. For this reason the responsorial psalm is formulated with these beautiful words: "Give us, O Lord, wisdom of heart." In fact, without that, how would it be possible to plan our lives, face its various difficulties, and still always preserve a deep feeling of peace and inner serenity? But to do this, as the first reading teaches, *humility is necessary, that is, the authentic sense of our own limits, joined to the intense desire for a gift from above with which to enrich ourselves from within*. Man of today, in fact, on the one hand finds it difficult to embrace and understand all the laws regulating the material universe, which are also the subject of scientific observation, while on the other hand, he confidently presumes to make laws on things of the spirit that by definition evade physical revelations: "We can hardly guess at what is on earth,...but who has traced out what is in the heavens,...unless you had sent your Holy Spirit from on high?" (Wis. 9:16-17)

Here the importance of being true disciples of Christ is symbolized, since through Baptism He has been made our wisdom (cf. 1 Cor. 1:30), hence the measure of all that forms the concrete texture of our lives.

The Gospel that was read brings out *precisely the necessary centrality of Jesus Christ in our existence.* And it does so with three conditional sentences: if we do not put Him above our dearest things, if we do not prepare to see our crosses in the light of His, *if we do not have the sense of the relativity of material goods, then we cannot be His disciples, that is, call ourselves Christians.* These things are essential to our identity as baptized; we must always reflect upon them a great deal, even if for now it suffices to mention them to you briefly.

FAMILY, WORK AND THE MADONNA

3. My very dear Velletrians, it is upon these solid evangelical bases that other important human and Christian values are engrafted and acquire even greater merit. I know that in Velletri it is said that three loves in particular are cherished: family, work and the Madonna. Well, if you permit, I want to tell you that I share them, and I would like to say a few words about each of them.

Above all, family: it is the first vital sphere that man encounters on coming into the world, and his experience remains forever decisive. For this reason it is important to care for and protect him, so that he may adequately discharge his specific tasks, which are made known and entrusted to him by nature and Christian revelation. It is the place of love and life, or rather the place where love generates life, since each one of these two realities would not be authentic if it were not accompanied by the other. This is why Christianity and the Church have always defended them and place them in mutual correlation. With regard to this, what my Predecessor, the great Pope Paul VI, proclaimed in his first Christmas radio message in 1963 is true: *we have "at times tried to turn to remedies that must be considered worse than the evil, if they consist in venturing to control the fecundity of life itself with means that human and Christian ethics must qualify as being illicit: instead of increasing the bread on the table of starving humanity, as today modern productive development can do, some are thinking of lessening, with procedures contrary to honesty, the number of table companions. This is not worthy of civilization"* (Teachings of Paul VI, I 1963, p. 419). *I fully agree with these words, and in fact would like to stress them even more*, seeing that from the time they were said until today the situation can be said to be aggravated and has need of responsible and effective commitment by all honest men at every level of civilized coexistence. Certainly you know that the imminent Synod of Bishops has as the theme of its studies precisely that of the family; let us pray the Lord that the Synod is fruitful of positive and lasting results for the good of the Church and human society itself.

4. In the second place, you love work. On these fertile hills your labor is certainly made real in the cheerful, serene image of the vineyard which produces that typical celebrated local wine, of which you are proud, and justly so. But I do not forget every other type of activity to which each one of you applies himself to earn daily bread for himself and for his loved ones.

The Church, as you know, devotes its most attentive care to the problems of labor and workers. In my apostolic journeys I have not failed to trace the main lines of this primary pastoral concern: and I remind you further how Vatican II stated that work *"proceeds immediately from the person, who as it were, impresses upon nature his seal and subjects it to his will"* (GS 67). Further, given its social importance, work needs to be not only promoted but also protected and defended, so that the duties of workers are justly balanced with their rights being recognized and respected. *From the Christian point of view it will never be right to enslave the human person either to an individual or to a system so as to render him a pure means of production.* He instead is always maintained to be superior to every profit and every ideology; never vice versa.

I hope your labor molds you to strong and tested virtue, makes you always more mature and conscientious builders of the common good and producers of that solidarity that, taking its origin from God the Creator, unites and cements your coexistence. Rather, I like to see in the produce of your good land an eloquent symbol of brotherhood and reciprocal communion, so that men are transformed into so many table companions, equal and joyful, seated at the banquet of this life as a prefiguration of the future and eternal feast shared by us with our only Lord.

5. Finally, you love the Mother of Jesus. I know that the Madonna of Grace is especially dear to you; her image is filially preserved and venerated in your beautiful cathedral. I am highly pleased, and I urge you to persevere in this devotion of yours that, if rightly understood and lived, will surely lead to the constantly

increasing penetration of the mystery of Christ, our only Savior. The heart of His Mother is great and tender enough to pour forth her own love also on each one of us, needful as we are of her protection every day. Therefore, let us invoke her with full trust. And therefore I also commend to her, my very dear Velletrians, all of you present here and those who could not participate in this wonderful meeting. In a special way I entrust to her maternal care the sick, the old, the children, whoever feels alone and weak, or in special need. We all have a place in her heart, and under her guidance we can courageously face the difficulties of life and above all reach a full Christian maturity.

This is also my warmest wish, with my cordial blessing. Amen!

THE KINGDOM OF GOD AND THE CHRISTIAN FAMILY

On November 15, 1980, the Holy Father visited Cologne during his pilgrimage to Germany, his eighth such pilgrimage beyond the boundaries of Italy. His first Mass on German soil was celebrated in the sports arena of Butzweiler Hof. The Pope delivered the following homily.

1. "The kingdom of heaven is like a net..." (Mt. 13:47).

Allow me, most Reverend Bishop of the ancient, venerable Church of Cologne, Reverend Confreres, Cardinals and bishops, allow me, all you beloved brothers and sisters, to try to clarify at this Eucharistic celebration the significance of our extraordinary meeting today, with the help of this parable, with the help of the Word of Christ, who repeatedly explained the kingdom of God by means of parables. With their help, He announced the presence of this kingdom in the midst of the world.

We, too, must meet in this dimension. This is, in a way, the essential premise of today's visit of the Apostle Peter's Successor in the Episcopal See of Rome to your Church in Germany, to you here in Cologne, who represent the Church of God as it has been formed in the course of many centuries round the Roman *Colonia Agrippina*. The outstanding symbol of this Church up to today has been your splendid cathedral, whose spiritual importance has been renewed in you thanks to the jubilee this year: the latter speaks eloquently of the kingdom of God among us.

*We who now form the Church of Christ on earth,
on this part of the German territory, must meet in the
dimension of the truth of the kingdom of God:* Christ
came to reveal this kingdom and launch it on this earth,
in every place of the earth, in men and among men.

This kingdom of God is in our midst (cf. Lk. 17:21),
as it was in all the generations of your fathers and ancestors. But like them, we too still pray in the "Our Father"
every day: "Thy kingdom come." *These words bear witness that the kingdom of God is still ahead of us, that we
are moving towards it, advancing along the confused
paths, and in fact sometimes even the wrong ones, of
our earthly existence.* We bear witness with these words
that the kingdom of God is being continually realized
and is approaching, even if we often lose sight of it and
no longer see its form, described by the Gospel. It often
seems that the one and only dimension of our existence
is "this world": the "kingdom of this world" with its
visible form, its breathtaking progress in science and
technology, in culture and in economy...breathtaking
and often also worrying! But if we kneel down to pray
every day, or at least from time to time, we always
utter, amid these circumstances of life, the same words:
"Thy kingdom come."

Dear brothers and sisters! These hours in which we
meet here, the time which, thanks to your invitation
and your hospitality, I can spend among you, is time of
the kingdom of God: of the kingdom which is "already
here," and of the one which is "still coming." For this
reason we must interpret the whole essential part, which
refers to this visit, with the help of the parable which we
listened to in today's Gospel: "The kingdom of heaven is
like...."

ANOTHER DIMENSION
OF MAN'S EXISTENCE

2. What is it like?

According to the words of Jesus, as the four evangelists transmitted them to us, this kingdom is explained with various parables and comparisons. Today's comparison is one of the many. It seems to us particularly closely connected with the work done by the Apostles of Christ, including Peter too, as well as by many of his listeners on the shores of the Sea of Galilee. Christ says: the kingdom of heaven is like "a net which was thrown into the sea and gathered fish of every kind" (Mt. 13:47). These simple words completely change the picture of the world: the picture of our human world, as we form it through experience and science. Experience and science cannot go beyond those boundaries of the "world" and of human existence in it, which are necessarily linked with the "sea of time": the boundaries of a world in which man is born and dies, in accordance with the words of Genesis: "You are dust, and to dust you shall return" (Gn. 3:1). The comparison of Christ, on the contrary, speaks of man's transference into another "world," into another dimension of his existence. The kingdom of heaven is precisely this new dimension, which opens above the "sea of time" and is at the same time the "net" which works in this sea for the final destiny of man and of all men in God.

Today's parable calls upon us to recognize the kingdom of heaven as the definitive fulfillment of that justice for which man longs with invincible nostalgia, which the Lord has put in his heart; that justice which Jesus Himself realized and proclaimed; that justice, finally, which Christ sealed with His own blood on the cross.

In the kingdom of heaven, the kingdom "of justice, love and peace" (the preface on the Feast of Christ the King), man, too, will be perfect. *For man is the being who springs from the depth of God and who conceals within himself such a depth that only God can fill. He, man, is in all his being an image of God and is like Him.*

FISHERS OF MEN

3. Jesus founded His Church on the twelve Apostles, several of whom were fishermen. The image of the net was very apropos. Jesus wanted to make them fishers of men. The Church, too, is a net, tied through the Holy Spirit, fastened through the apostolic mission, effective through unity in faith, life, and love.

I am thinking at this moment of the farspread net of the whole universal Church. At the same time, I see before my eyes every single church in your land, especially the great church of Cologne and the neighboring dioceses. And finally I see before my eyes the smallest of these churches, the *"Ecclesiola,"* the domestic church, to which the very recent Synod of Bishops in Rome gave such great attention in its subject on "the role of the Christian family."

The family: the domestic Church, the unique and irreplaceable community of persons, of which St. Paul speaks in today's second reading. Here he has before his eyes, of course, the Christian family of his time; but what he says must also be applied to the problems of the families of our time: what he says to husbands, what he says to wives, to children and to parents. And finally what he says to us all: "Put on, then...compassion, kindness, humility, meekness, and patience, forbearing one another and...forgiving each other.... And above all these put on love, which binds everything together in perfect harmony. And let the peace of Christ rule in your hearts, to which indeed you were called in the one body. And be thankful!" (Col. 3:12-15) What a great lesson of matrimonial and family spirituality!

REDISCOVER THE VALUE
OF MARRIAGE

4. We, however, cannot close our eyes to the other side either; the Synod Fathers in Rome gave their earnest attention to it, too: *I mean the difficulties to which the high ideal of the Christian concept of the family and of family life is exposed.* Modern industrial society has fundamentally changed the conditions of life for marriage and the family. Marriage and the family were previously not only communities of life, but also communities of production and economy. They have been ousted from many public functions. *Public opinion is not always favorable to marriage and the family.* And yet, in our anonymous mass civilization, they prove to be a place of refuge in the search for a haven and happiness. *Marriage and the family are more important than ever: cells of reproduction for the renewal of society, springs of strength, because of which life becomes more human.* I can draw inspiration from the image: the net, which gives support and unity and raises from the currents of the deep.

Let us not allow this net to break. *The state and society are on the way to their own decline if they do not support marriage and the family more effectively, and do not protect them more, and if they put them on the same level as other non-matrimonial communities of life.* All men of good will, particularly we Christians, are called to rediscover the dignity and value of marriage and the family and to live them before men in a convincing way. The Church, with the light of faith, offers her advice and her spiritual service for this purpose.

PERSONAL BOND OF FIDELITY

5. Marriage and the family are very deeply connected with man's personal dignity. They are not derived only from instinct and passion, nor only from feeling; they are derived in the first place from a decision of the free will, from a personal love, because of which spouses become not only one flesh, but also one heart and one soul. *Physical and sexual communion is something great and beautiful. But it is fully worthy of man only if it is integrated in a personal union, recognized by the civil and ecclesiastical community.* Full sexual communion between man and woman is legitimate, therefore, only within the exclusive and definitive personal bond of fidelity in marriage. *The indissolubility of conjugal fidelity, which is no longer understandable to many people today, is likewise an expression of man's unconditional dignity. One cannot live only on trial, one cannot die only on trial. One cannot love only on trial, accept a person only on trial and for a limited time.*

THE RIGHT TO LIFE

6. Thus marriage is geared to duration, to the future. It looks beyond itself. Marriage alone is suitable for procreation and the upbringing of children. Therefore matrimonial love is by its very nature geared also

to fertility. In this role of handing down life, spouses are collaborators with the love of God the Creator. I know that here, too, in today's society, the difficulties are great. Burdens, particularly for the woman. Small houses, economic and health problems, and often even a declared prejudice against large families, are an obstacle to greater fertility. I appeal to all those responsible, to all forces of society: do everything to bring help. I appeal first of all, however, to your conscience and to your personal responsibility, dear brothers and sisters. *You must make the decision about the number of your children in your conscience, in the presence of God.*

As spouses you are called *to responsible parenthood. This, however, means a family planning that respects ethical norms and criteria, as was also stressed by the recent Synod of Bishops.* In this connection I wish to recall emphatically to your memory today only the following: the killing of unborn life is not a legitimate means of family planning. I repeat what I said on May 31st of this year to workers in the Parisian suburb of Saint-Denis: *"The first right of man is the right to life. We must defend this right and this value. In the contrary case, the whole logic of faith in man, the whole program of really human progress, would be shaken and collapse."*

As a matter of fact, it is a question of this: to serve life.

MYSTERY OF MARRIAGE AND THE FAMILY

7. Dear brothers and sisters! On the indispensable foundation and premises of what has been said, we wish to turn now to the deepest mystery of marriage and the

family. From the point of view of our faith, marriage is a sacrament of Jesus Christ. *Love and conjugal fidelity are understood and sustained by the love and fidelity of God in Jesus Christ.* The power of His cross and of His resurrection sustains and sanctifies Christian spouses.

As the recent Synod of Bishops stressed in its "Message to Christian Families in the Modern World," the Christian family is called in particular to collaborate in God's salvific plan, since it helps its members *"to become agents of the history of salvation and at the same time living signs of God's loving plan for the world"* (Sect. III, no. 8).

As a "Church in miniature," sacramentally founded, or domestic Church, marriage and the family must be a school of faith and a place of common prayer. I attribute great significance precisely to prayer in the family. It gives strength to overcome the many problems and difficulties. In marriage and in the family, the fundamental human and Christian attitudes, without which the Church and society cannot exist, must grow and mature. *This is the first place for the Christian apostolate of the laity and of the common priesthood of all the baptized.* Such marriages and families, imbued with the Christian spirit, are also the real seminaries, that is, seedbeds for spiritual vocations for the priestly and religious state.

Dear spouses and parents, dear families! What could I more heartily wish you on the occasion of today's Eucharistic meeting than this: that all of you and every single family may be such a "domestic Church," a Church in miniature! That the parable of the kingdom of God may be realized in you! That you may experience the presence of the kingdom of God, in that you are yourselves a living "net," which unites and supports and gives refuge for yourselves and for many around you.

This is my good wish and blessing, which I express as your guest and pilgrim and as the servant of your salvation.

REFLECTION ON
ST. ALBERT THE GREAT

8. And now allow me, at the end of this fundamental reflection on the kingdom of God and on the Christian family, to turn again to St. Albert the Great, the celebration of whose seventh centenary has brought me to your city. Here, in fact, is the tomb of this famous son of your country, who was born in Lauingen, and who, in his long life, was at once a great scientist, a spiritual son of St. Dominic, and the teacher of Saint Thomas Aquinas. He was one of the greatest intellects of the thirteenth century. More than any other, he wove the "net" that unites faith and reason, God's wisdom and worldly knowledge. At least in spirit I also visit the city in which he was born, Lauingen, while today, here in Cologne, close to his tomb, I stop to meditate together with you on the words with which today's liturgy celebrates him:

"If the great Lord is willing,
he will be filled with the spirit of understanding;
he will pour forth words of wisdom
and give thanks to the Lord in prayer.
He will direct his counsel and knowledge aright,
and meditate on his secrets.
He will reveal instruction in his teaching,
and will glory in the law of the Lord's covenant.

Many will praise his understanding, and it will never be
  blotted out;

his memory will not disappear, and his name will live
  through all generations.

Nations will declare his wisdom, and the congregation
  will proclaim his praise" (Sir. 39:6-10).

There is nothing to be added to these words of the
wise son of Sirach. But neither must any be left out.
They describe perfectly, in fact, the figure of that man
on whom your country, your city, rightly pride themselves, and who is a joy for the whole Church. *Albertus
Magnus, doctor universalis*—Albert the Great, of vast
learning: a real "disciple of the kingdom of God"! If we
have reflected together today on the vocation of the
Christian family to build up the kingdom of God on
earth, the words of Christ's parable must also give us
the deepest significance of this saint, whom we are solemnly commemorating today. Christ says, in fact:
"Every scribe who has been trained for the kingdom of
heaven is like a householder who brings out of his treasure what is new and what is old" (Mt. 13:52).

St. Albert, too, is like this householder! May his
example and his intercession accompany me, while I try
on my pilgrimage through your country, as a fisher of
men, to knot the net more tightly and throw it out further, in order that the kingdom of God may come.
Amen.

THE CHURCH'S TEACHING ON MARRIAGE

About one million persons assisted at the Mass concelebrated by Pope John Paul in Cebu, the second city of the Philippines visited by the Pope in the course of his ninth apostolic journey. The celebration, dedicated especially to families, took place on February 19, 1981, on the large esplanade of the old international wharf.

During the Liturgy of the Word the Holy Father gave the following homily.

Dear brothers and sisters in Christ,

1. Finding myself in this important city known as ᵗhe cradle of Christianity in the Philippines, I want to express my deep joy and profound thanksgiving to the Lord of history. The thought that for 450 years the light of the Gospel has shone with undimmed brightness in this land and on its people is cause for great rejoicing. Four and a half centuries of fruitful interaction between the local culture and the Christian message have resulted in this harmonious blending called "Filipino Christian culture." Any Christian coming here from any part of the world finds himself at home among people sharing the same aspirations and the same hope that are central in Jesus Christ. Praised be the name of Jesus for what His love has wrought!

God's Providence in the Philippines has been truly wonderful.

The Christianization that took place in the sixteenth century was not something merely accidental. Divine grace was at work when the people of this region had their first contact with the image of the Santo Niño. It is an important historical fact, rich in religious meaning, that on January 1, 1571, the village kingdom of Sugbu was renamed the "Villa del Santo Niño," and thus the first city of the Philippines was placed under the patronage of the Child Jesus.

GREAT HOPE FOR THE FUTURE

2. Divine Providence has made it possible for us to be together here today, in order to offer a sacrifice of praise and thanksgiving to our Father in heaven for the four and a half centuries of Christianity in this country. The whole Church thanks God that the people who "were once far off have been brought near in the blood of Christ" (Eph. 2:12-13). She thanks God for the 450 years that His name has been glorified here, that true worship has been offered to Him, that the Blessed Virgin Mary has been devoutly and lovingly venerated, and that millions of people have been reborn in Christ. The unforgettable ceremonies held yesterday in Manila honoring the Filipino Protomartyr, Blessed Lorenzo Ruiz, forcefully illustrate that the Christian Faith has taken deep root in the Filipino soul.

In a particular way the Church thanks God that the tiny Christian community of Sugbu, under the patronage of the Infant Jesus, has now become a flourishing archdiocese of two million people, almost all of whom are Catholics, with an active and zealous clergy, both diocesan and religious, with dedicated men and women religious, and with an encouraging number of seminarians. I am also deeply gratified to know that there are numerous Catholic institutions and organizations and movements of the laity. It can truly be said that growth in faith and Christian living has been until now a constant feature of the Church in Cebu as well as in the whole of the Philippines. The glorious past gives great hope for the future. The harmonious relationship—under the leadership of Cardinal Julio Rosales, of the Coadjutor Archbishop and of the Auxiliary Bishop—between the hierarchy and the diocesan and religious clergy; the deep commitment to evangelization by priests, religious and laity; the existence of a solid ecclesial sense and the profound religiosity of the people—all this constitutes a great spiritual force for the building up of a dynamic Church in Cebu.

3. Beloved brothers and sisters in Christ, the centuries-old veneration of the Santo Niño here in Cebu prompts me *to speak to you today about the family. The Infant Jesus Himself was born of the Virgin Mary and lived in a family*, and it was in the Family of Nazareth that He began the mission which the Father had entrusted to Him. "For to us a child is born, to us a son is given" (Is. 9:6). *In Him a new era dawned, in Him the world was recreated, in Him a new life was offered to humanity, a life redeemed by and in Christ.*

Because the Creator wills that life should take its origin from the love of a man and a woman joined in a covenant of sharing in marriage, and because Christ elevated this union of spouses to the dignity of a sacrament, we must look at the family, at its nature and mission, in the bright light of our Christian Faith. *With legitimate pride one can state that whatever the Church teaches today on marriage and the family has been her constant teaching in fidelity to Christ.* The Catholic

Church *has consistently taught*—and I repeat here with the conviction that springs from my office as chief Pastor and Teacher—that *marriage was established by God;* that marriage is a covenant of love between one man and one woman; that the bond uniting husband and wife is *by God's will indissoluble;* that marriage between Christians is a sacrament symbolizing the union of Christ and His Church; and that *marriage must be open to the transmission of human life.*

FAITHFUL AND FRUITFUL

4. When Jesus was going about, teaching and healing, He was one day confronted by some Pharisees who wanted to test Him about marriage. Jesus answered, clearly and firmly, by reaffirming what Scripture had said: "From the beginning of creation, God made them male and female. For this reason a man shall leave his father and mother, and be joined to his wife, and the two shall become one. So they are no longer two but one. What therefore God has joined together, let no man put asunder" (Mk. 10:6-9). *By making them male and female God established the complementarity of the sexes,* for a man leaves his father and mother in order to be joined to his wife in that union of love that permeates all levels of human existence. *This union of love enables man and woman to grow together and to care properly for their children. The union that makes them one cannot be broken by any human authority; it is permanently at the service of the children and of the spouses themselves.* Thus the love between a man and a woman in marriage is a love that is both faithful and fruitful. It is a holy love, sacramentally symbolizing the union of

love between Christ and the Church, as St. Paul wrote to the Ephesians: "This is a great mystery, and I mean in reference to Christ and the Church" (Eph. 5:32).

CONTRACEPTION AND ABORTION

5. For these reasons, *the Church will never dilute or change her teaching on marriage and the family.* For these reasons, the Church condemns any attempt through the practice of polygamy to destroy the unity of marriage, and any attempt through divorce to destroy the marriage bond. *For these reasons also the Church states clearly that marriage should be open to the transmission of human life. God willed the loving union of husband and wife to be the source of new life.* He wishes to share, as it were, His creative power with husbands and wives, endowing them with procreative power. *God desires that this tremendous power to procreate a new human life should be willingly and lovingly accepted by the couple when they freely choose to marry.* Parenthood has a dignity all of its own, guaranteed by God Himself. *On my part I owe it to my apostolic office to reaffirm as clearly and as strongly as possible what the Church of Christ teaches in this respect, and to reiterate vigorously her condemnation of artificial contraception and abortion.*

6. Yes, *from the moment of conception and through all subsequent stages, all human life is sacred, for it is created in the image and likeness of God.* Human life is precious because it is a gift of God, whose love knows no limit; and *when God gives life, it is forever. Whoever attempts to destroy human life in the*

womb of the mother, not only violates the sacredness of a living, growing and developing human being, and thus opposes God, but also attacks society by undermining respect for all human life. I want to repeat here what I stated when visiting my homeland: "If a person's right to life is violated at the moment in which he is first conceived in his mother's womb, an indirect blow is struck also at the whole moral order, which serves to ensure the inviolable goods of man. *Among those goods, life occupies the first place.* The Church defends the right to life, not only in regard to the majesty of the Creator, who is the first giver of this life, but also in respect to the essential good of the human person" (June 8, 1979).

TO REFLECT CHRIST'S SACRIFICIAL LOVE

7. When the Church holds up before you the ideals of Christian marriage and the Christian family, when she insists that the love of husband and wife and the love of parents should be marked by generosity, *she knows that there are many factors today that threaten family life and tempt the human heart.* The selfish pursuit of pleasure, sexual permissiveness and the fear of a permanent commitment are destructive forces. As a good mother, the Church stands by her children in difficult times; she stands by the couples who experience difficulties in abiding by her teachings. With love and with an understanding of human weakness, but also with an understanding of the power of Christ's grace in individual human hearts, *the Church constantly challenges her children.* She challenges them to be con-

scious of the dignity of their Baptism and of the gift of sacramental grace that they have been given precisely in order that they might be able to reflect Christ's sacrificial love in their lives, develop their own love in a faithful and indissoluble union, and respond with generosity to the gift of parenthood. As the Second Vatican Council declared: "Authentic married love is caught up into divine love and is governed and enriched by Christ's redeeming power and the saving activity of the Church. Thus this love can lead the spouses to God with powerful effect and can aid and strengthen them in the sublime role of being a father or a mother" (GS 48). To all of you Christian couples—spouses and parents—I offer the invitation: walk with Christ! It is He who reveals to you the dignity of the covenant you have made; it is He who gives immense value to your conjugal love; it is He, Jesus Christ, who can accomplish in you immeasurably more than you can ask for or imagine (cf. Eph. 3:21).

EVERYONE RESPONSIBLE

8. *In a Christian community, everyone has a responsibility for families.* Programs that focus on the family and on the dignity of marriage are of great importance: programs to prepare those who are getting married, and programs for those who are already married. In regard to their children, parents have an irreplaceable role to play, not only as the first educators in the Faith and as models of virtue, but also as examples of faithful conjugal love. In the community of love and trust that each family ought to be, parents and children can be evangelized and at the same time instruments of

evangelization. Sincere respect for life and human dignity, unselfish charity and the sense of duty and justice rooted firmly in the Gospel, come from a family where wholesome relations between parents and children prevail, and where each member of the family tries to be a servant to each other. *A family where prayer, loving support and formation in the Faith are a constant concern will bring untold benefits not only to the members of the family themselves, but also to the Church and to society.*

THE FAMILY APOSTOLATE

9. I am most happy to know that all over the Philippines the Family Apostolate has received enthusiastic endorsement and support. I wish to praise the Catholic Bishops Conference of the Philippines for having declared the present decade, 1981 to 1990, "The Decade of the Family," and for having prepared a comprehensive pastoral program for this purpose. I commend most heartily the different organizations and movements, which in close collaboration with the hierarchy, devote their zealous efforts to the family. *I encourage all Catholic educators, but especially parents themselves, to devote great attention to the proper formation of the young in regard to human sexuality, placing in proper perspective the purpose of the Creator from the beginning, the redemptive power of Christ, and the influence of a true sacramental life.* The delicate responsibility for sex education belongs principally to the families, where an atmosphere of loving reverence will be conducive to a fully human and Christian understanding of the meaning of love and life.

A MEMORABLE TIME FOR ME

10. And so, my brothers and sisters in Christ, my friends of Cebu city and the surrounding areas, I am taking leave of you. This has been a memorable time for me: to be with you, to share with you the teachings of our Lord Jesus Christ on the Christian family, and to experience and reciprocate your love in the midst of God's family—the Church. May the Santo Niño bless you. May Mary the Mother of Jesus and St. Joseph her spouse assist you and all the families in the Philippines to reflect the holiness and joy and love of the Holy Family of Nazareth.

Pagpalain kayo nang Poong Maykapal! (May Almighty God bless you!)

POPE JOHN XXIII,
A MAN SENT BY GOD!

On April 26, 1981, tens of thousands, including many relatives of John XXIII, participated in a Mass celebrated by Pope John Paul II at Sotto il Monte, where Angelo Roncalli was born a hundred years ago. The Holy Father delivered the following homily.

Beloved brothers and sisters!

1. "We have contemplated, O God, the marvels of Your love!"

These words of the liturgy are well suited to this *"Domenica in Albis,"* on which, commemorating in his own native village the centenary of the birth of Pope John XXIII, we contemplate the marvelous gift that the Lord bestowed on us with his life and his teaching.

My heart is full of joy and emotion at being here at Sotto il Monte today for this solemn and significant ceremony, celebrated with you, to whom I extend my affectionate greeting.

I was driven here by the deep desire to bestow on my venerated Predecessor an honor and recognition that are due to him not only from the Church, but from all men who enjoyed his goodness and his wisdom.

A great many of you, inhabitants of Sotto il Monte and of Bergamo, knew Pope John, saw him, met him, spoke to him, heard his warm, loving and persuasive voice, sensitive to every joy and to every human suffering. And I too remember him with deep emotion at the first session of the Second Vatican Council, and above all, at its final meeting, when he greeted us in what was meant to be an *au revoir*, but was instead the final farewell.

And I am particularly happy to recall the affection that Pope John always felt for my country, Poland. On September 17, 1912, on the occasion of the Eucharistic Congress of Vienna, he visited Krakow and celebrated in the cathedral at the altar of the miraculous cross of Wavel, as he liked to recall with extreme precision of detail. He also many times visited the Marian sanctuary of Jasna Gora, discovering in the deep religious sentiments of my people something kindred, which touched him and comforted him.

It was only right, therefore, that on such an extraordinary and solemn occasion, his Successor in Peter's See should come to his birthplace to meditate on his message and breathe his spirituality.

POPE OF GOODNESS

2. As you very well know, Angelo Giuseppe was born on Friday, November 25, 1881, into the Roncalli family, the fourth of thirteen children, and that very evening the bell of the parish church rang out to announce his baptism.

And so today we commemorate not only little "Angelino's" birth to the light of the sun, but also the spiritual birth to the life of grace and faith of him who was to become, as Paul VI said, "the Pope of the goodness, meekness and pastoral nature of the Church" (*Insegnamenti di Paolo VI*, vol. I, p. 534); the Pope who was able to love everyone and who was loved by all for his characteristics of fatherhood, serenity, and human and priestly sensitivity. In fact, the reason for his extraordinary success in the esteem and affection of the whole world, then and today, was his goodness: mankind is in great need of goodness, and for this reason it loved Pope John and still venerates and invokes him.

We seem to see him in these streets, through these hills, among these houses, in this landscape of his, so ardently loved and remembered with tenderness to the last days of his life, "his dear nest of Sotto il Monte," where he came every year, when it was possible, as a priest, as a bishop and as a Cardinal, to take refuge, to fortify his spirit *in gratia et fide,* as his parents and his godfather, his great uncle Zaverio, had trained him.

3. If we ask ourselves where and how Pope John acquired such gifts of goodness and fatherliness, together with a Christian Faith that was always complete and pure, we can easily answer: *from his family.*

He himself, throughout his long life and in a very great number of writings, private and official, recalls, with emotion and gratitude, his family home, the years of his childhood and adolescence, spent in a crystal-clear and serene environment, in which *the pattern was the grace of God, lived with simplicity and consistency; the rule of life was the catechism and parish instruction; the comfort was prayer, especially Mass on feast days, and the evening rosary; and the daily commitment was charity:* "We were poor," Pope John wrote, "but content with our condition, confident in the help of Providence. When a beggar appeared at the kitchen door, where a score of boys and girls were waiting for a bowl of soup, there was always an extra place. My mother hastened to give the guest a seat beside us" (Giornale dell'anima, IV ed. Appendix).

The family and parish catechesis was his spiritual nourishment; faithfulness to the practices of piety and to the rites of the Church was his constant commitment, because he had in his parents an example, a stimulus and his first school of theology. With sweet affability he recalled in an address: "The dear image of our Lady, under the title 'Help of Christians,' was for many years familiar to our eyes as a boy and an adolescent in the house of our parents" (Discorsi, Messaggi, Colloqui del Santo Padre Giovanni XXIII, vol. XIV, p. 307). And in the address he delivered for his eightieth birthday, he said: "It was from these memories that there began and was nourished with veneration all that referred to religious life, to the sanctuary of our families, modest, hard working, God-fearing and serene" (ibid., vol. IV, p. 23).

On Christmas night, 1959, he went back with deep nostalgia to those distant times and with simplicity and wisdom traced the lines of Christian Doctrine concerning the family: *"How well the great realities of the Christian family were lived! Engagement in the reflection of God's light, marriage sacred and inviolable in respect to its four characteristic notes: fidelity, chastity, mutual love and holy fear of the Lord; the spirit of prudence and sacrifice in the careful upbringing of the children; and always in every circumstance, love of neighbor, forgiveness, the spirit of endurance, trust, respect for others. It is in this way that you build a house that does not collapse"* (ibid., vol. II, p. 96).

GENUINE AND TRANSPARENT FAITH

4. His faith, which originated in the family, and was enlightened and confirmed by the serious and methodical study carried out in the seminary in the wake of Holy Scripture, the Magisterium of the Church, patris-

tics and qualified and approved theology, subsequently accompanied throughout the course of the years by reading and meditation on the great masters of asceticism and mysticism, remained in this way always complete and profound, without suffering the errors of modernism, without ever deviating from the straight path of truth. In 1910 he noted in the "Journal of a Soul": "I thank the Lord on my knees for having kept me unharmed in the midst of such seething and agitation of tongues and brains.... I must always recall that the Church contains within her the eternal youth of truth and of Christ who is of all times.... *The first treasure of my soul is faith, the holy, sincere and ingenuous faith of my parents and my good old relatives.*"

From this genuine and transparent faith, instilled in him by the family, there sprang also his complete and confident abandonment to Providence, expressed in the motto that inspired his life: *Obedientia et Pax;* from it there arose the supernatural and eschatological view of existence and of all history, through which he walked in the light of "the last things" and of the "theology of the beyond." *This faith, enjoyed in his heart as absolute truth and as the meaning of human existence, was expressed with sweetness and confidence in the practices of piety which nourish Christian life—the many beautiful devotions that have blossomed throughout the centuries on the fertile trunk of dogma*—the union with the Eucharistic and crucified Christ, with the Sacred Heart; devotion to the Blessed Virgin, to the angels, to the saints; the constant remembrance of souls in purgatory; and naturally the visits to the Blessed Sacrament, regular confession, the recitation of the rosary, retreats and spiritual exercises, meditation and pilgrimages.

It is a faith rightly and soundly traditional, which, however, is not static, petrified, unduly conservative in the demanding and sweeping changes of times and situations; on the contrary, it is marvelous, youthful, fearless, open, farsighted, to the extent of planning and initiating the Second Vatican Council and of feeling, with keen intelligence, all the problems that accompany the modern era, as the Encyclicals *Mater et magistra* and *Pacem in terris* clearly show.

FIVE "KEY POINTS" OF HIS TEACHING

5. Pope John was truly a man sent by God! He has left us an immensely rich and precious heritage. But in this birthplace of his, where he received from his family the first seeds of the Faith which subsequently developed in such a surprising and fruitful way, I wish to recall and welcome in particular what he tells us about the family.

He had already given a warning about the dangers looming over it: "This sanctuary," he said with an anguished heart, "is threatened by so many snares. Propaganda, sometimes uncontrolled, uses the powerful media of the press, the theater and entertainment to spread, especially among the young, the fatal germs of corruption. *The family must defend itself...taking advantage also, when necessary, of the protection of the civil law"* (Discorsi..., vol. I, p. 172, March 1, 1959). Therefore, his teaching remains valid and perennial, because it is the voice of truth and what the soul of every person hopes for and expects deep down. I am happy to sum up that teaching in the five following "key points."

—In the first place the sacredness of the family, and therefore also of love and sexuality: "The family is a gift of God," he said. "It implies a vocation that comes from above, which cannot be improvised" *(Discorsi...,* vol. III, p. 67). "In the family there is the most admirable and close cooperation of man with God: the two human persons, created in the divine image and likeness, are called not only to the great task of continuing and prolonging the work of creation by giving physical life to new beings, in whom the life-giving Spirit infuses the mighty principle of immortal life, but also the nobler charge, which perfects the first one, of the civil and Christian education of their offspring" *(ibid.,* vol. II, p. 519). Owing to this essential characteristic, Jesus willed that marriage be a "sacrament."

—The morality of the family. "Let us not be deceived, blinded, deluded," he admonished with Christian and fatherly wisdom. *"The cross is always the only hope of salvation; the law of God is always there with its ten commandments, to remind the world that in this law alone is the safeguarding of consciences and families, that the secret of peace and tranquillity of conscience lies only in its observance.* Anyone who forgets it, even if he seems to shun any serious commitment, builds up, sooner or later, his own sadness and misery" *(ibid.,* vol. II, pp. 281-282). And on another occasion he added: "The cult of purity is the most precious honor and treasure of the Christian family" *(ibid.,* vol. IV, p. 897).

—The responsibility of the family. Pope John had confidence in the educational work of parents, sustained by divine grace. Addressing mothers he said: "The mother's voice, when it encourages, invites, beseeches, remains carved in the depths of her children's hearts, and is never forgotten. Oh, only God knows the good done by this voice, and its services to the Church and to human society" *(ibid.,* vol. II, p. 67). And to fathers he added: *"In families in which the father prays and has a joyful and conscious faith, attends catechetical instructions and takes his children there, there will not be the storms and desolation of a rebellious and estranged youth.* Our word wishes to be always one of hope; but we are certain that, in some discouraging expressions of youthful life, the greatest responsibility is to be sought first of all in those parents, especially in the fathers of families, who shirk the precise and serious duties of their state" *(ibid.,* vol. IV, p. 272).

—The purpose of the family. On this point, Pope John was clear and straightforward: *the aim for which we are born is holiness and salvation, and the family is willed by God for this purpose.* Twenty years ago, in the letter-testament, written on the occasion of his eightieth birthday, recalling one by one the beloved members of his family, he said: "This is what is most important: to secure eternal life, trusting in the goodness of the Lord who sees everything and provides for everything" (December 3, 1961). And commenting on the individual mysteries of the rosary, he said that he prayed at the third joyful mystery for children of all human races who had been born to the light of day in the last twenty-four hours *(ibid.,* vol. IV, p. 241).

—The good example of the Christian family. Pope John warmly exhorted Christian parents and children to be an example of faith and virtue in the modern world, on the model of the Holy Family: "The secret of true peace," he said, "of mutual and lasting harmony, of the docility of children, of the flourishing of noble morals, lies in the continuous and generous imitation of the sweetness and the modesty of the Family of Nazareth" (*ibid.*, vol. II, pp. 118-119). Pope John is sure that from these exemplary families there can spring many choice priestly and religious vocations, despite the difficulties of the times.

This is in summary the doctrine of the great and lovable Pontiff about the family, a doctrine which is an open condemnation of theories and practices which are contrary to the institution of the family.

May the good and smiling figure of Pope John, so close to the hearts of all Italians, help to cause to emerge once more in their souls that heritage of goodness and solidarity, characteristic of a people that wants life, and not the death of man, the advancement and not the destruction of the family.

LISTENING TO HIS WORD

6. Beloved brothers and sisters! Meeting with Pope John here today at Sotto il Monte to commemorate the centenary of his birth is certainly a great joy for everyone and a sweet consolation; but it must also be an incentive to keep his example always in mind and to listen to his word: "Every believer," he wrote in *Pacem in terris*, "must be a spark of light, a center of love, a vivifying ferment in the mass" (no. 57).

This is the commitment I leave to you in his name! I leave it to you, inhabitants of Sotto il Monte and of the whole region of Bergamo, which he loved so much, following the indications of the pastoral plan drawn up in such an excellent way by your bishop.

I leave it to all the faithful of the Church, priests and lay people, and I extend it to all men of good will, who were attracted and moved by the fatherly figure of Pope John.

May the tender devotion to the Blessed Virgin, which always marked his life, be also the precious heritage of everyone. "It aims at nothing other than making our faith more sturdy, ready and active," are his words. "Mary will help us all, who are pilgrims here below: with her supreme support we will overcome the inevitable sorrows and adversities, and we will acquire the habit of looking to heaven, with serenity and joy" (ibid., vol. II, p. 707).

May Pope John accompany us with his example and his prayer along the laborious ways of our lives. He is a good friend: let us listen to him! His heritage is truly a blessing!

V. Addresses and Homilies to the Synod, Roman Offices, and National Bishops on Human Life and the Family

a) "The Need To Restore Confidence to Christian Families," Address to Members of the Family Movements Gathered for the Synod on the Family, October 12, 1980.

b) "Role of the Family in Charity and Truth," Concluding Address to the Synod of Bishops on the Family, October 25, 1980.

c) "Safeguard the Values of Marriage," Address to the Sacred Roman Rota, The Roman Ecclesiastical Marriage Tribunal, January 24, 1981.

d) "Fidelity to the Truth in Love," Address to the United States Episcopal Conference in Chicago, October 5, 1979.

e) "The Apostolate of the Family: a Priority in the Task of Bishops," Address to a Group of Argentine Bishops, October 28, 1979.

f) "At the Service of Life," Address to the Bishops of Kenya on Their Ministry in the Service of Human Life, May 7, 1980.

g) "On Human Sexuality and Personhood,"
Message to a Workshop of United States Bishops
Meeting in Dallas, February 10, 1981.

h) "In the Service of the Church, Family and
Society," Address to the Italian Federation of Nur-
sery Schools, January 17, 1981.

THE NEED TO RESTORE CONFIDENCE TO CHRISTIAN FAMILIES

On October 12, 1980, the day dedicated to families, there was a special afternoon audience attended by representatives of about sixty Church Family Movements and the Synod Fathers. The Holy Father delivered the following message to the assembly.

Most reverend Archbishops and Bishops,
Beloved brothers and sisters,

1. The testimonies that we have all listened to with attention and a sense of deep participation offer us—it seems to me—a faithful and inspiring portrait of the family in these times of ours.

Lights and shadows, expectations and concerns, serious problems and firm hopes, are part of this portrait. Looking at it, the thought occurs to me that in the future, scholars will really be able to say that ours was the century of the family. In fact, *never as in this century has the family been conscious of so many threats, aggressions, and erosions.* But, at the same time, never as in this century has the family received so much assistance, both on the ecclesial and on the civil plane. In particular, theological reflection as well as pastoral activity in the various parishes tirelessly offer the family reference points and concrete ways to overcome the difficulties and seek improvement. If we can say what my Predecessor Pius XII affirmed immediately after the Second World War, namely that in our suffering society the family is the great invalid, it must also be said that *there are many who wish to offer the family valid remedies and assistance.* The Church, in conformity with her mission—the Synod which is going on in these days bears witness to this—is ready to offer it the *medicina evangelii*, the *remedium salutis*.

APPRECIATION
OF WITNESS STORIES

2. We have all followed with emotion and gratitude the words of those who have wished to bear their real-life witness here. They were short narratives, which, however, enabled us to catch, behind the necessarily concise sentences, a glimpse of real poems of love and dedication, the individual chapters of which we will get to know thoroughly in the kingdom of God, and this, too, will be part of the perfect joy of that time. I am sorry not to be able to take up again and develop all the subjects which have been recalled here with the liveliness, the freshness, the forcefulness characteristic of all testimonies rooted in personal experience.

I cannot pass over in silence, however, the appreciation with which I listened, for example, to the two young fiancés speaking of the priority they had given to spiritual values over material ones, in the preparation for their marriage. And in the same way, I was struck by the clarity with which stress was laid, in the various testimonies, on the positive impact that the commitment to live love chastely had on its growth and its development. *In the midst of so many voices which in our permissive society exalt sexual "freedom" as a factor of human fullness, it is right that there should also be raised the voice of those who, in daily experience of serene and generous self-control, have been able to discover a new source of mutual knowledge, deeper understanding, and true freedom.*

I also noted with deep joy that the various couples showed that they felt it a "natural" requirement of their love to open to brothers, in order to offer to those in need understanding, advice, and concrete aid: the altruistic dimension is part of true love which, giving itself, instead of becoming impoverished and dispersed, finds itself enriched, enlivened, and strengthened.

A LOVE THAT ENCOUNTERS GOD

A fact that emerged in the various experiences presented was the awareness, perceptible in the words of all, that *true love is the key to solve all problems, even the most tragic ones, such as the failure of the marriage, the death of the partner or of a child, the war.* The way out—it was said—is always and only love; a love stronger than death.

Human love is, therefore, a frail and menaced reality: everyone recognized this, explicitly or implicitly. To survive without drying up, it needs to transcend itself. Only a love that encounters God can avoid the risk of losing itself along the way. From different standpoints, those who spoke bore witness to us of the decisive importance that dialogue with God, prayer, had in their lives. In the experience of each one there have been moments in which it was only through God's face that it was possible to rediscover the real features of the face of the loved one.

These are some of the beautiful things that these brothers and sisters of ours said to us today. *We are grateful to them because now, after listening to them, we feel richer.*

We are fully aware, in fact, that we have a lot to learn from those who are trying to live consistently the unfathomable riches of a sacrament. It is in the wake of the testimonies that we have just listened to that I want to express some thoughts of mine now, pursuing, as it were, a dialogue.

NECESSITY OF RESTORING CONFIDENCE

3. And first and foremost I am anxious to say: *it is necessary to restore confidence to Christian families.* In the storm now raging over it, under indictment as it is, the Christian family is more and more tempted to give way to discouragement, lack of confidence in itself, and fear. *We must, therefore, tell it, with true and convincing words, that it has a mission and a place in the modern world and that, to carry out this task, it has formidable resources and lasting values.*

These values are above all of a spiritual and religious order: there is a sacrament, a *sacramentum magnum*, at the root and at the base of the family, a sacrament which is a sign of the active presence of the risen Christ within the family, just as it is also an inexhaustible source of grace.

But these values are also of a natural order: to illuminate them when they are dimmed, to strengthen them when they are weakened, and to rekindle them when they are almost extinguished, is a noble service rendered to man. *These values are love, faithfulness, mutual help, indissolubility, fecundity in its fullest meaning, intimacy enriched by opening towards others, the awareness of being the original cell of society,* etc.

The family is the steward and privileged transmitter of these values. The Christian family is so in a new and special way. These values strengthen it in its being and make it dynamic and efficacious in the community as a whole at every level. But the family must believe in these values, it must proclaim them fearlessly and live them serenely, transmit them and spread them.

COMMITMENT
OF EVERYONE NEEDED

4. My second thought is this: the more the "passion" of the family in the conditions of our modern world is extensive and takes on varied faces (we perceived this clearly on listening to the testimonies!), the more universal must be "compassion" for the family.

What, therefore, is the Christian family suffering from today? It is suffering, of course, in poor countries and in the poor areas of rich countries; it is suffering serious harm from regrettable situations of work and wages, of hygiene and housing, of food and education.... But this is not the only suffering: even the well-to-do family is not protected from other difficulties. The difficulty that comes from lack of preparation for the high responsibilities of marriage; that of misunderstanding among members of the family, which may lead to serious breaks; that of the deviation, in various forms, of one or several children, etc....

No man, no human group alone can remedy these different forms of suffering. That calls for the commitment of everyone: the Church, the state, intermediary bodies, the various human groups are called, in respect for the personality of each one, to effective service of the family. *Above all, the commitment of each of the spouses is necessary, and, for this purpose, it is greatly to be hoped that husband and wife have from the outset, or endeavor to have, the same view about the essential values of the family.*

FAMILY MOVEMENTS

5. My third thought concerns the Christian family and the pastoral help that the Church owes to it.

A short time ago, as I was listening to the various testimonies, I was struck not only by the content of each one and the special petition that came out of it; I was also struck by the fact that they were all coming from lay people, from Christian husbands and wives who actually live family life. This factor is a significant one in the Church's present pastoral action regarding the family.

In this regard, I cannot fail to mention the importance of family movements. They are numerous and flourishing, and in the present century they are one of the signs of the Church's never-failing vitality and pastoral creativity. An essential aspect of these movements is the fact that they are an active principle for the interior perfecting of many families at the different levels of family life; and at the same time they constitute dynamic centers of apostolic zeal.

One cannot fail to be grateful to these movements for all they are doing for the family. One cannot fail to rejoice that they are seeking to widen their own horizons with a view to service which will be ever more powerful, ever more intelligent, ever more in harmony with the complex realities and problems of the present time. Nevertheless, one must express the hope that the family movements will not water down what is their fundamental inspiration—an inspiration that is also their charisma and therefore their strength—into an activity that, however praiseworthy, could become merely generic and indiscriminate. *A just and legitimate social preoccupation must not cause these movements to fall into a false sociology that would empty them of the full content that is proper to them as long as they remain true ecclesial movements.*

To be totally effective, all family movements must take into account that fundamental structure of the Church which is the parish, and find integration in it. In this regard also it is useful to recall what I mentioned last year in the context of catechesis: *"The parish is still a major point of reference for the Christian people"* (RH 67). Through its coordinated pastoral activity, the parish is entirely oriented to the good of the family, to the family's well-being. *The family in its turn is called to support the parish in its essential mission of building up the kingdom of God by bringing the Word of God into the lives of all.*

In offering my encouragement and my support to all those who, in the different parishes of the world, collaborate in promoting the pastoral care of families, I express the hope that everyone will take advantage of the opportunities to be had for families at the parish level, and I pray that every parish will itself truly become a united and loving family.

FAMILY SPIRITUALITY

6. A last thought brings me to an invisible dimension, which cannot be expressed in numbers, but which has to be considered among the most important, if not the most important one of the family reality. *I am referring*—you will have already guessed—*to family spirituality*. All considerations on the Christian family should always converge towards this reference point as towards their own root and their own summit. *In fact, the Christian family springs from a sacrament—that of marriage—which, like all sacraments, is a bewildering divine initiative at the heart of a human existence.* Then, too, one of the purposes of this sacrament is to construct with living cells the Body of Christ which is the Church. The family can be understood only in the field of attraction of these two poles: a call from God which is binding on each one of the Christians who compose it, the response of each one in the great community of faith and salvation on its pilgrimage towards God.

Nevertheless, a Christian family embodies and lives all this in the context of elements which belong specifically to the family reality: human love between husband and wife and between parents and children, mutual understanding, forgiveness, reciprocal help and service, the education of the children, work, joys and sufferings.... *All these elements, within Christian marriage, are enveloped and, as it were, impregnated by grace and by the virtue of the sacrament, and become a way of evangelical life, a search for the face of the Lord, a school of Christian charity.*

Then there is a specific form of living the Gospel within the framework of family life. To learn it and put it into practice is to live marriage and family spirituality fully. In the hour of trial and hope that the Christian family is living, it is necessary for a larger number of families every day to discover and carry out a sound family spirituality in the midst of the daily fabric of their own existence. The effort made by Christian couples who, inside or outside family movements, endeavor to spread, under the guidance of enlightened pastors, the main lines of a true marriage and family spirituality, is more necessary and providential than ever. The Christian family needs this spirituality to find its balance, its complete fulfillment, its serenity, its dynamism, its opening to others, its joy and its happiness.

Christian families need someone to help them to live a real spirituality. The fact that the present Synod is concerned also with this dimension is a cause of joy for us all.

MANY FAMILIES WALKING WITH YOU

7. These are some considerations by which I set particularly great store. I entrust them to you and invite you to study them more deeply through personal reflection and in common conversation with your partner, and to draw suitable conclusions from them for yourselves and your married and family life. Always be aware that as a Christian family you are never alone and abandoned with your joys, needs, and difficulties. *In the large community of the faithful many other families are walking at your side, your pastors and bishops assist you, by order of Jesus Christ, and the Pope too thinks of you in tireless pastoral concern, and prays for you in love of the Lord.*

In this vast brotherly community of the Church, I therefore greet in you also all married couples and families in your respective homelands, for whom it was impossible to take part in this Day of the Family personally. We are sure that they too have participated, individually and with the members of their family, in today's worldwide prayer of the Church for the family. We have prayed here at the center of Christendom for them too, and for all families in the world. We feel united with them in the same way and pray for the special protection and assistance of God for them as for all the families represented here.

Many families from my country too are taking part in today's unusual meeting, characterized by the dimension of a testimony, before God, the Church and the world, on the Christian family and its tasks in the modern world. And this gives me particular joy. I welcome you and cordially greet you all at St. Peter's tomb, at the heart of the Church. In you, present here—and through you—I greet every Polish family, both in the homeland and outside its frontiers: every father, every mother, every child who is the hope and the future of the world and the Church. Take this greeting and my blessing to the thresholds of every home, to every family. And also take this experience and this testimony of the family which you have given here in Rome, and those that the Church gives on the family.

From Rome, from the present Synod of Bishops, and from all that you are experiencing in the course of these days, *you draw the conviction, the confidence, and the certainty that it is a right and duty of the Church to cultivate and carry out her doctrine in pastoral guidance on marriage and the family.*

She does not intend to impose this doctrine and guidance on anyone, but is ready to propose them freely and to safeguard them as a reference point that cannot be renounced for those who style themselves Catholics and who wish to belong to the ecclesial community.

The Church considers, therefore, that she can proclaim her convictions on the family, certain that she is rendering a service to all men. She would betray man if she passed over in silence her message on the family. Be sure, therefore, that you are sowing good whenever you announce the Good News about the family with freedom, humility, and love.

May our families be strong with the strength of God; may the divine law, grace, and love guide them; may the face of the earth be renewed in them and for them.

ROLE OF THE FAMILY
IN CHARITY AND TRUTH

On October 25, 1980, in the Sistine Chapel, the solemn rite for the closing of the Fifth General Assembly of the Synod of Bishops began.

After an address of homage to the Pope by one of the delegate presidents, Cardinal Primatesta, the "Message to the Christian Family in the Modern World" was read; then, ending with the singing of Terce, John Paul II delivered the following homily in Latin.

Venerable Brothers,

1. We have heard how St. Paul the Apostle thanked God for the Church of Corinth, "because it had become rich in Christ Jesus, in every word and in all knowledge" (cf. 1 Cor. 1:5). We now also feel compelled to express thanks above all to the Father, Son and Holy Spirit, before we bring an end to this Synod of Bishops; to celebrate this occasion, we who were members of this assembly or who participated in its work *have been brought together, in the mystery of that highest unity which is proper to the most Holy Trinity.* To this ceremony, therefore, we bring a sense of gratitude that we have completed the Synod, which is an outstanding indication of the vigor of the Church and which has great importance for the life of the Church. For the Synod of Bishops—let us use the words of the Council, according to whose direction the Sovereign Pontiff Paul VI established the Synod—"as an instrument of the entire Catholic episcopate, signifies that all bishops are participants in a hierarchical communion of solicitude for the universal Church" (CD 5).

We are also grateful for these four weeks in which we have worked together. Indeed, this space of time, even before the last resolutions were offered—that is, the message and the propositions—was fruitful for us, insofar as truth and love seemed to grow more and more as the days and weeks went by.

This progress must surely be brought to light, and the characteristics which made it outstanding should be briefly described. In this way it will be evident how rightly and clearly there were manifested in it both freedom and responsible concern regarding the subject which was treated.

Today, above all, we want to offer thanks to Him "who sees in secret" (Mt. 6:4), and is active as a "hidden God," in that He directed our thoughts, our hearts and our consciences, and indeed endowed us with them so that we would focus on a spiritual work in fraternal peace and joy. Such was His gift that we scarcely felt the work or the fatigue. Nevertheless, how much fatigue there really was! You have truly spared no effort.

A SINGULARLY FRUITFUL SYNOD

2. It is likewise fitting that we give thanks among ourselves. Before all else, this must be said: that progress by which, in a gradually maturing manner, "we bore the truth in charity," we should all attribute to the constant prayers which the entire Church—standing around us, as it were—poured out at this time. This prayer was offered for the Synod and for families: for the Synod, insofar as it had reference to families; and for families, in regard to the roles which they must exercise in the Church and in the modern world. By reason of these prayers, perhaps, the Synod was singularly fruitful.

God was besieged with constant and copious prayers: this was most evident on October 12th, when husbands and wives, who represented families throughout the world, came before St. Peter's Basilica to celebrate the sacred rites and pray together with us.

But if we ought to thank one another, this duty must at the same time be extended to so many benefactors who are unknown, but who helped us by their prayers throughout the whole world, offering also their sufferings to God for the intention of this synod.

EXPRESSION OF GRATITUDE

3. Now we come to that expression of gratitude in which we embrace all those who contributed to the celebration of this synod; there are the Presidents, the General Secretary, the General Relator, the members themselves in a special way, the Special Secretary and his helpers, the men and women auditors, the communications media assistants, and all the others, from the ushers to the technicians and typists.

We are all grateful, because we could complete this Synod, which was a singular manifestation of the collegial solicitude of the bishops of the whole world for the Church. *We are grateful because we could see the family as it really is in the Church and in the modern world*, as we considered the many different conditions which face the family; the traditions which, flowing from various forms of culture, touch it; the elements of a more sophisticated life which affect it and to which it is subjected; and other things of this type. We are grateful because, *with the outlook of faith, we could reexamine the eternal plan of God concerning the family, manifested in the mystery of creation and confirmed by the blood of the Redeemer*, the Spouse of the Church; finally, we are grateful that we could define, according to the eternal plan concerning life and love, the roles of the family in the Church and in the modern world.

FRUIT OF THE SYNOD

4. The fruit which this synod of 1980 has already brought forth is contained in the propositions accepted by the assembly, the first of which says: "How to know the plan of God on the pilgrimage of the People of God. The sense of faith."

We have now received this rich treasure of propositions, which number forty-three, as a singularly precious fruit of the labors of the Synod.

At the same time, we confirm the joy which the assembly itself, in offering its message, has addressed to the universal Church, which message the General Secretariat, with the help of the offices of the Holy See, will take care to send to all to whom it is of interest, likewise using the help of the Episcopal Conferences.

NECESSITY OF SYNODS

5. Those things which the Synod of 1980 has pointedly considered and enunciated in its propositions make us see the Christian and apostolic roles of the family in the modern world and make us in some way elicit those responses from the whole abundance of things which the Second Vatican Council has taught. Thus we go forward along the way which will enable the doctrinal and pastoral proposals of the Synod to be effectively carried out.

In its achievements, this year's Synod is connected with past Synods and is their continuation—we speak of the 1971 Synod and especially of the 1977 Synod which served, and ought to serve, to draw the conclusion from the Second Vatican Council regarding life. These Synods help the work pertaining to this, so that the Church might in an appropriate way address itself to the conditions of our age.

ACCURATE EXAMINATION

6. Among the labors of this synod, of the greatest usefulness must be considered *the accurate examination of doctrinal and pastoral questions which certainly needed such scrutiny and, consequently, the sure and insightful judgment concerning each of these questions.*

In the abundance of interventions, reports and conclusions of this Synod, which have aroused our admiration, there are two hinges on which the discussion has turned: namely, *fidelity toward the plan of God for the family, and a pastoral way of acting, proper to which is merciful love and reverence shown to all men and women, embracing them totally, touching their "being" and their "living"*—in such abundance, we say, there are certain parts which were singularly taken to heart by the Fathers of the Synod, because they were conscious that they were interpreters of the expectations and hopes of many spouses and families.

Therefore, among the labors of the Synod, it is appropriate to remember these questions and to acknowledge this useful examination, which has been pointedly done: namely, *the doctrinal and pastoral examination of questions,* which, although they were not the only things treated in the Synod discussions, *nevertheless had a special place there, insofar as their consideration was undertaken in a very sincere and free manner.*

From this results the importance which is attributed to the opinions, which the Synod clearly brought forth concerning these questions, retaining at the same time *that truly Christian perspective, according to which marriage and the family are considered gifts of divine love.*

Therefore, the Synod, commenting on the pastoral ministry of those who have entered a new union after divorce, deservedly praised those spouses, who, although faced with great difficulties, nevertheless witness in their own life to the indissolubility of marriage; in their life there is carried the beautiful message of faithfulness to the love which has in Christ its strength and foundation. Besides, the Fathers of the Synod, affirming once again the indissolubility of marriage and the practice of the Church of not admitting to Eucharistic Communion those who have divorced and have— against the rule—attempted another marriage, exhort pastors and the whole Christian community to help these brothers and sisters, who are not to be considered separate from the Church, but by virtue of their Baptism can and ought to participate in the life of the Church by praying, by hearing the Word, by assisting at the Eucharistic Celebration of the community, and by fostering charity and justice. *Although it must not be denied that such persons can be received to the Sacrament of Penance, eventually and finally to Eucharistic Communion, when they open themselves with a sincere heart to live in a manner which is not opposed to the indissolubility of marriage: namely, when a man and*

woman in this situation, who cannot fulfill the obliga-
tion to separate, take on themselves the duty to live in
complete continence, that is, by abstinence from acts in
which only married couples can engage, and when they
avoid giving scandal; nevertheless, the deprivation of
sacramental reconciliation with God should not prevent
them from persevering in prayer, penance, and works of
charity that they might find the grace of conversion and
salvation. It is fitting that the Church present herself as
a merciful mother by pouring forth prayers for these
persons and by strengthening them in faith and in hope.

A PROMISE AND A GRACE

7. *The Fathers of the Synod are not removed in*
mind and heart from the grave difficulties which many
spouses feel in their consciences about moral laws which
pertain to transmitting and fostering human life. Knowing that the divine precept carries with it both a promise
and a grace, they have openly confirmed the validity
and clear truth of the prophetic message—profound in
meaning and pertaining to today's conditions—contained
in the Encyclical letter *Humanae vitae.* The same Synod
urged theologians to join their talents with the work of
the hierarchical Magisterium so that the biblical foundation and so-called "personalistic" reasons for this doctrine might be continually illustrated, *explaining it so*
that the whole doctrine of the Church might be clearer
to all persons of good will, and so that understanding
might grow deeper by the day.

Directing their attention to those things which concern pastoral ministry for the good of spouses and of
families, the Fathers of the Synod rejected any type of
division or "dichotomy" between a pedagogy which

takes into account a certain progression in accepting the plan of God, and doctrine, proposed by the Church, with all its consequences, in which the precept of living according to the same doctrine is contained—*in which case there is not a question of a desire of keeping the law as merely an ideal to be achieved in the future, but rather of the mandate of Christ the Lord that difficulties constantly be overcome. Really, the "process of gradualness," as it is called, cannot be applied unless someone accepts divine law with a sincere heart and seeks those goods which are protected and promoted by the same law.* Thus, the so-called *lex gradualitatis* (law of gradation) or gradual progress cannot be the same as *gradualitas legis* (the gradation of the law), *as if there were in divine law various levels or forms of precept for various persons and conditions.*

All spouses are called to sanctity in marriage according to God's plan; but this vocation takes effect insofar as the human person responds to the precept of God, and with a serene mind has confidence in divine grace and one's own will. Therefore, for spouses, if both are not bound by the same religious insights, it will not be enough to accommodate oneself in a passive and easy manner to existing conditions, but they must try, so that, with patience and good will, they might find a common willingness to be faithful to the duties of Christian marriage.

CONSIDERING CULTURES

8. The Fathers of the Synod have sought a deeper awareness and consciousness either of the riches, which are found in various forms in people's cultures, or of the benefits which every culture brings with it—through

which the unfathomable mystery of Christ is more fully understood. Besides, they have acknowledged, even within the purposes of marriage and the family, a vast field of theological and pastoral research, so that the accommodation of the message of the Gospel to the character of each people might be fostered, and *so that it might be perceived in what ways their customs, outstanding characteristics, the sense of life and the genius peculiar to each human culture are compatible with those things known from divine revelation* (cf. AG 22).

This inquiry, if it is instituted according to the principle of communion with the universal Church and under the impetus of local bishops, who are joined among themselves and with St. Peter's Chair, "which presides over the universal assembly of charity" (LG 13), will bear fruit for families.

DIGNITY OF WOMAN

9. In words both opportune and persuasive, the Synod has spoken of woman with reverence and a grateful spirit, especially of her dignity and vocation as a daughter of God, as a wife, and as a mother. *Therefore, it commendably asked that human society be so constituted that women not be forced to engage in external work proper to a certain role or, as they say, profession, but rather, so that the family might be able to live rightly, that the mother might devote herself fully to the family.*

TRUTH IN CHARITY

10. If we have remembered these outstanding questions and the responses which the Synod gave to them,

we would not wish to think less of other matters which the Synod treated; for it has been shown how, in many interventions through these weeks, useful and fruitful, worthy questions were treated, which are explained either in the teaching or in the pastoral ministry of the Church, with great reverence and love, full of mercy toward men and women, our brothers and sisters, who come to the Church to receive words of faith and hope. Therefore, taking the example of the Synod, pastors should address these problems as they exist in married and family life with the same care and firm will so that we all might "bear the truth in charity."

We now wish to add something as the fruit of labors which we have undertaken for more than four weeks: namely that *no one can exercise charity other than in truth.* This principle can be applied to the life of families no less than to the life and work of pastors who really intend to serve families.

Therefore, the fruit of this Synod Session has been found in precisely this: that the roles of the Christian family, of which charity itself is the heart, are not fulfilled except in full charity. Moreover, all on whom it has been proposed to confer responsibility for a role of this type in the Church—whether lay people or clerics or religious of either sex—can do it in no other way than in truth. For truth is that which frees; truth is that which provides order; truth shows the way to holiness and justice.

It has been shown to us how great is the love of Christ and how great is the charity conferred on all those who establish any family in the Church and in the world: not only to the men and women joined in marriage, but also to children and young people, to widows

and orphans, and to each and every person who partici-
pates in family life in any way.

To all of these, the Church wants to be and to remain a witness and, as it were, a portal to the fullness of that life of which St. Paul speaks at the beginning of the words just read: that we have become rich in all things in Christ Jesus, in every word and in all knowledge (cf. 1 Cor. 1:5).

And now we announce to you that we have appointed to help the general Secretary of the Synod of Bishops, three prelates whose nomination originates with the Roman Pontiff, to add to the twelve members of the same secretariat elected by you. They are: Cardinal Ladislaus Rubin, Prefect of the Sacred Congregation for Oriental Churches; Archbishop Paulos Tzadua, Metropolitan Archbishop of Addis Abeba of the Ethiopians; Archbishop Carlo Maria Martini, Archbishop of Milan.

Finally, we wish you all well in the Lord.

SAFEGUARD THE VALUES
OF MARRIAGE

On January 24, 1981, the Holy Father received in audience the judges of the Sacred Roman Rota, at the beginning of the new judicial year. In reply to an address by Mons. Heinrich Ewers, Dean of the Sacred Roman Rota, John Paul II spoke as follows.

Very Reverend Dean,
Dear prelates and officials of the Sacred Roman Rota!

1. I am happy to meet you today, on the occasion of the opening of the new judicial year of your court. I heartily thank the dean for the noble words addressed to me and for the wise methodological resolutions formulated. I greet you all with fatherly affection, while I express my sincere appreciation for your work, so delicate and yet so necessary, which is an integral and qualified part of the pastoral office of the Church.

The specific competence of the Sacred Roman Rota with regard to matrimonial cases touches very closely the topical theme of the family, which has been the subject of study by the recent Synod of Bishops. Well, I now intend to speak to you about the juridical safeguarding of the family in the judicial activity of the ecclesiastical courts.

MARRIAGE PROBLEMS

2. With a deep evangelical spirit the Second Vatican Ecumenical Council has accustomed us *to look to man, in order to know him in all his problems and to*

help him to solve his existential problems by the light of the truth revealed to us by Christ and with the grace that the divine mysteries of salvation offer us.

Among the problems that most affect man's heart today—and consequently the human environment, both family and social, in which he lives and works—the preeminent and indispensable one is that of conjugal love, which binds two human beings of different sex, making them a community of life and love, that is, uniting them in marriage.

Marriage gives rise to the family, "where," Vatican II emphasizes, "different generations come together and help one another to grow wiser and harmonize the rights of individuals with other demands of social life"; and as such "the family constitutes the basis of society" (GS 52). In fact, the Council adds, "the well-being of the individual person and of both human and Christian society is closely bound up with the healthy state of conjugal and family life" *(ibid.,* no. 47). But with the Council itself we must recognize that "this happy picture of the dignity of these partnerships is not reflected everywhere, but is overshadowed by polygamy, the plague of divorce, so-called free love, and similar disfigurements; furthermore, married love is very often dishonored by selfishness, hedonism, and unlawful contraceptive practices" *(ibid.).*

Also owing to the serious difficulties that arise, sometimes with violence, from the deep changes in society today, the institution of marriage plainly shows its irreplaceable value, and the family still remains "a school for human enrichment" *(ibid.,* no. 52).

In the face of grave evils which nearly everywhere today beset this great good, which is the family, it has been suggested that *there should be drafted a charter of the rights of the family, universally recognized, in order to ensure this institution just protection, in the interest also of the whole of society.*

3. The Church on her part, and within the sphere of her competence, has always tried to protect the family also with appropriate legislation, as well as encouraging it and helping it with various pastoral initiatives. I have already mentioned the recent Synod of Bishops. But it is well known that, right from the beginning of her Magisterium, the Church, encouraged by the word of the Gospel (cf. Mt. 19:5; 5:32), has always taught and explicitly reiterated the precept of Jesus on the unity and indissolubility of marriage, without which it is never possible to have a secure, healthy family, a real vital cell of society. Contrary to the Graeco-Roman and Judaic practice, which greatly facilitated divorce, the Apostle Paul already declared: "To the married I give charge, not I but the Lord, that the wife should not separate from her husband...and that the husband should not divorce his wife" (1 Cor. 7:10-11). There followed the preaching of the fathers, who, before the spread of divorce, affirmed emphatically that marriage is, by divine will, indissoluble.

Respect, therefore, for the laws willed by God for the meeting between man and woman and for the continuation of their union, was the new element that Christianity introduced into the institution of marriage. "The intimate partnership of life and the love which constitutes the married state"—Vatican II will subsequently say—"has been established by the Creator and endowed by Him with its own proper laws: it is rooted in the contract of its partners, that is, in their irrevocable personal consent. It is an institution confirmed by the divine law and receiving its stability, even in the eyes of society, from the human act by which the partners mutually surrender themselves to each other" (GS 48).

This doctrine immediately guided the apostolate, the behavior of Christian spouses, the ethics of marriage and its juridical discipline. And the catechetical and pastoral activity of the Church, supported and strengthened by the witness of Christian families, introduced changes even in Roman legislation, which, with Justinian, no longer admitted divorce *sina causa*, and gradually came to accept the Christian institution of marriage. It was a great achievement for society, since the Church, having restored dignity to woman and to marriage through the family, contributed to saving the best of Graeco-Roman culture.

DANGER IN EASY DECLARATIONS OF NULLITY

4. In the present-day social framework, the original effort, doctrinal and pastoral, of conduct and praxis, as well as legislative and judicial, is again proposed to the Church today.

The good of the human person and of the family, in which the individual realizes a great part of his dignity, and the good of society itself, require that the Church, today even more than in the recent past, surround the institution of marriage and the family with particular protection.

The pastoral effort, urged also by the recent Synod of Bishops, might turn out to be almost in vain if it were not accompanied by a corresponding legislative and judicial action. For the comfort of all pastors, we can say that the new codification of Canon Law is making provision with wise juridical norms to express what has emerged from the recent Ecumenical Council in favor of marriage and the family. The voice heard at the recent Synod of Bishops about the alarming increase of matrimonial cases in the ecclesiastical courts, will certainly be evaluated during the revision of the Code of Canon Law. It is likewise certain that the pastors, also in response to the requests of the above-mentioned Synod, will be able, with increased pastoral commitment, to promote the adequate preparation of engaged couples for the celebration of marriage. The stability of the conjugal bond and the happy continuation of the family community depend, in fact, to a great extent on the way in which fiancés prepare for their marriage. But it is also true that the very preparation for marriage would be negatively influenced by the pronouncements or sentences of matrimonial nullity, if these were obtained too easily. *If, among the evils of divorce, there is also that of making the celebration of marriage less serious and binding, to the extent that today it has lost due consideration among a good many young people, it is to be feared that also the sentences of the declaration of matrimonial nullity would lead to the same existential and psychological perspective, if they were multiplied as easy and hasty pronouncements.* "Hence the ecclesiastical judge"—my venerated Predecessor Pius XII already admonished—"must not prove to be easy in declaring the nullity of marriage, but must rather endeavor first and foremost to bring it about that what has been contracted invalidly should be made valid, especially when the circumstances of the case make it particularly advisable." And in explanation of this admonishment he had first stated: "As for declarations of nullity of marriages, everyone knows that the Church is wary and averse to encouraging them. If, in fact, the tranquillity, stability and security of human dealings in general demand that contracts should not lightly be proclaimed null, this applies even more to a contract of such importance as is marriage, whose firmness and stability are required by the common good of human society and by the private good of spouses and their offspring, and whose dignity as a sacrament forbids that what is sacred and sacramental should be easily exposed to the danger of profanation" (Address to the Sacred Roman Rota, October 3, 1941, *AAS* [1941], pp. 423-424). With its wise and prudent work of vigilance, the Supreme Court of the Apostolic Signatura is contributing in a praiseworthy way to warding off this danger. The judicial action of the Court of the Sacred Roman Rota seems to me likewise valid. The equally wise and responsible work of the lower courts must correspond to the vigilance of the Signatura and the sound jurisprudence of the Rota.

FULL CONFORMITY
TO CHURCH DOCTRINE

5. No small contribution to the necessary protection of the family is made by the attention and prompt availability of the diocesan and regional courts in following the directive of the Holy See, the constant jurisprudence of the Rota, and faithful application of the norms, both of substantial and of process law,

already codified, without having recourse to presumed or probable innovations, to interpretations which do not objectively correspond to the canonical norm and which are not borne out by any qualified jurisprudence. *Any innovation in law, whether substantial or regarding process law, which does not find verification in the jurisprudence or praxis of the courts and departments of the Holy See, is, in fact, rash.* We must be convinced that a serene, attentive, well pondered, complete and exhaustive examination of matrimonial cases calls for full conformity with the precise doctrine of the Church, Canon Law, and sound canonical jurisprudence, which has been developing above all through the contribution of the Sacred Roman Rota; all that must be considered, as Paul VI of venerated memory already said to you, a "wise means" and "a railroad track, as it were, whose central line of direction is precisely the pursuit of objective truth, and whose terminal point is the correct administration of justice" (Paul VI, Jan. 28, 1978, *AAS* [1978], p. 182).

In this pursuit, all the ministers of the ecclesiastical tribunal—each one with due respect for his own role and that of others—must take into particular, constant and conscientious consideration, the formation of free and valid matrimonial consent, always combined with the concern, equally constant and conscientious, for protection of the Sacrament of Marriage. To the attainment of knowledge of the objective truth, that is, the existence of the matrimonial bond validly contracted, or its nonexistence, there contribute both attention to the problems of the person and attention to the laws on which—by divine or natural law, or the positive law of the Church—the valid celebration of marriage and its continuation depend. Canonical justice, which, according to the fine expression of St. Gregory the Great, we call more significantly sacerdotal justice, emerges from all the proofs of the process as a whole, evaluated conscientiously in the light of the doctrine and law of the Church, and with the support of the most qualified jurisprudence. *The good of the family demands this, keeping in mind the fact that all protection of the legitimate family is always in favor of the person; while unilateral concern with the individual can lead to injury of the human person himself, in addition to harming marriage and the family, which are goods both of the person and of society.* The provisions of the marriage code which is in force must be seen in this perspective.

COURTS MUST HELP PERSONS SEEK TRUTH

6. In the Synod's message to Christian families, stress is laid on the great good that the family, especially the Christian one, constitutes and realizes for the human person. The family "helps its members to become promoters of the history of salvation and at the same time living signs of the plan that God has for the world" no. 8). Also judicial activity, being an activity of the Church, must keep in mind this reality—which is not only natural but also supernatural—of marriage and of the family which springs from marriage. Nature and grace reveal to us, though in different ways and to different degrees, a divine plan for marriage and the family, which must always be taken into consideration, protected and, according to the roles peculiar to each activity of the Church, promoted so that it may be accepted by human society as widely as possible.

The Church, therefore, also with her law and exercise of *potestas iudicialis*, can and must safeguard the values of marriage and the family, in order to promote man and emphasize his dignity.

The judicial action of the ecclesiastical matrimonial courts, like the legislative one, will have to help the human person in the search for objective truth and then to affirm this truth, so that the same person may be able to know, live, and carry out the loving plan that God has assigned to him.

The invitation that Vatican II addressed to all, particularly to "everyone who exercises an influence in the community and in social groups," responsibly involves, therefore, also the ministers of the ecclesiastical courts for matrimonial cases, so that they too, while serving truth and administering justice well, may devote themselves "to the welfare of marriage and the family" (GS 52).

FOR A SERENE AND PROFITABLE WORK

7. Therefore I offer to you, Very Reverend Dean, to the Prelate Auditors and to the Officials of the Sacred Roman Rota, my cordial wishes for serene and profitable work, carried out in the light of these considerations today.

And, while I am happy to renew the expression of my appreciation for the valuable and tireless activity of your court, I willingly impart to you all the special apostolic blessing, invoking divine assistance for your delicate office and as a sign of my constant favor.

FIDELITY TO THE TRUTH IN LOVE

On the Pope's last day in Chicago, October 5, 1979, he met the bishops of the Episcopal Conference of the United States at Quigley South Seminary, and delivered the following address.

Dear brothers in our Lord Jesus Christ,

1. May I tell you very simply how grateful I am to you for your invitation to come to the United States? It is an immense joy for me to make this pastoral visit, and in particular, to be here with you today.

On this occasion I thank you, not only for your invitation, not only for everything you have done to prepare for my visit, but also for your partnership in the Gospel from the time of my election as Pope. I thank you for your service to God's holy people, for your fidelity to Christ our Lord, and for your unity with my Predecessors and with me in the Church and in the College of Bishops.

I wish at this time to render public homage to a long tradition of fidelity to the Apostolic See on the part of the American hierarchy. During the course of two centuries, this tradition has edified your people, authenticated your apostolate, and enriched the universal Church.

Moreover, in your presence today, I wish to acknowledge with deep appreciation the fidelity of your faithful and the renowned vitality that they have shown in Christian life. This vitality has been manifested not only in the sacramental practice of communities but also in abundant fruits of the Holy Spirit. With great zeal your people have endeavored to build up the kingdom of God by means of the Catholic school and through all catechetical efforts. An evident concern for others has been a real part of American Catholicism, and today I thank the American Catholics for their generosity. Their support has benefited the dioceses of the United States, and a widespread network of charitable works and self-help projects, including those sponsored by Catholic Relief Services and the Campaign for Human Development. Moreover, the help given to the missions by the Church in the United States remains a lasting contribution to the cause of Christ's Gospel. *Because your faithful have been very generous to the Apostolic See, my Predecessors have been assisted in meeting the burdens of their office;* and thus, in the exercise of their worldwide mission of charity, they have been able to extend help to those in need, thereby showing the concern of the universal Church for all humanity. For me then this is an hour of solemn gratitude.

AN HOUR OF ECCLESIAL COMMUNION

2. But even more, this is an hour of ecclesial communion and fraternal love. I come to you as a brother Bishop: one who, like yourselves, has known the hopes and challenges of a local Church; one who has worked within the structures of a diocese, who has collaborated within the framework of an Episcopal Conference; one who has known the exhilarating experience of collegiality in an Ecumenical Council as exercised by bishops together with him who both presided over this collegial assembly and was recognized by it as *totius Ecclesiae Pastor*—invested with "full, supreme and universal power over the Church" (cf. LG 22). I come to you as one who has been personally edified and enriched by participation in the Synod of Bishops; one who was

supported and assisted by the fraternal interest and self-giving of American bishops who traveled to Poland in order to express solidarity with the Church in my country. I come as one who found deep spiritual consolation for my pastoral activity in the encouragement of the Roman Pontiffs with whom, and under whom, I served God's people, and in particular in the encouragement of Paul VI, whom I looked upon not only as Head of the College of Bishops, but also as my own spiritual father. And today, under the sign of collegiality and because of a mysterious design of God's Providence, I, your brother in Jesus, now come to you as Successor of Peter in the See of Rome, and therefore as Pastor of the whole Church.

Because of my personal pastoral responsibility, and because of our common pastoral responsibility for the people of God in the United States, *I desire to strengthen you in your ministry of faith as local pastors*, and to support you in your individual and joint pastoral activities by encouraging you to stand fast in the holiness and truth of our Lord Jesus Christ. And in you I desire to honor Jesus Christ, the Shepherd and Bishop of our souls (cf. 1 Pt. 2:25).

Because we have been called to be shepherds of the flock, we realize that we must present ourselves as humble servants of the Gospel. Our leadership will be effective only to the extent that our own discipleship is genuine—to the extent that the beatitudes have become the inspiration of our lives, to the extent that our people really find in us the kindness, simplicity of life and universal charity that they expect.

We who, by divine mandate, must proclaim the duties of the Christian law, and who must call our people to constant conversion and renewal, know that St. Paul's invitation applies above all to ourselves: "You must put on the new man created in God's image, whose justice and holiness are born of truth" (Eph. 4:24).

PERSONAL CONVERSION

3. The holiness of personal conversion is indeed the condition for our fruitful ministry as bishops of the Church. *It is our union with Jesus Christ that determines the credibility of our witness to the Gospel and the supernatural effectiveness of our activity.* We can convincingly proclaim "the unsearchable riches of Christ" (Eph. 3:8) only if we maintain fidelity to the love and friendship of Jesus, only if we continue to live in the faith of the Son of God.

God has given a great gift to the American hierarchy in recent years: the canonization of John Neumann. An American bishop is officially held up by the Catholic Church to be an exemplary servant of the Gospel and shepherd of God's people, above all because of his great love of Christ. On the occasion of the canonization, Paul VI asked: "What is the meaning of this extraordinary event, the meaning of this canonization?" And he answered, saying: "It is the celebration of holiness." And this holiness of St. John Neumann was expressed in brotherly love, in pastoral charity, and in zealous service by one who was the bishop of a diocese and an authentic disciple of Christ.

During the canonization, Paul VI went on to say: "Our ceremony today is indeed the celebration of holiness. At the same time, it is a prophetic anticipation— for the Church, for the United States, for the world—of a renewal of love: love for God, love for neighbor." As bishops, we are called to exercise in the Church this prophetic role of love and, therefore, of holiness.

Guided by the Holy Spirit, we must all be deeply convinced that holiness is the first priority in our lives and in our ministry. In this context, as bishops we see the immense value of prayer: the liturgical prayer of the Church, our prayer together, our prayer alone. In recent times many of you have found that the practice of making spiritual retreats together with your brother bishops is indeed a help to that holiness born of truth. May God sustain you in this initiative so that each of you, and all of you together, may fulfill your role as a sign of holiness offered to God's people on their pilgrimage to the Father. May you yourselves, like St. John Neumann, also be a prophetic anticipation of holiness. The people need to have bishops whom they can look upon as leaders in the quest for holiness —bishops who are trying to anticipate prophetically in their own lives the attainment of the goal to which they are leading the faithful.

CONSECRATED IN TRUTH

4. St. Paul points out the relationship of justice and holiness to truth (cf. Eph. 4:24). Jesus Himself, in His priestly prayer, asks His Father to consecrate His disciples by means of truth; and He adds: "Your word is truth"—*Sermo tuus veritas est* (Jn. 17:17). And He goes on to say that He consecrates Himself for the sake of the disciples, so that they themselves may be consecrated in truth. Jesus consecrated Himself so that the disciples might be consecrated, set apart, by the communication of what He was: the Truth. Jesus tells His Father: "I gave them your word"—"Your word is truth" (Jn. 17:14, 17).

The holy Word of God, which is truth, is communicated by Jesus to His disciples. *This Word is entrusted as a sacred deposit to His Church, but only after He had implanted in His Church, through the power of the Holy Spirit, a special charism to guard and transmit intact the Word of God.*

With great wisdom, John XXIII convoked the Second Vatican Council. Reading the signs of the times, he knew that what was needed was a Council of a pastoral nature, a Council that would reflect the great pastoral love and care of Jesus Christ the Good Shepherd for His people. But he knew that a pastoral Council—to be genuinely effective—would need a strong doctrinal basis. And precisely for this reason, precisely because the Word of God is the only basis for every pastoral initiative, John XXIII on the opening day of the Council— October 11, 1962—made the following statement: "The greatest concern of the Ecumenical Council is this: that the sacred deposit of Christian doctrine should be more effectively guarded and taught."

This explains Pope John's inspiration; this is what the new Pentecost was to be: this is why the bishops of the Church—in the greatest manifestation of collegiality in the history of the world—were called together: *"so that the sacred deposit of Christian doctrine should be more effectively guarded and taught."*

In our time, Jesus was consecrating anew His disciples by truth; and He was doing it by means of an Ecumenical Council; He was transmitting by the power of the Holy Spirit His Father's Word to new generations. And, what John XXIII considered to be the aim of the Council, I consider as the aim of this postconciliar period.

SAFEGUARD DOCTRINE

For this reason, in my first meeting last November with the American bishops on their *ad limina* visit I stated: *"This then is my own deepest hope today for the pastors of the Church in America, as well as for all the pastors of the universal Church: that the sacred deposit of Christian doctrine should be more effectively guarded and taught."* In the Word of God is the salvation of the world. By means of the proclamation of the Word of God, the Lord continues in His Church and through His Church to consecrate His disciples, communicating to them the truth that He Himself is.

For this reason the Vatican Council emphasized the bishop's role of announcing *the full truth of the Gospel* and proclaiming "the whole mystery of Christ" (CD 12). This teaching was constantly repeated by Paul VI for the edification of the universal Church. It was explicitly proclaimed by John Paul I on the very day he died, and I too have frequently reaffirmed it in my own Pontificate. And I am sure that my Successors and your successors will hold this teaching until Christ comes again in glory.

"I AM RESOLVED"

5. Among the papers that were left to me by Paul VI there is a letter written to him by a bishop, on the occasion of the latter's appointment to the episcopacy. It is a beautiful letter; and in the form of a resolution it includes a clear affirmation of the bishop's role of guarding and teaching the deposit of Christian doctrine, of proclaiming the whole mystery of Christ. Because of the splendid insights that this letter offers, I would like to share part of it with you.

As he pledged himself to be loyal in obedience to Paul VI and to his Successors, the bishop wrote: "I am resolved:

—"To be faithful and constant in proclaiming the Gospel of Christ.

—"To maintain the content of Faith, entire and uncorrupted, as handed down by the Apostles and professed by the Church at all times and places."

And then with equal insight, this bishop went on to tell Paul VI that, with the help of Almighty God, he was determined:

—"To build up the Church as the Body of Christ, and to remain united to it by your link, with the order of bishops, under the authority of the Successor of Saint Peter the Apostle.

—"To show kindness and compassion in the name of the Lord to the poor and to strangers and to all who are in need.

—"To seek out the sheep who stray and to gather them into the fold of the Lord.

—"To pray without ceasing for the People of God, to carry out the highest duties of the priesthood in such a way as to afford no grounds for reproof."

This then is the edifying witness of a bishop, an American bishop, to the episcopal ministry of holiness and truth. These words are a credit to him and a credit to all of you.

A challenge for our age—and for every age in the Church—*is to bring the message of the Gospel to the very core of our people's lives*—*so that they may live the full truth of their humanity, their redemption and their adoption in Jesus Christ*—*that they may be enriched with "the justice and holiness of truth."*

RELEVANCE OF GOD'S WORD

6. In the exercise of your ministry of truth, as bishops of the United States you have, through statements and pastoral letters, collectively offered the Word of God to your people, showing its relevance to daily life, pointing to the power it has to uplift and heal, and at the same time upholding its inherent demands. Three years ago you did this in a very special way through your pastoral letter, so beautifully entitled "To Live in Christ Jesus." This letter, in which you offered your people the service of truth, contains a number of points to which I wish to allude today. With compassion, understanding and love, you transmitted a message that is linked to revelation and to the mystery of faith. And so with great pastoral charity you spoke of God's love, of humanity and of sin—and of the meaning of redemption and of life in Christ. You spoke of the Word of Christ as it affects individuals, the family, the community and nations. You spoke of justice and peace, of charity, of truth and friendship. And you spoke of some special questions affecting the moral life of Christians: the moral life in both its individual and social aspects.

You spoke explicitly of the Church's duty to be faithful to the mission entrusted to her. And precisely for this reason you spoke of certain issues that needed a clear reaffirmation, because Catholic teaching in their regard had been challenged, denied, or in practice violated. You repeatedly proclaimed human rights and human dignity and the incomparable worth of people of every racial and ethnic origin, declaring that "racial antagonism and discrimination are among the most persistent and destructive evils of our nation."

You forcefully rejected the oppression of the weak, the manipulation of the vulnerable, the waste of goods and resources, the ceaseless preparations for war, unjust social structures and policies, and all crimes by and against individuals and against creation.

DIVORCE, CONTRACEPTION, HOMOSEXUALITY

With the candor of the Gospels, the compassion of pastors and the charity of Christ, you faced the question of the indissolubility of marriage, rightly stating: "The covenant between a man and a woman joined in Christian marriage is as indissoluble and irrevocable as God's love for His people and Christ's love for His Church."

In exalting the beauty of marriage *you rightly spoke against both the ideology of contraception and contraceptive acts*, as did the Encyclical *Humanae vitae.* And I myself today, with the same conviction of Paul VI, ratify the teaching of this encyclical, *which was put forth by my Predecessor "by virtue of the mandate entrusted to us by Christ"* (AAS, 60, 1968, p. 485).

In portraying the sexual union between husband and wife as a special expression of their covenanted love, you rightly stated: "Sexual intercourse is a moral and human good only within marriage, outside marriage it is wrong."

As "men with the message of truth and the power of God" (2 Cor. 6:7), as authentic teachers of God's law and as compassionate pastors you also rightly stated: *"Homosexual activity...as distinguished from homosexual orientation, is morally wrong."* In the clarity of this truth, you exemplified the real charity of Christ; you did not betray those people who, because of homosexuality, are confronted with difficult moral problems, as would have happened if, in the name of understanding and compassion, or for any other reason, you had held out false hope to any brother or sister. Rather, by your witness to the truth of humanity in God's plan, you effectively manifested fraternal love, upholding the true dignity, the true human dignity, of those who look to Christ's Church for the guidance which comes from the light of God's Word.

RIGHT TO LIFE OF THE UNBORN

You also gave witness to the truth, thereby serving all humanity, when, echoing the teaching of the Council—*"From the moment of conception life must be guarded with the greatest care"* (GS 51)—you reaffirmed the right to life and the inviolability of every human life, including the life of unborn children. You clearly said: "To destroy these innocent unborn children is an unspeakable crime.... Their right to life must be recognized and fully protected by the law."

And just as you defended the unborn in the truth of their being, so also you clearly spoke up for the aged, asserting: "Euthanasia or mercy killing...is a grave moral evil.... Such killing is incompatible with respect for human dignity and reverence for life."

And in your pastoral interest for your people in all their needs—including housing, education, health care, employment, and the administration of justice—you gave further witness to the fact *that all aspects of human life are sacred.* You were, in effect, proclaiming that the Church will never abandon man, nor his temporal needs, as she leads humanity to salvation and eternal life. *And because the Church's greatest act of fidelity to humanity and her "fundamental function in every age and particularly in ours is to direct man's gaze, to point the awareness and experience of the whole of humanity toward the mystery of God"* (RH 10)—because of this you rightly alluded to the dimension of eternal life. It is indeed in this proclamation of eternal life that we hold up a great motive of hope for our people. Against the onslaughts of materialism, against rampant secularism and against moral permissiveness.

RESPONSIBLE PASTORAL INITIATIVES

7. A sense of pastoral responsibility has also been genuinely expressed by individual bishops in their ministry as local pastors. To the great credit of their authors I would cite but two recent examples of pastoral letters issued in the United States. Both are examples of responsible pastoral initiatives. One of them deals with the issue of racism and vigorously denounces it. The other refers to homosexuality and deals with the issue, as should be done, with clarity and great pastoral charity, thus rendering a real service to truth and to those who are seeking this liberating truth.

Brothers in Christ: as we proclaim the truth in love, *it is not possible for us to avoid all criticism; nor is it possible to please everyone.* But it is possible to work for the real benefit of everyone. And so we are humbly convinced that God is with us in our ministry of truth, and that He "did not give us a spirit of timidity but a spirit of power and love and self-control" (2 Tm. 1:7).

One of the greatest rights of the faithful is to receive the Word of God in its purity and integrity as guaranteed by the Magisterium of the universal Church: the authentic Magisterium of the bishops of the Catholic

Church teaching in union with the Pope. Dear brothers: we can be assured that the Holy Spirit is assisting us in our teaching if we remain absolutely faithful to the universal Magisterium.

In this regard I wish to add an extremely important point which I recently emphasized in speaking to a group of bishops making their *ad limina* visit: "In the community of the faithful—*which must always maintain Catholic unity with the bishops and the Apostolic See*—there are great insights of faith. The Holy Spirit is active in enlightening the minds of the faithful with His truth, and in inflaming their hearts with His love. *But these insights of faith and this* sensus fidelium *are not independent of the Magisterium of the Church, which is an instrument of the same Holy Spirit and is assisted by Him.* It is only when the faithful have been nourished by the Word of God, faithfully transmitted in its purity and integrity, that their own charisms are fully operative and fruitful. Once the Word of God is faithfully proclaimed to the community and is accepted, it brings forth fruits of justice and holiness of life in abundance. But the dynamism of the community in understanding and living the Word of God depends on its receiving intact the *depositum fidei;* and for this precise purpose a special apostolic and pastoral charism has been given to the Church. It is one and the same Spirit of truth who directs the hearts of the faithful and who guarantees the Magisterium of the pastors of the flock."

CUSTODIANS OF THE CHURCH'S UNITY

8. One of the greatest truths of which we are the humble custodians is the doctrine of the Church's unity —that unity which is tarnished on the human face of the

Church by every form of sin, but which subsists inde-
structibly in the Catholic Church (cf. LG 8; UR 2, 3). A
consciousness of sin calls us incessantly to conversion.
The will of Christ impels us to work earnestly and per-
severingly for unity with all our Christian brethren,
being mindful that the unity we seek is one of perfect
faith, a unity in truth and love. We must pray and
study together, knowing however that intercommunion
between divided Christians is not the answer to Christ's
appeal for perfect unity. And with God's help we will
continue to work humbly and resolutely to remove the
real divisions that still exist, and thus to restore that full
unity in faith which is the condition for sharing in the
Eucharist (cf. Address of May 4, 1979). The commitment of the Ecumenical Council belongs to each of us;
as does the testament of Paul VI, who writing on ecu-
menism stated: "Let the work of drawing near to our
separated brethren go on, with much understanding,
with much patience, with great love; but without deviating from the true Catholic doctrine."

SACRAMENT OF PENANCE
AND GENERAL ABSOLUTION

9. As bishops who are servants of truth, we are
also called to be servants of unity, in the communion of
the Church.

In the communion of holiness we ourselves are
called, as I mentioned above, to conversion, so that we
may preach with convincing power the message of
Jesus: "Reform your lives and believe in the Gospel."
We have a special role to play in safeguarding the Sacrament of Reconciliation, so that, in fidelity to a divine

precept, we and our people may experience in our innermost being that "grace has far surpassed sin" (Rom. 5:20). I, too, ratify the prophetic call of Paul VI, who urged the bishops to help their priests to "deeply understand how closely they collaborate through the Sacrament of Penance with the Savior in the work of conversion" (Address of April 20, 1978). In this regard I confirm again the norms of *Sacramentum paenitentiae* which so wisely emphasize the ecclesial dimension of the Sacrament of Penance and indicate the precise limits of general absolution, just as Paul VI did in his *ad limina* address to the American bishops.

Conversion by its very nature is the condition for that union with God which reaches its greatest expression in the Eucharist. Our union with Christ in the Eucharist presupposes, in turn, that our hearts are set on conversion, that they are pure. This is indeed an important part of our preaching to the people. In my encyclical I endeavored to express it in these words: "The Christ who calls to the Eucharistic banquet is always the same Christ who exhorts us to penance and repeats His 'Repent.' Without this constant and ever-renewed endeavor for conversion, partaking of the Eucharist would lack its full redeeming effectiveness..." (RH 20). In the face of a widespread phenomenon of our time, namely, that many of our people who are among the great numbers who receive Communion make little use of Confession, we must emphasize Christ's basic call to conversion. We must also stress that the personal encounter with the forgiving Jesus in the Sacrament of Reconciliation is a divine means which keeps alive in our hearts and in our communities, a consciousness of sin in its perennial and tragic reality, and which actually brings forth, by the action of Jesus and the power of His Spirit, fruits of conversion in justice and holiness of life. By this sacrament we are renewed in fervor, strengthened in our resolves and buoyed up by divine encouragement.

CHRIST'S REAL PRESENCE IN THE EUCHARIST

10. As chosen leaders in a community of praise and prayer, it is our special joy to offer the Eucharist and to give our people a sense of their vocation as an Easter people, with the "alleluia" as their song. And let us always recall that the validity of all liturgical development and the effectiveness of every liturgical sign presupposes the great principle *that the Catholic liturgy is theocentric, and that it is above all "the worship of divine majesty" (cf. SC 33), in union with Jesus Christ. Our people have a supernatural sense whereby they look for reverence in all liturgy, especially in what touches the mystery of the Eucharist.* With deep faith our people understand that the Eucharist—in the Mass and outside the Mass—is the body and blood of Jesus Christ, and therefore deserves the worship that is given to the living God and to Him alone.

As ministers of a community of service, it is our privilege to proclaim the truth of Christ's union with His members in His Body, the Church. Hence we commend all service rendered in His name and to His brethren (cf. Mt. 25:45).

In a community of witness and evangelization may our testimony be clear and without reproach. In this regard the Catholic press and the other means of social communication are called to fulfill a special role of great dignity at the service of truth and charity. The Church's aim in employing and sponsoring these media is linked to her mission of evangelization and of service to humanity; through the media the Church hopes to promote ever more effectively the uplifting message of the Gospel.

11. And each individual Church over which you preside and which you serve is a community founded on the Word of God and acting in the truth of this Word. *It is in fidelity to the communion of the universal Church that our local unity is authenticated and made stable.* In the communion of the universal Church local churches find their own identity and enrichment ever more clearly. But all of this requires that the individual churches should maintain complete openness toward the universal Church.

And this is the mystery that we celebrate today in proclaiming the holiness and truth and unity of the episcopal ministry.

Brothers: this ministry of ours makes us accountable to Christ and to His Church. Jesus Christ, the chief Shepherd (1 Pt. 5:4), loves us and sustains us. It is He who transmits His Father's Word and consecrates us in truth, so that each of us may say in turn of our people: "I consecrate myself for their sake now, that they may be consecrated in truth" (Jn. 17:19).

Let us pray for and devote special energy to promoting and maintaining vocations to the sacred priesthood, so that the pastoral care of the priestly ministry may be ensured for future generations. I ask you to call upon parents and families, upon priests, religious and laity to unite in fulfilling this vital responsibility of the entire community. And to the young people themselves let us hold up the full challenge of following Christ and of embracing His invitation with full generosity.

As we ourselves pursue every day the justice and holiness born of truth, let us look to Mary, Mother of Jesus, Queen of Apostles, and Cause of our Joy. May St. Frances Xavier Cabrini, St. Elizabeth Ann Seton and St. John Neumann pray for you, and for all the people whom you are called to serve in holiness and truth and in the unity of Christ and His Church.

Dear brothers: "Grace be with all who love our Lord Jesus Christ with unfailing love" (Eph. 5:24).

THE APOSTOLATE
OF THE FAMILY:
A PRIORITY
IN THE TASK OF BISHOPS

On October 28, 1979, the Holy Father received in audience a group of bishops from Argentina on their visit "ad limina Apostolorum." After listening to a sincere address of loyalty by Archbishop Jorge Manuel Lopez of Corrientes, John Paul II delivered the following discourse.

Beloved brothers in the episcopate,

1. I thank the Lord for granting me this desired meeting with you, bishops of the Church in Argentina. It is a meeting the joy of which is dimmed by the recent death of Cardinal Antonio Caggiano, who, during his long life, left so many examples of virtue and such fruitful works.

Today is the culminating point of your visit *ad limina,* which is at the same time a complement, as it were, to that of the other Argentine prelates who preceded you.

In this way I have been able to meet each of you personally and, through you, your collaborators: priests, religious men and women and laymen of each of the dioceses of a country that is far away geographically, but very close to my heart as Pastor of the universal Church.

I want to express right now my gratitude and appreciation for your apostolic commitment, and I want to tell you how pleased I am with the Christian spirit that is reflected in the ecclesial communities entrusted to your responsibility.

2. I am following with special interest the commendable solicitude with which you have been set-

ting up an organic apostolate of the family, and I look hopefully to the full development of the "Program of Pastoral Action for Marriage and the Family," which your Episcopal Conference—as the Archbishop of Corrientes has just mentioned—set going with a special emphasis some years ago, for all the various Churches of Argentina.

I am happy that, in view of this aim, you have been able to arrive at a joint apostolate, capable of uniting and fully exploiting the apostolic forces, at all levels, making them converge harmoniously towards nation-wide goals. In this way an effective contribution is made to that happy result that only the concentration of intentions, actions and methods can yield in a work of such importance as that of forming and guiding families in the whole sphere of a really Christian life.

3. Your decision to offer to the Blessed Virgin Mary the results of your work at the National Marian Congress, which you will celebrate at Mendoza next year, is also a reason of joy for me. I am sure that it will be a fruit most pleasing to the Lord, because it will ripen under the assistance of His Mother, devotion to whom you are endeavoring to stimulate in your ecclesial communities and families, as a guarantee for the success of your intentions.

I encourage you to continue your action along this way, as widely and deeply as possible, since its beneficial effects will be felt not only in the Church but also in civil society.

In this way you will walk along the paths laid down by Vatican Council II, which stressed, in its documents, the importance of marriage and of the family (cf.

LG 11, 41; GS 47-52; AA 11; GE 3). It is likewise a subject to which I have referred on so many occasions, in this first year of my Pontificate.

4. Speaking to Latin American bishops, I do not wish to fail to indicate that at the opening address of the Puebla Conference I pointed out the subject of the family as one of the priority tasks to be carried out (IV, a). I also dedicated my homily at Palafox Seminary to it. I commend to your reflection what I said there.

It is a necessary duty of pastors to teach and defend the doctrine of the Church with regard to marriage and the institution of the family, in order to safeguard their constituent elements, their requirements and perennial values.

In your people, thank God, the sense of the family remains very deeply rooted; but we cannot fail to recognize that the permissive trends of modern society have a growing impact on this important area, which the Church must protect with all her energies.

Marriage, on which the family is based, is a community of life and love, instituted by the Creator for the continuation of mankind, which has not only an earthly destiny, but also an eternal one (cf. GS 48). Strive, therefore, to defend its unity and undissolubility applying to family life the central thought of the Puebla Conference: communion and participation.

Communion, that is, an interior disposition of understanding and love of the parents for each other and for their children. Participation, namely, mutual respect and giving, both in happy moments and in times of trial.

Within this unity, vivified by love, marriage shines forth as a source of human life, in harmony with the laws established by God Himself. This indicates to us the necessity of stressing the Christian sense of responsible parenthood, in line with Paul VI's Encyclical *Humanae vitae. Do not hesitate either to proclaim a fundamental right of the human being: that of being born* (cf. Opening Address at Puebla, II, 5).

An adequate family apostolate will have to take into great consideration the three dimensions which Latin American families must have: "education in the Faith, formation of persons, promotion of development" (Homily at Puebla Seminary, 2).

In fact, the Christian home must be the first school of faith, where baptismal grace opens to knowledge and love of God, Jesus Christ and the Blessed Virgin, and where experience of Christian truths, that have become norms of behavior for parents and children, is gradually deepened. Family catechesis, at all ages and with various pedagogical approaches, is extremely important. *It must become operative with Christian initiation from before First Communion and it will have to have a special development by means of conscious and responsible reception of the other sacraments.* In this way the family will really be a domestic Church (cf. LG 11; AA 11).

In the formation of persons, *the family has a special role which gives it a certain sacred character, with its own rights founded in the last resort on the dignity of the human person, and consequently they must always be respected.* I said so in my address to the Organization of American States: "When we speak of the right to life, to physical and moral integrity, to nourishment, to housing, to education, to health care, to employment, to shared responsibility in the life of the nation, we speak of the human person. It is this human person whom faith makes us recognize as created in the image of God and destined for an eternal goal" (*L'Osservatore Romano*, Oct. 8-9, 1979).

The family apostolate must, then, watch over the defense of these rights. In this way it contributes at the same time to making the family a real and effective agent of development.

On the other hand, it is evident that to be able to work efficaciously in this field, it is necessary to make a serious effort to eliminate the deep causes from which there spring so many factors that upset the balance of society and, consequently, of the family. Everyone can see, in this connection, the enormous repercussion, not only of a moral nature, that certain situations of clear social injustice have, or situations that affect likewise the area of labor relations.

Consequently, as part of your ministry, do not fail to preach and stimulate a sound public moral doctrine, in full harmony with the line marked by the social teaching of the Church. If the latter is put into practice faithfully and without tergiversations of any tendency, the exigencies of a human and evangelical nature that it intends to safeguard will become a fruitful reality.

5. If with rightful concern for the safeguarding of these human rights, you stress clearly the principles set forth above, you will find in lack of due respect for these principles the root of the unleashing of violence.

In order to contribute, to the best of your ability, to ending the fatal spiral of violence, proceed, venerable brothers, with all zeal in the accomplishment of your pastoral duties, endeavoring to bring it about that society and the first cell of this society, that is, the family, will take its place in that civilization of love, which my Predecessor Paul VI desired so much.

6. If in the light of the requirements of your vast and difficult program, the number of the collaborators at your disposal might seem inadequate—in spite of the recent increase in vocations—let the following promising assertion of the Council serve as an encouragement: "The greatest contribution is made by families which are animated by a spirit of faith, charity and piety and which provide, as it were, a first seminary" (cf. OT 2).

God wished to leave us a model very close to us in the Holy Family of Nazareth. May Jesus, Mary and Joseph inspire, accompany and encourage your family apostolate and the task of all your collaborators.

7. Before concluding this meeting, I wish to refer to the gratitude you expressed to me for the task of mediator that I have accepted, to contribute to peace and friendship between two brother peoples: Argentina and Chile. Rest assured that I really appreciate the fact that you are facilitating my work with your pastoral action, which, based on prayer and on the teachings of the Gospel, contributes effectively to creating the right atmosphere for the desired solution, for the good of everyone.

Finally, I charge you with a particular task: to take to your priests, deacons, religious men and women, seminarians, agents of the apostolate and all your diocesans, the greeting and blessing of the Pope, who thinks of everyone and prays for everyone with great affection and deep hope. With them I bless you all.

AT THE SERVICE OF LIFE

The Holy Father's final engagement on May 7, 1980, was a meeting with the Kenyan bishops in the Nunciature at Nairobi. John Paul II spoke to them as follows:

Venerable and dear brothers in our Lord Jesus Christ,

1. Today during this Easter season it is a cause of deep joy and a source of pastoral strength for us to assemble in Nairobi, to gather together in the name of Jesus who said: "I am the resurrection and the life" (Jn. 11:25).

We are extremely conscious that our ministry in Africa and our service to the universal Church is placed under the sign of the risen Christ. For, together with all our brother bishops throughout the world, we are Successors of the body of Apostles that was chosen to witness to the resurrection. The knowledge that "with great power the apostles gave their testimony to the resurrection of the Lord Jesus" (Acts 4:33) truly strengthens us and uplifts us, because we know that we have received the inheritance of the Apostolic College. For us bishops this is an hour of trust in the risen Lord, an hour of Easter joy, an hour of great hope for the future of Africa.

AMECEA'S INSTITUTE

2. On this occasion my thoughts go to all the bishops of Africa, and I note with deep satisfaction that the members of the Episcopal Conference of Kenya are resolutely engaged in many programs of collabora-

tion and joint action with their fellow bishops from the AMECEA countries of Tanzania, Uganda, Zambia, Malawi, the Sudan and Ethiopia. In the abundant strength that comes from charity and mutual support, your ministry is sustained and enriched. Be assured of my admiration and esteem for the unity that you express in diversity and in fraternal collaboration, and for your concerted efforts on behalf of the evangelization of those countries that have so much in common.

An initiative worthy of particular mention is AMECEA'S Pastoral Institute at Eldoret. This Institute offers special opportunities to reflect on the Church's mission to guard and teach ever more effectively the Word of God. *The Holy Spirit Himself is directing the Church in Africa to scrutinize "the signs of the times" in the light of the sacred deposit of God's Word as it is proclaimed by the Magisterium.* It is only on this sound basis that true answers can be found to the real problems that touch people's lives. It is in judging according to this sacred norm that the bishops will exercise their personal responsibility to evaluate what pastoral activities and solutions are valid for Africa today.

MINISTRY OF SERVICE

3. Venerable brothers, the episcopal ministry is a ministry at the service of life, bringing the power of the resurrection to your people, so that they may "walk in newness of life" (Rom. 6:4), so that they may be ever more aware of the Christian life to which they are called by virtue of their baptism, and so that in their daily lives—in the setting of Africa—they may have fellowship with the Father and His Son Jesus Christ in the

unity of the Holy Spirit. *And because this fellowship is fully achieved only in heaven, your ministry likewise involves a clear proclamation of eternal life.*

PASTORS OF THE FLOCK

4. As Successor of Peter in the See of Rome and as your brother in the College of Bishops, I have come to Africa to encourage you in your efforts as pastors of the flock: in the efforts of each of you to offer to Christ a local Church in which unity reigns between the bishop and the priests, the religious and the laity; in your efforts to enlighten communities with the Gospel and make them vibrant with the life of Christ; *in your efforts to bring the dynamic power of the resurrection into human life and by it to transform and elevate all levels of society.*

I have come to confirm you in your total acceptance of God's holy Word as it is authentically proclaimed by the Catholic Church at all times and in all places. I wish to support you in the conviction, so splendidly expressed by the bishops of Kenya in their Pastoral Letter of April 27, 1979, that fidelity to the teachings of Christ and the Magisterium of His Church is truly in the interests of the people. By following your clear insights of faith you showed yourselves true pastors of the flock, exercising real spiritual leadership when you declared: "We, your bishops, would do a disservice to the people if we did not expect of them the goodness and the fidelity that they are capable of by the grace of God" (Pastoral Letter, p. 10). *Your greatest contribution to your people and to all Africa is indeed the gift of God's Word, the acceptance of which is the basis for all community and the condition for all progress.*

RESPECT FAMILY VALUES

5. As the *Servus Servorum Dei* I have come to uphold with you the priorities of your ministry. In the first place I offer my support for your pastoral efforts on behalf of the family—the African family. The great African tradition is faithful to so many family values, and to life itself, which takes its origin in the family. A profound respect for the family and for the good of children is a distinctive gift of Africa to the world. It is in the family that each generation learns to absorb these values and to transmit them. And the whole Church appreciates everything you do to preserve this heritage of your people, to purify it and uplift it in the sacramental fullness of Christ's new and original teaching. Hence we see the great value of presenting the Christian family in its relationship to the most Holy Trinity, and of maintaining the Christian ideal in its evangelical purity. *It is the divine law proclaimed by Christ that gives rise to the Christian ideal of monogamous marriage, which in turn is the basis for the Christian family.* Only a week before he died, my Predecessor John Paul I spoke to a group of bishops in these words, which I consider very relevant here today in Africa: "Let us never grow tired of proclaiming the family as a community of love: conjugal love unites the couple and is procreative of new life; it mirrors the divine love, is communicated, and in the words of *Gaudium et spes*, is actually a sharing in the covenant of love of Christ and His Church" (*AAS* 70 [1978], p. 766).

Be assured of my solidarity with you in this great task involving the diligent preparation of the young for marriage, the repeated proclamation of the unity and indissolubility of marriage, and the renewed invitation to the faithful to accept and foster with faith and love the Catholic celebration of the Sacrament of Marriage. Success in a pastoral program of this nature requires patience and perseverance and a strong conviction that Christ has come to "make all things new" (Rev. 21:5).

THE ENCYCLICAL
HUMANAE VITAE

Know also that in all your efforts to build up strong united families, in which human love reflects divine love and in which the education of children is embraced with a true sense of mission, you have the support of the universal Church. With the love and sensitivity of pastors, you have illustrated well the great principle that any pastoral approach that does not rest on the doctrinal foundation of the Word of God is illusory. Hence with true pastoral charity you have faced various problems affecting human life, and repeated the Church's teaching at the true service of man. You have clearly insisted, for example, *on the most fundamental human right: the right to life from the moment of conception;* you have effectively reiterated the Church's position on abortion, sterilization and contraception. Your faithful upholding of the Church's teaching contained in the Encyclical *Humanae vitae* has been the expression of your pastoral concern and your profound attachment to the integral values of the human person.

Every effort to make society sensitive to the importance of the family is a great service to humanity. When the full dignity of parents and children is realized and is expressed in prayer, a new power for good is unleashed throughout the Church and the world. John Paul I expressed this eloquently when he said: "The holiness of the Christian family is indeed a most apt means for producing the serene renewal of the Church which the Council so eagerly desired. Through family prayer, the *ecclesia domestica* becomes an effective reality and leads to the transformation of the world" *(ibid.,* p. 767). Upon you, brethren, rest the hope and trust of the universal Church for the defense and promotion of the African family, both parents and children. The Holy Spirit of truth, who has implanted so many values in the hearts of the African people, will never cease to assist you as pastors in bringing the teaching of Jesus ever more effectively into the lives of your brothers and sisters. *We need never be afraid to preach the fullness of His message in all its evangelical purity,* for, as I stated on another occasion: "Let us never fear that the challenge is too great for our people: they were redeemed by the precious blood of Christ; they are His people. Through the Holy Spirit, Jesus Christ reserves to Himself the final responsibility for the acceptance of His Word and for the growth of His Church. *It is He, Jesus Christ, who will continue to give the grace to His people to meet the requirements of His Word, despite all difficulties, despite all weaknesses.* And it is up to us to continue to proclaim the message of salvation in its entirety and purity, with patience, compassion and the conviction that what is impossible with man is possible with God" *(ASS* 71, [1979], pp. 1424f.).

CATECHESIS—A PRIORITY

6. Another great priority of your ministry is catechesis: developing the initial faith of your people and bringing them to the fullness of Christian life. I am close to you, in praise and encouragement, in every undertaking of yours to communicate Christ, to make His Gospel incarnate in the lives and culture of your people. In union with the universal Church, and in openness to the patrimony of her long history, you are striving to lead your people in the reality of their daily lives to look to Christ for light and strength. *The aim of your local Churches is to have the faithful living through, with and in Christ. Your efforts,* in which you rightfully endeavor to associate the whole community— and in a special way the catechists—*must have constant reference to Christ: to His divine Person, His Spirit, and His Gospel.*

The "acculturation" or "inculturation" which you rightly promote *will truly be a reflection of the Incarnation of the Word, when a culture, transformed and regenerated by the Gospel, brings forth from its own living tradition original expressions of Christian life, celebration and thought* (cf. CT 53). By respecting, preserving and fostering the particular values and riches of your people's cultural heritage, you will be in a position to lead them to a better understanding of the mystery of Christ, which is to be lived in the noble, concrete and daily experiences of African life. There is no question of adulterating the Word of God, or of emptying the cross of its power (cf. 1 Cor. 1:17), but rather of bringing Christ into the very center of African life and of lifting up all African life to Christ. *Thus not only is Christianity relevant to Africa, but Christ, in the members of His Body, is Himself African.*

PROPER FORMATION

7. Again, with good reason, you attribute great pastoral importance to the proper formation of priests and religious, as well as to fostering these vocations in the Church. This attitude is an expression of your deep understanding of the needs of the Body of Christ.

Since the beginning of my Pontificate I have striven to point out the importance of religious consecration in the Church and the value of religious life as it affects the whole community of the faithful. Religious have the task of showing forth the holiness of the whole Body of Christ and of bearing witness to a new and eternal life acquired by the redemption of Christ (cf. LG 44). At the same time they are called to many different apostolates in the Church. Their service in the Gospel is very necessary for the life of the Church. Missionary religious in Kenya have labored with great fidelity in the cause of the Gospel; only the Lord Jesus can adequately thank them and reward them for what has been accomplished for the implantation of the Church. Their mission now goes on side by side with their Kenyan fellow religious, who have heard the call of Christ and are working generously for the cause of the Gospel. The future of evangelization in this land will continue to owe much to the men and women religious, both autochthonous and from abroad.

I have likewise sought to draw attention to the essential nature, role and function of the priesthood in

its unchanging relationship to the Eucharist, which is
the summit of all evangelization (cf. PO 5).

In particular I wish to confirm the vital importance
for the Christian people of having their priests properly
trained in the Word of God, in the knowledge and love
of Jesus Christ and His cross. In the divine plan, the
transmission of the life-giving Gospel of Christ is linked
with the preparation of the priests of this generation. To
provide this proper seminary training is one of our
greatest responsibilities as bishops of the Church of
God; it can be one of our most effective contributions to
the evangelization of the world.

UNITY AND COOPERATION

8. An important element that affects every community in the Church is the unity and cooperation
between bishops and priests. By reason of his ordi-
nation, the priest is "a co-worker with the order of
bishop," and to live out the truth of this vocation he is
called to collaborate with the bishop and to pray for
him. To explain the unity of the priests with the bishop,
St. Ignatius of Antioch compared it to the relationship between the strings and the lute (Letter to the Ephesians, IV).

On the part of the bishop this relationship requires
that he should be close to his priests as a brother and
father and friend. As such he must love them and
encourage them, not only in their pastoral activities, but
in their lives of personal consecration. The bishop is
called to strengthen his priests in faith and to urge them
to look constantly to Christ the Good Shepherd, in
order that they may realize ever more their priestly
identity and dignity.

The Church renews her debt of gratitude to all the missionary and *Fidei Donum* priests who are laboring in the cause of Christ's Gospel. Their generosity is an expression of the power of Christ's grace, and their ministry is a great proof of Catholic unity.

9. In the building up of the Church I am aware of your sustained work to build small Christian communities in which the Word of God is the guideline of action and in which the Eucharist is the true center of life. The whole community of the faithful benefits from these initiatives that make it possible for people to recognize the Church in her concrete expression and human dimension as a visible sacrament of God's universal love and saving grace. It is certainly the will of Jesus Christ that the love of Christians should be manifested in such a way that individual communities exemplify the universal norm: "By this will all men know that you are my disciples, if you have love for one another" (Jn. 13:35). In your pastoral zeal you know the wise criteria laid down by Paul VI and which remain a sure guide for the effectiveness of these communities (cf. EN 58). At this time I would just stress the great power which those communities have to fulfill an active ecclesial role in the evangelization of Africa. May they go forward with you, their pastors, and with the priests, to communicate "the unsearchable riches of Christ" (Eph. 3:8).

10. Before concluding my words to you today, my dear brethren in Christ Jesus, I wish to emphasize once more the great need for holiness in our lives. To exercise fruitfully our role as pastors of God's people, we must know Christ and love Him. In a word, we are called to friendship with the Lord, just as the Apostles were. Like Jesus we are the object of the Father's love, and the Holy

Spirit is alive in our hearts. The effectiveness of everything we do depends on our union with Jesus, on our holiness of life. There is no other way to be a worthy bishop, a good shepherd of the flock. There is no pastoral leadership without prayer, for only in prayer is union with Jesus maintained. Only by being like Jesus, Son of Mary, who is the Mother of us all, can we fulfill our mission in the Church.

May Mary Queen of Apostles sustain you in holiness and love, in prayer and pastoral charity, and help you to bring Jesus to all your people, to all Kenya, to all Africa.

Praised be Jesus Christ, "the chief Shepherd" (1 Pt. 5:4) of God's people, "the Bishop and Shepherd of our souls" (1 Pt. 2:25).

ON HUMAN SEXUALITY AND PERSONHOOD

On February 10, 1981, John Paul II sent the following message to the bishops taking part in the Dallas (U.S.A.) "Workshop on Human Sexuality and Personhood."

Dear brothers in our Lord Jesus Christ,

I am pleased to have this occasion to speak to you, a large number of my brother bishops of North America who have gathered in Dallas for the "Workshop on Human Sexuality and Personhood." Once again this year, aided by the generous assistance of the Knights of Columbus and urged on by your own pastoral zeal for proclaiming the Gospel of our Lord Jesus Christ, you have come together for the purpose of improving your understanding of important questions with which our episcopal ministry is vitally concerned at the end of the twentieth century.

You have wisely chosen to examine both *the subject of human sexuality and the subject of personhood. This simultaneous treatment is not only praiseworthy, it is necessary.* The subject of human sexuality cannot be brought into proper focus without reference to the human person. And likewise, if we were to study the human person without reference to sexuality, we would be overlooking a fundamental truth revealed to us in the book of Genesis, overlooking the fact that "God created them male and female" (Gn. 1:27).

The topic you have selected is of particular interest at this present moment in the Church's history. For this reason I have spoken about certain aspects of it during my Wednesday audiences in Rome over the course of the past year and a half. And as you know, the recent Synod of Bishops also gave it considerable attention.

Obviously, it is not possible for me today to speak exhaustively on the topic nor even to summarize what I have said previously. I would, however, like to indicate some important elements which should be included in pastoral and theological discussions dealing with this subject.

In his Encyclical *Humanae vitae*, Pope Paul VI underscored the importance of referring to the "total vision of man" (no. 7). I wish to draw attention to this emphasis of my Predecessor, for *we live in an age in which, for a variety of reasons, this total vision can easily be dismissed or ignored.* It can also be replaced by a number of partial viewpoints which, although they may be a faithful representation of one or another aspect of the complete truth, do not express a fully integrated vision of the human being.

In this light I am happy to note how your workshop is seeking to bring together the latest insights of the medical and behavioral sciences with the truths of faith contained in the Sacred Scriptures and in the Church's tradition. *You have rightly seen the need to incorporate into your deliberations both the truth of revelation and the truth of human experience.*

Human sexuality and personhood can be fully understood *only when studied within the framework of the mystery of creation and the mystery of redemption.* Following the example of Jesus (cf. Mt. 19:4), we need to look at what God the Creator intended from the beginning. Thus in the book of Genesis we read: "In the beginning.... God created man in the image of himself, in the image of God he created him, male and female he created them" (Gn. 1:1, 17). Examining the plan of God as it existed in the beginning we discover the nuptial meaning of the body; we see that, *in the mystery of creation, man and woman are made to be a gift to each other and for each other.* In their very existence, as male and female, *by their sexuality and freedom as persons, man and woman are capable of mirroring the creative activity of God.* And in the mystery of redemption, through the grace won by the Savior on the cross, man and woman receive, not the power to return to the state of original innocence prior to the fall of Adam, *but the strength to live, in Christ and through Christ, a new ethos of redemptive love.*

An examination of moral norms and a quest for appropriate pastoral approaches to the various problems of human sexuality would be incomplete if reference were not made to the teaching of Christ found in the Sermon on the Mount, especially to the Lord's words: "You have heard that it was said, 'You shall not commit adultery.' But I say to you that everyone who looks at a woman lustfully has already committed adultery with her in his heart" (Mt. 5:27f.). As we examine this teaching, which reminds us of the importance of purity of heart, as well as the need for lifelong fidelity to one's spouse, we must continually recall that the words of our Savior are not words of accusation or condemnation. Rather they are words of invitation, words of truth spoken in love and compassion, *words which lead men and women to the fullness of life and freedom. For they invite men and women to live in accordance with the truth of their own personhood and sexuality as revealed by God from the beginning.* We, on our part, must help our people to see moral teaching on sexuality as part of the total Christian ethos of redemption, as part of their calling in Christ to "walk in newness of life" (Rom. 6:4).

All pastoral charity that is authentic, all human compassion that is genuine, all fraternal support that is real, embraces and communicates the whole truth as revealed to us by the eternal Word and proclaimed by His Church.

My brother bishops: may God sustain the Pope John XXIII Medical-Moral Research and Educational Center in its important role of assisting the Magisterium of the Church. And may the Spirit of God be with you to direct your deliberations during these days. May you be renewed in your zealous pastoral service to humanity and in your desire to lead all men and women to the fullness of truth in our Lord Jesus Christ.

To Him, and to Him alone, we say with Peter: "You have the words of eternal life" (Jn. 6:68).

IN THE SERVICE OF THE CHURCH, FAMILY AND SOCIETY

On January 17, 1981, the Holy Father received in audience the participants in the third National Congress of the "Italian Federation of Nursery Schools" (F.I.S.M.). The group, composed of religious and lay people, represented over ten thousand nursery schools in Italy.
John Paul II delivered the following address.

Beloved brothers and sisters!

1. I am truly happy with this meeting, which gives me the joyful opportunity of cordially greeting the representatives of the "Italian Federation of Nursery Schools," gathered in Rome these days for the third National Congress.

I bid a hearty welcome to you and, through you, to the twenty-five thousand sisters in Italy who dedicate themselves zealously to such an important mission, and to the parents who have shown their confidence in the validity and importance of your tireless work and have entrusted their children to you to be educated and formed during that very delicate period between the ages of three and six.

The brief words which I address to you at this audience are intended to be words of approval, gratitude, encouragement and good wishes, in order that, in this sector, so important from the religious and social point of view, you may be able to carry out in full serenity that work which is indeed humble, discreet and hidden, but so valuable and meritorious for the Church, the family and society, and which corresponds to the desire of Jesus: "Let the children come to me" (cf. Lk. 18:16).

TEN THOUSAND CHRISTIAN
NURSERY SCHOOLS

2. Today I wish to express to your federation, to you who represent it, to all sisters, educators, and those who carry out their activity in the field of the nursery school, my congratulations and those of the Apostolic See for your effective presence, so widespread and vast throughout the nation: it is a question, in fact, of as many as ten thousand nursery schools of Christian inspiration, with about one million children who attend them, and therefore there are also a million families who are involved, stimulated and jointly interested in the complex and daily educational activity in the service of the child, who must be the real center of all affection, attention, interests and plans: the child, who is beginning to take his first uncertain, cautious steps in the fascinating adventure of life; *who expresses his own identity and personality in an original way*; who presents himself in need of love and protection; who is open to the beauty of nature; who asks himself and others so many questions about the world and the persons who surround him; who deeply feels the religious sense and is capable, with extraordinary spontaneity, of dialoguing intensely with the heavenly Father.

We can never sufficiently express our sincere gratitude to those who have dedicated the best of their energies, their time, their whole life, to this truly evangelical apostolate for little children, who are the concrete sign of the fruitful love of families, the finest hope of the nations, the constant reminder of the goodness, innocence and charity which should animate relations among men.

DEVELOPMENT OF THE CHILD'S PERSONALITY

3. When the Church, especially through the work of the congregations and religious institutes, dedicates herself to the spread of nursery schools, working out an overall educational project, inspired by Christian values, she actually operates for the advancement of the whole man and every man. She intends to collaborate actively with families in the education, the formation and, in particular, the initiation of children to faith. *The school of Christian inspiration is chosen and preferred by the parents precisely for the formation and religious education integrated into the education of the pupils.* Nursery schools too, like all Catholic schools, therefore have the serious duty of proposing a religious formation adapted to the circumstances, often very different, of the pupils. Formation is an essential work, which calls for great love and deep respect for the child, who has the right to a simple and true presentation of Christian faith, as I stressed in the apostolic exhortation on catechesis in our time (cf. CT 36 and 69).

For this purpose a continual contact and dialogue with the parents is necessary, to examine together, analyze, and compare educational methods and approaches, in order to avoid possible differences, however unimportant they may seem, which might, however, have a negative influence on the development of the human and Christian personality of the child.

4. In this way the nursery school can and must become a very special meeting place, particularly for young couples, both for their own growth in faith, and for the correct and complete education of their children.

In this perspective the nursery school of Christian inspiration represents an area of specific and committed pastoral action for sisters, as well as for priests and laymen.

I wish to renew to sisters the grateful recognition of the Church for all they accomplish in this field in a spirit of motherly dedication, and also urge them not to let themselves be discouraged by objective difficulties, which might induce them to abandon this area for other types of apostolic activity; but let them continue with renewed vigor in this work, assigning to it adequate means and specifically qualified personnel, even if that may involve great sacrifices.

To the priests, especially parish priests, who have built a nursery school alongside their church at the cost of so many sacrifices, I intend to address the expression of my satisfaction, together with encouragement for this pastoral choice of theirs, which is truly ecclesial.

To men and women educators belonging to the laity, who, through their specific qualification, wish to contribute to the education and formation of children, I wish to hold out also the possibility that they may choose the nursery school as a field of evangelization and human advancement.

To all these I recall the consoling and demanding words of the conciliar Declaration on Christian Education: "Splendid, therefore, and of the highest importance is the vocation of those who help parents in carrying out their duties, and act in the name of the community by undertaking a teaching career. This vocation requires special qualities of mind and heart, most careful preparation, and a constant readiness to accept new ideas and to adapt the old" (GE 5).

I hope, therefore, that all the faithful will feel that their nursery schools are schools of the Christian community, which must therefore be encouraged and helped; and I also trust that civil societies will recognize *the social value of nursery schools of Christian inspiration*, ensuring them due support by means of adequate contributions, in order to guarantee the actual freedom of choice of parents in the field of education.

With these wishes I invoke on you personally, and on all those working for the nursery schools, the abundance of the Lord's gifts, and I willingly impart my apostolic blessing.

VI. Addresses to Various Specialists Concerned with Life and the Family

a) "The Inviolability of Human Life in the Sanctity of the Family," to the First International Congress for the Family of Africa and Europe, January 15, 1981.

b) "The Process of Urbanization and the Family," to the Conference on Population and Urban Future, September 4, 1980.

c) "Moral Aspect of Solving Problems of Married Couples," to Confederation of Family Advisory Bureaus of Christian Inspiration, November 29, 1980.

d) "Help the Modern Family To Rediscover the Real Meaning of Life," to Union of Women Major Superiors of Italy, October 11, 1980.

e) "The Person, Not Science, Is the Measure," Address to Congresses on Medicine and Surgery, October 27, 1980.

f) "Freedom of Conscience and the Defense of Life," to Italian Doctors, December 28, 1978.

g) "You Are the Guardians of Human Lives," to Participants in a Meeting for Midwives, January 26, 1980.

h) "Art Must Not Violate the Right of Privacy," General Audience, April 29, 1981.

THE INVIOLABILITY
OF HUMAN LIFE
IN THE SANCTITY
OF THE FAMILY

On January 15, 1981, the Holy Father received in audience the participants in the first Congress for the Family of Africa and Europe. The Pope delivered the following message to the group assembled in the Clementine Hall.

1. I am very happy to receive this morning the participants in so important an event as the first Congress for the Family of Africa and of Europe, which you are attending here in Rome at the Faculty of Medicine of the Catholic University of the Sacred Heart. I greet you all with heartfelt affection and I express to you my esteem and appreciation.

Your congress comes soon after the recent Synod of Bishops, which set out to specify "the role of the Christian family in the modern world in accordance with the eternal plan concerning life and love" (Address at the concluding Mass of the Synod, October 3-25, 1980).

With regard to respect for human life, which has been the principal subject for your consideration, the Synod "openly confirmed the validity and clear truth of the prophetic message contained in the Encyclical *Humanae vitae*, a message profound in meaning and pertinent to modern conditions," while at the same time it made an appeal that the "biblical and 'personalistic' reasons for the teaching be continually clarified with the aim of making the whole of the Church's teaching clear to all people of good will and better understood day by day" *(ibid., 8)*.

I find it truly encouraging to see you here for this congress, following on a similar one for the family of the Americas. You are a group of experts in various fields and from different walks of life: bishops and theologians, philosophers and medical experts, as well as many religious and laity who are working "in the field"; *and you have come together to seek the best manner of placing the enriching teaching of Christ at the service of couples who wish to live out the authentic vision of the human person and of human sexuality.*

A special word of thanks is due to Sister Doctor Anna Cappella, who in the midst of so many other duties, has had to bear the greatest responsibility for the organization of this impressive congress. I know also that many of the delegates present, especially those from almost twenty African countries, have been chosen and sponsored in various ways by their episcopal conferences and ecclesiastical authorities. I appreciate the sacrifices that this has involved and I wish to thank your bishops for this sign that they give of the priority of the family apostolate in their pastoral activity.

NEED TO RECALL
SACREDNESS OF LIFE

2. I have carefully studied the content of the program of your congress. I wish to recall for you the words that I addressed recently to the members of the College of Cardinals concerning the very questions that you are considering. These words sum up my own pastoral program concerning the family: a theme which must receive priority today, if the Church is to render an authentic service to our tormented world; and I repeat them to you today, as the representatives of the

families of Africa and of Europe: *"In the face of contempt for the supreme value of life, which goes so far as to ratify the suppression of the human being in the mother's womb; in the face of the disintegration of family unity, the only guarantee for the complete formation of children and young people; in the face of the devaluation of clear and pure love, unbridled hedonism, the spread of pornography*, it is necessary to recall emphatically the holiness of marriage, the value of the family and the inviolability of human life. I will never tire of carrying out this mission, which I consider cannot be deferred" (Address to College of Cardinals, December 22, 1980).

This is the message that I have taught clearly on the occasion of my pastoral visits to the nations of Africa and Europe. It is the message that I direct to each of you, who come from various parts of these two continents, but are united by *your desire to follow the authentic teaching of Christ concerning the family and concerning human life.* Your contribution to the development of your own culture, your own society and your own nation depends greatly on the manner in which you live your vocation as families and to the extent that you help other families to do likewise. I stressed this point in addressing the families of Kenya, when I said: "The strength and vitality of any country will only be as great as the strength and vitality of the family within that country. For this reason Christian couples have an irreplaceable role in today's world. The generous love and fidelity of husband and wife offer stability and hope to a world torn by hatred and division. By their lifelong perseverance in life-giving love they show the unbreakable and sacred character of the sacramental marriage bond. At the same time, it is the Christian family that most simply and most profoundly promotes the dignity and worth of human life from the moment of its conception" (Homily at Uhuru Park, Nairobi, May 7, 1980).

TO REALIZE VALUES OF FAMILY LIFE

3. *It is only in this broad context of God's design for the family and for the creation of new life that one can consider the more specific question of the regulation of births.* The wisdom of the Creator has enriched human sexuality with great values and a special dignity (cf. GS 49). The vocation of Christian couples is to realize these values in their lives.

Perhaps the most urgent need today is to develop *an authentic philosophy of life and of the transmission of life, considered precisely as "procreation," that is, as discovering and collaborating with the design of God the Creator.*

The design of the Creator has provided the human organism with structures and functions to assist couples in arriving at responsible parenthood. "In fact, as experience bears witness, not every conjugal act is followed by new life. God has wisely disposed natural laws and rhythms of fecundity which, of themselves, cause a separation in the succession of births" (HV 11).

The plan of the Creator is impressed not only on the human body but also on the human spirit. How sad it is to note that the spirit of so many men and women has drifted away from this divine plan! *For so many men and women of our time new life is looked on as a threat and something to be feared; others, intoxicated with the technical possibilities offered by scientific prog-*

ress, wish to manipulate the process of the transmission of life and, following only the subjective criteria of personal satisfaction, are prepared even to destroy newly conceived life.

The Christian vision and attitude must be quite different: inspired by objective moral standards based on an authentic and all-embracing vision of the human person, *the Christian stands in awe of all the laws that God has impressed on the body and spirit of man.* Your task as Christian experts is to discover, understand better and treasure these laws, and to assist couples and all men and women of good will to appreciate the life-giving faculty which God has given them in trust, to be used according to His design.

Seen in this profound context of God's design for marriage and of the vocation to married life, your task will never be reduced to a question of presenting one or other biological method, much less to any watering down of the challenging call of the infinite God. *Rather your task is, in view of the situation of each couple, to see which method or combination of methods best helps them to respond as they ought to the demands of God's call.*

Your task then is above all to lead the men and women of our time to that true communion of life, love and grace which is the rich ideal of Christian marriage, appreciating *the essential inseparability of the unitive and procreative aspects of the conjugal act.*

In his Encyclical *Humanae vitae,* referred to so often during the recent synod as "a prophetic encyclical," Paul VI noted that he believed "that people of our day are particularly capable of grasping the deeply reasonable and human character of this principle" (HV 12).

It is our task as apostles of human life, to assist the men and women of our time to arrive at this authentic vision through a solid and consistent catechesis of life.

Upon all of you in your efforts I invoke the grace and strength of our Lord Jesus Christ.

POPE'S ADDRESS IN ITALIAN

Then speaking in Italian, the Holy Father continued:

As a tribute to the Catholic University of the Sacred Heart, which organized this congress, and in consideration of the large numbers of Italian-speaking participants, I would now like to add a word in their language. I express in the first place my congratulations on the useful initiative, which has gathered persons highly qualified as regards scientific commitment and generous service to life. I am happy to testify to my deep appreciation for the work that each of you, ladies and gentlemen, carries out in this field, and I willingly take the opportunity to encourage all efforts aimed at assisting the family in the very noble task of being the cradle of a new life.

The Second Vatican Council opportunely recalled that *"children are really the supreme gift of marriage and contribute very substantially to the welfare of their parents"* (GS 50). It is necessary, therefore, to offer married couples all opportune help, so that they may adequately respond to their vocation, namely "to cooperate with the love of the Creator and the Savior, who through them will enlarge and enrich His own family day by day" *(ibid.)*.

That will be beneficial, moreover, for the fuller realization of their mutual love. *Not living their union, in fact, just for themselves, but also for others, that is, for their children, they will discover a new way of understanding and mutual presence: the children will become testimonies of their love and each partner will be able to recognize in them the living presence of the other.*

May this congress, therefore, serve to confirm and strengthen in each of you the resolution to dedicate yourselves with renewed enthusiasm to this well-deserving and worthy cause. This is a wish that I willingly accompany with my conciliatory apostolic blessing.

THE PROCESS OF URBANIZATION AND THE FAMILY

The mayors of sixty of the most populous cities in the world took part in an International Conference on the theme "Population and Urban Future," held in Rome from the 1st to the 4th of September, 1980. In an audience with them on September 4th, the Holy Father delivered the following address.

Ladies and gentlemen,
Dear friends,

1. I am pleased to extend a warm welcome to all of you who have come from many different countries, and who are participating in the International Conference on Population and the Urban Future being held in Rome. I greet you, not as one who is an expert in the economic, social and political aspects of the subject of your discussions, but as one vitally interested in every human dimension of your theme—as one eager to proclaim with you, from the perspective of man and his inviolable dignity, the great relevance of your topic.

2. It was almost a decade ago that my Predecessor Paul VI, in a well-known document of his Pontificate, made the following reflection: "A major phenomenon draws our attention, as much in the industrialized countries as in those which are developing: urbanization." He then went on to raise the following questions: "Is not the rise of an urban civilization...a true challenge to the wisdom of man, to his capacity for organization and to his farseeing imagination?... Urbanization, undoubtedly an irreversible stage in the development of human societies, confronts man with difficult problems. How is he to master its growth, regulate its organization and successfully accomplish its animation for the good of all?" (OA 9-10)

3. And today, moved by humanitarian concern, you are endeavoring to share useful experiences and to shed light on many issues involved in this vast topic of the urban future; you are hoping, moreover, to focus your attention on policies and programs, and to gain insights into those means which are best adapted to your goals.

The attention that you devote to this subject is patently justified by reason of its importance. Who could contest that the phenomenon of urbanization, and consequently of urbanism itself, is intimately linked to the progress of tomorrow's world? *By reason of its power to effect social, economic and political changes, and to influence man, urbanization must be counted among the more significant factors of this century affecting human affairs.* Permit me therefore to express the conviction that you do well to ponder, from the viewpoint of total human well-being—a viewpoint which respects in man a scale of spiritual and material values—different ramifications of the phenomenon such as health, education, employment, food and housing. On her part, *the Catholic Church considers the question from a religious viewpoint, which can never prescind from, but which must rather take into account, all the other truly human dimensions of an issue that is eminently human.*

4. In the aforementioned document, Paul VI also spoke explicitly of the many and various evils that spring from a "disordered growth" of the city: "Behind the facades, much misery is hidden...; other forms of misery spread where human dignity founders: delinquency, criminality, abuse of drugs and eroticism. It is in fact the weakest who are the victims of dehumanizing

living conditions, degrading for conscience and harmful for the family institution" *(ibid.,* 10). Because of his understanding of the consequences of disordered urbanization, Paul VI could not but conclude: "It is the grave duty of those responsible to strive to control this process and to give it direction" *(ibid.,* 11).

5. The challenge is indeed formidable, but the ingenuity of man is great. Even the prediction for the future, based on projections of the past, are subject to the causality of man and to his concrete interventions. By reason of this principle we have a confirmation of the importance of the discussions that you have undertaken in the hope of promoting the true good of man. *For those of us who are the heirs of the Judaeo-Christian or other religious traditions, there emerges also the great element of God's providence in the world and the reality of His action.* The ancient Psalmist expressed this, saying: "Unless the Lord builds the house, those who build it labor in vain" (Ps. 127:1).

6. *The good of man—man seen in the totality of his nature and in the full dignity of his person—is indeed a determining factor for all human interventions in this field.* Those who would serve man must be motivated by a love and a fraternal compassion that effectively takes into account man in his origin, in his composition, in the laws that govern his nature, in the incomparable role that is his at the present time, as well as in the grandeur of his destiny. It is this last factor which, far from negating the value of the present moment or that of the future, seeks to put it in full and final perspective. *The sacredness of human life and its transmission, the inviolability of all human rights, the importance of each individual person*—all of this together is the perspective

from which every intervention in the field of population and the urban future is rightfully evaluated; these are the criteria of its utility and its success.

7. *Society today and tomorrow exists for man and for the advancement of his personal dignity.* A contribution before the witness of history to a true and genuine city of man is a great contribution, and one to be accomplished with God's help. It is a contribution worthy of you all. It is indeed a splendid initiative and a weighty responsibility that your congress assumes in endeavoring to promote the urban future in the city of tomorrow. Through your efforts, and through the upright and enlightened contribution of countless other men and women of good will who have understood what is at stake, may this city of tomorrow be a city of human dignity and fraternal service, a city of justice, of love and of peace.

MORAL ASPECT
OF SOLVING PROBLEMS
OF MARRIED COUPLES

On November 29, 1980, the Holy Father received in audience participants in the Second National Meeting of the Confederation of Family Advisory Bureaus of Christian Inspiration, and delivered the following address.

Dear brothers and sisters,

1. My cordial greeting to you all, who are celebrating the national meeting sponsored by the Confederation of Family Advisory Bureaus of Christian Inspiration, to which you belong. I am happy to take advantage of the occasion to express to you my appreciation: you are engaged in an action of great value both on the human and on the ecclesial plane.

The family is a fundamental chapter of the apostolate, to which the whole Christian community is called to give attention particularly at the present historical moment. It is no mere chance that the recent Synod of Bishops stopped to reflect on the "role of the Christian family in the modern world," in order to detect its problems, analyze the elements, and indicate solutions. The urgency of a more adequate and precise intervention in this area of human experience, which the cultural changes of our age have shaken up and put in a state of crisis in a particularly deep way, has never been felt so much as today.

"Models" of interpretation of the conjugal reality, which exclude any reference to the superior values of ethics and religion, are proposed on many sides. The practical behavior which is deduced from them is conse-

quently in contrast not only with the Christian message, but also with a truly human view of that "intimate partnership of life and love," which marriage is (cf. GS 48).

REDEEMED HUMAN LOVE

2. *It is the task of the Christian community to proclaim forcefully, before present-day society, the joyful announcement of redeemed human love. Christ has "freed" man and woman for the possibility of loving each other in truth and fullness.* The great danger for family life, in a society in which pleasure, comforts and independence are idols, lies in the fact that men may be induced to close their hearts to such a possibility, resigning themselves to a "reduced ideal" of the life of the couple. The Christian community must contest a view of the conjugal relationship which, instead of unreserved mutual dedication, proposes the mere coexistence of two loves, concerned, when all is said and done, only with themselves.

"If Christian marriage"—I said in the course of my pilgrimage in Africa—"is comparable to a very high mountain which places spouses in the immediate vicinity of God, it must be recognized that its ascent calls for a great deal of time and effort. But is that a reason for suppressing or lowering this summit?" (Kinshasa, Homily at the Mass for Families, May 3, 1980)

It is necessary to help individual couples to interpret their love correctly and to strengthen their own convictions, by studying the intrinsic reasons that justify the Christian view of marriage and the family, and grasping its deep connections with the essential requirements of a really human anthropology.

For this purpose the community must take its place beside the couple with the offering of concrete help along the way that it traverses, to arrive at ever fuller realization of the ideal glimpsed with that depth of intuition that love gives to the eyes of the heart. *Man is a historical being, who becomes and constructs himself day after day thanks to a multiple and progressive commitment.* Also conjugal life is a way, and a way that is not without obstacles. It is important that spouses should be sustained and encouraged, so that they will not have to submit to a narrow perspective, which does not know "the dilated spaces of charity" (Augustine).

BENEFICIAL INFLUENCE

3. One of the concrete ways with which the Christian community really becomes present beside the couple in its growth and progress towards maturity is certainly constituted by the institution of Family Advisory Bureaus. In recent years they have multiplied, and your confederation now includes ninety or so. Still more will come, as I hope. I am happy to acknowledge to you, beloved in Christ, the really important task which you are called to carry out in the service of the family, "the first and vital cell of society," "the domestic sanctuary of the Church" (AA 11).

Yours is a commitment which well deserves the title of mission, so noble are the aims that it pursues and so decisive—for the good of society and of the Christian community itself—are the results derived from it.

In order, however, to be able to carry out their function effectively, Advisory Bureaus of Christian Inspiration will have to be strictly consistent with their identity, which is that of contributing to the formation of Christian families, aware of their specific vocation. In their approach to their work, open as it is to *the total reality of marriage and the family*, they cannot fail to give special attention to the ethical and religious aspect which characterizes it.

In fact, it is only by giving the moral aspect priority over all others that the problems of the couple can be solved. *The reminder of the ethical norm which must regulate the behavior of spouses is a "conditio sine qua non" of the ecclesial service to which the Advisory Bureaus are called. This reminder, moreover, must be carried out in full conformity with the teaching of the Magisterium, which has been repeatedly expressed on this matter, excluding among other things both premarital intercourse and extramarital intercourse, and condemning contraception and abortion.* The task of the Advisory Bureaus is to help to overcome the difficulties, not to support surrender to them.

NOBLE COMMITMENT

4. In this perspective I wish to stress the urgency of an unmistakable testimony of service to life. *Members of the Advisory Bureaus must not only undertake to take an interest in, and assist, those who have recourse to their help, but they must also feel it their duty to exclude any form of participation in procedures geared to abortion.* The Italian bishops have spoken clearly in this connection: it is necessary to follow them, without being led astray by other teachers.

Such an attitude of steadfast consistency falls, moreover, into the sphere of that autonomous freedom of policy which also the civil law recognizes.

Christian inspiration must, moreover, stimulate each of you to do his utmost to contribute to make the Advisory Bureau an exemplary institution of its kind, capable, that is, of carrying out its activity in a highly qualified way. That will not fail to win for you the appreciation and sympathy of the persons and couples in need of help, and will also exercise, as time goes on, a beneficial influence on similar organizations, inducing them to assume criteria of intervention more in keeping with a fully human view of conjugal reality.

Continue, therefore, with confidence and enthusiasm in your highly meritorious action. The Pope encourages you, and, with him, your bishops and the whole Christian community encourage you. All that you succeed in doing in support of the family is destined to have an efficacy which, going beyond its own sphere, will also reach other persons and have an impact on society. *The future of the world and of the Church passes through the family.*

With these wishes, I am happy to grant to you, as a token of abundant heavenly favors, my apostolic blessing, which I willingly extend to your dear ones and to all those who collaborate with you in the Family Advisory Bureaus.

HELP THE MODERN FAMILY TO REDISCOVER THE REAL MEANING OF LIFE

On October 11, 1980, the Holy Father received in audience 650 participants in the twenty-eighth Assembly of the Union of Women Major Superiors of Italy treating the subject "Religious Life and the Family." John Paul II delivered the following address.

Beloved sisters in the Lord!

1. At the end of your annual assembly you have desired this audience, reserved completely for you, Mothers general and provincials of the many congregations and religious houses scattered in all the regions of Italy.

I greet you warmly and through you I wish to extend my affectionate greeting to all your fellow sisters in Italy who, in the frantic metropolises as well as in remote mountain villages, are living with love and joy their consecration to Christ and to souls. *Yes, beloved sisters, take to all the sisters entrusted to your responsibility the greeting of the Pope; tell them that he remembers them, follows them, esteems them, prays for them, suffers with them, is concerned about their human and spiritual experiences, and would like them to be always joyful and generous, even in inevitable tribulations.*

I wish furthermore to express to you my satisfaction with this general assembly of yours, in which you have wanted to participate in such large numbers to study the subject: "Religious Life and the Family," which echoes the theme dealt with in the Synod of Bishops now in progress, and to talk about it among yourselves, exchanging your experiences.

GREAT RESPONSIBILITY

2. It is an important subject because the relations of sisters with family communities are frequent. Sisters, in fact, are in continual contact with children in nursery schools and are acquainted with the background of every home; they approach boys and girls in schools, oratories, Catholic associations, and in the various ecclesial groups; they take part in pastoral councils and in parish and diocesan catechesis. Above all, sisters are present in orphanages, hospitals, homes for the aged, clinics, places of assistance and care for the handicapped, visits to the sick in the homes, and also to places of aid for drifters, those excluded from society, drug addicts, etc.

It can be said that the sister, in a certain way, accompanies families on their existential way, and therefore her responsibility is great, but great must be also her consolation, being able in this way to make her concrete contribution of faith and charity to what is the masterpiece of the love of God, the Creator and Redeemer.

RELATIONS WITH FAMILIES

3. *Today more than ever, many persons are tormented by the problem of existence and of their own identity. They feel the longing to go beyond the limits of history and time, they feverishly look for truth! So the first task and the first duty of the sister in her relations with the family is to bear witness to truth, that is, to help the modern family rediscover the real meaning of life and history.*

Dear sisters, bring to families *the truth as it was revealed by Christ and as it is taught by the Church! Do not let yourselves be disturbed by the sensation made by the many insistent ideologies which confuse and depress.* Always sow the good seed of truth, following the teaching of the Church and the example of the saints.

Hence the necessity of a serious and authentic updating in the various fields of doctrine on the part of the sister, overcoming the dangers of superficiality and emotion. It is necessary, therefore, *to watch carefully over the various means of aggiornamento and guidance (books, newspapers, reviews, courses of study, etc.), in order not to be disconcerted by false ideas, and then misdirect the persons that have to be approached. Every family wants the truth from those who are consecrated to God:* therefore be faithful and happy to be able to proclaim it and bear witness to it!

FIRST POSSESS PEACE

4. Then bring to the family peace! The spirit must be firm and staunch in truth, but the heart must be full of understanding and compassion. *The family needs above all spiritual help and encouragement, great support and affection.* Never so much as now does the family need to feel the Divine Master close and consoling, willing to bestow His forgiveness, certainty, hope and love! *Certainly, evil must be combatted and error condemned, but every person must be understood and loved; the oil of kindness and mercy must be spread on every wound,* as was done by the Good Samaritan in the parable.

But to bring peace it is necessary to possess it! *Therefore your houses must be oases of serenity, achieved through the school of patience and mutual charity.*

Bring peace to families with your faith and your love! Bring it especially where suffering groans, where loneliness reigns, where division weighs, where the hope of a life after death is lacking! Bring peace, pointing to the crucified Christ and our real country which is in heaven! (cf. Phil. 4:20)

GOD IN MY SOUL

5. Beloved sisters, Sister Elizabeth of the Holy Trinity wrote: "Let us live with God as with a friend; let us make our faith alive in order to communicate with God through everything that makes saints. We bear in us our heaven, because He who satisfies the glorified in the light of vision gives Himself to us in faith and in mystery. It is the same thing. It seems to me that I have found my heaven on earth, because heaven is God, and God is in my soul. The day when I understood this, everything was illuminated in me and I would like to whisper this secret to those I love, in order that they, too, through everything, may always adhere to God and that Christ's prayer: 'Father, let them be consummated in one,' may be realized" (Servant of God, Sister Elizabeth of the Holy Trinity, *Scritti*, Roma, *Post. gener. dei Carmelitani Scalzi*, 1967).

You too, live this secret and proclaim it to families, with the help and assistance of the Blessed Virgin and St. Joseph: it is the secret that illuminates, comforts, and saves!

With these wishes, imploring from the Lord an abundance of heavenly favors, I warmly impart to you the conciliatory apostolic blessing, which I gladly extend to all your fellow sisters.

THE PERSON, NOT SCIENCE, IS THE MEASURE

On October 27, 1980, the Holy Father received about three thousand participants in two medical congresses: the 81st Congress of the Italian Society of Internal Medicine, and the 82nd Congress of the Italian Society of General Surgery. John Paul II delivered the following address.

1. I welcome you with deep satisfaction, eminent representatives of the Italian Society of Internal Medicine and of the Italian Society of General Surgery, who, on the occasion of the celebration of your respective national congresses, kindly wished to pay me a visit.

In fact, I consider your presence particularly significant not only because of the qualified medico-scientific activity in which each of you is engaged, but also because of the implicit and yet clear witness that it expresses in favor of moral and human values. What induced you, in fact, to request this audience, but watchful and attentive awareness of the highest reasons of life and action, reasons which you know are part of the daily solicitude of Peter's Successor?

To all of you, therefore, with the expression of my gratitude, the most respectful and cordial greeting, with a special grateful thought for the presidents of your two societies, Prof. Alessandro Beretta Angussola and Prof. Giuseppe Zannini. I then wish to greet the collaborators, students and relatives who have accompanied you here, together with the zealous and well-deserving bishop, Most Rev. Fiorenzo Angelini.

THE NEW APPROACH

2. You are gathered in Rome, ladies and gentlemen, to discuss some particularly topical aspects of the disciplines in your sphere of competence. In the last few years medical skill has made significant breakthroughs, which have considerably increased the possibilities of therapeutic intervention. That has brought about a slow modification of the very concept of medicine, extending its role from its original function of combatting disease to that of the overall promotion of the human being's health. The consequence of this new approach has been the progressive evolution of the relationship between doctor and patient towards more and more complex organized forms, aimed at safeguarding the citizen's health from birth to old age.

The protection of childhood and of old age, school medicine, factory medicine, the prevention of occupational diseases and accidents at work, mental hygiene, protection of the handicapped and of drug addicts, of the mentally ill, prevention of pollution diseases, control of the territory, etc., are as many chapters of the present way of conceiving "service for man," to which your skill is called.

There is no reason not to rejoice at this, since it can well be said that, from this standpoint, man's right over his life has never been so fully recognized. It is one of the qualifying features of the extraordinary acceleration of history, which characterizes our age. Because of this extraordinary development, medicine is playing an outstanding role in shaping the face of society today.

FORMS OF VIOLATION

A serene and attentive examination of the present situation as a whole must, however, lead to the recognition that insidious forms of violation of the right to a decent life, to which every human being is entitled, have not at all disappeared. In some ways it could even be said that negative aspects have emerged, as I wrote in the Encyclical *Redemptor hominis:* "If therefore our time...appears as a time of great progress, it is also seen as a time of threat in many forms for man.... This is why all phases of present-day progress must be followed attentively. Each stage of that progress must, so to speak, be x-rayed from this point of view.... Indeed there is already a real perceptible danger that, while man's dominion over the world of things is making enormous advances, *he should lose the essential threads of his dominion, and in various ways let his humanity be subjected to the world, and become himself something subject to manipulation in many ways*—even if the manipulation is often not directly perceptible" (no. 16).

SCIENCE, NOT THE HIGHEST VALUE

3. The truth is that technological development, characteristic of our time, is suffering from a fundamental ambivalence: while on the one hand it enables man to take in hand his own destiny, *it exposes him, on the other hand, to the temptation of going beyond the limits of a reasonable dominion over nature, jeopardizing the very survival and integrity of the human person.*

Just consider, to remain in the sphere of biology and medicine, the implicit danger to man's right to life represented by the very discoveries in the field of artificial insemination, the control of births and fertility, hibernation and "retarded death," genetic engineering, psychic drugs, organ transplants, etc. *Certainly, scientific knowledge has its own laws by which it must abide. It must also recognize, however, especially in medicine, an impassable limit in respect for the person and in protection of his right to live in a way worthy of a human being.*

If a new method of investigation, for example, harms or threatens to harm this right, it is not to be considered lawful simply because it increases our knowledge. Science, in fact, is not the highest value to which all others must be subordinated. *Higher up in the scale of values is precisely the individual's personal right to physical and spiritual life, to his psychic and functional integrity.* The person, in fact, is the measure and criterion of good or evil in all human manifestations. Scientific progress, therefore, cannot claim to lie in a kind of neutral ground. The ethical norm, based on respect for the dignity of the person, must illuminate and discipline both the research phase and the phase of the application of the results reached in it.

MEDICINE VERSUS MAN

4. For some time, alarmed voices have been raised in your field, denouncing the harmful consequences derived from a medicine concerned more with itself than with man, whom it should serve. I am thinking, for example, of the pharmacological field. There is no doubt that the amazing success of modern therapy is based on the wealth of drugs at our disposal and their

effectiveness. It is a fact, however, that, among the chapters of pathology today, there has been added a new one, the iatrogenetic one. There are more and more frequent morbid manifestations due to the indiscriminate use of drugs: diseases of the skin, of the nervous system, of the digestive system, above all, diseases of the blood. It is not only a question of unsuitable use of drugs, or of abuse of them. It is often a question of real and proper intolerance of the organism.

The danger is not to be neglected, because even the most careful and conscientious pharmacological research does not completely exclude a potential risk: the tragic example of thalidomide is a proof of this. Even with the intention of being beneficial, the doctor, therefore, may involuntarily harm the individual's right over his own life. Pharmacological research and therapeutic application must, therefore, be highly attentive to the ethical norms responsible for safeguarding this right.

ON EXPERIMENTATION

5. The discourse has led us to touch on a subject that is much debated today, that of experimentation. Here, too, recognition of the dignity of the person, and of the ethical norm derived from it, as a superior value by which scientific research must be inspired, has precise consequences at the deontological level. *Pharmacological and clinical experimentation cannot be initiated without having taken all precautions to guarantee the harmlessness of the intervention.* The preclinical phase of the research must therefore provide the most abundant pharmaco-toxicological documentation.

It is obvious, moreover, that the patient must be informed of the experimentation, of its purpose and any risks it involves, so that he may give or refuse his consent in full awareness and freedom. *The doctor, in fact, has only that power and those rights over the patient which the patient himself confers on him.*

Consent on the part of the patient is not, furthermore, without any limitation. To improve his own conditions of health remains, apart from particular cases, the essential purpose of collaboration on the part of the patient. *Experimentation, in fact, is justified* in primis *with the interest of the individual, not with that of the collectivity.* That does not exclude, however, that without detriment to his own substantial integrity, *the patient can legitimately assume a proportionate part of risk, in order to contribute with his initiative to the progress of medicine and, in this way, to the good of the community.* Medical science, in fact, has its place in the community as a force to set man free from infirmities that handicap him and from psychosomatic weaknesses that humiliate him. *To give something of oneself, within the limits laid down by the moral norm, may constitute a highly meritorious witness of charity and an occasion of spiritual growth so significant as to be able to compensate for the risk of a slight physical disability.*

RE-PERSONALIZE MEDICINE

6. The considerations set forth on the matter of pharmacological research and medical therapy can be extended to other fields of medicine. More often than is thought, in the very sphere of care for the sick person, his personal right to psycho-physical integrity can be harmed, with the exercise of what is actually violence:

in the diagnostic investigation by means of complex procedures which are not infrequently traumatizing, in surgical treatment which now goes so far as to carry out the boldest interventions of destruction and reconstruction, in the case of organ transplants, in applied medical research, in the hospital organization itself.

It is not possible to deal completely now with such subjects, whose examination would take us far, forcing us to question ourselves on the type of medicine towards which we wish to move: whether that of a medicine in keeping with man or, on the other hand, a medicine under the sign of pure technology and organizational efficiency.

It is necessary to make an effort for a "re-personalization" of medicine which, leading once more to a more unified consideration of the patient, will stimulate the establishment of a more humanized relationship with him, such, that is, as not to tear the bond between the psycho-affective sphere and his suffering body. *The patient-doctor relationship must be based once more on a dialogue made up of listening, respect, and interest; it must become once more a real meeting between two free people or*, as has been said, between a "trust" and a "conscience."

This will make it possible for the patient to feel understood for what he really is: *an individual who has difficulties in the use of his body or in the exercise of his faculties, but who preserves intact the deep essence of his humanity, and expects to see his rights to truth and good respected, both on the human and on the religious plane.*

7. Ladies and gentlemen, in proposing these reflections to you, my thought spontaneously goes to Christ's

words: "I was sick and you visited me" (Mt. 25:36). What a stimulus to the desired "personalization" of medicine can come from Christian charity, *which makes us discover in the features of every sick person the adorable face of the great, mysterious Patient*, who continues to suffer in those over whom your profession, wise and useful, bends!

My prayer goes to Him at this moment, to invoke on you, on your dear ones, and on all your patients, the abundance of heavenly favors, as a token of which I willingly impart to you the conciliatory apostolic blessing.

FREEDOM OF CONSCIENCE AND THE DEFENSE OF LIFE

On December 28, 1978, John Paul II received in audience the Association of Italian Catholic Doctors and delivered the following address.

Gentlemen and beloved sons of the Italian Catholic Doctors Association,

Welcoming you heartily to this house, which has now become mine, I want to express to you in the first place my joy at this meeting where I can make the acquaintance of so many persons eminent for their scientific merits, admirable for their high sense of duty, and exemplary for their courageous profession of Christian faith. I am sincerely grateful to you for the courtesy and affection of which this visit of yours is a manifest and consoling sign, and I am happy, therefore, to address my greeting to your zealous ecclesiastical assistant, our revered brother, Mons. Fiorenzo Angelini; to your illustrious president, Prof. Pietro de Franciscis, efficiently assisted by the three vice-presidents; to the indefatigable secretary general, Prof. Domenico Di Virgilio; to the members of the national council; to the regional delegates and presidents of the diocesan sections; to representatives of the members of the association, as well as to the group of Catholic nurses whose presence today wishes to be a testimony of the close collaboration which they intend to carry out with you doctors in the service of the patients.

ESTEEM FOR MEDICAL PROFESSION

I am glad to take the opportunity to express publicly my great esteem for a profession such as yours, always considered by everyone more as a mission than as ordinary work. The dignity and responsibility of such a mission will never be sufficiently understood, or adequately expressed. To assist, treat, comfort and cure human pain is a commitment which, in its nobility, usefulness and ideality, is very close to the priest's vocation. In both offices, in fact, there is a more direct and evident manifestation of the supreme commandment of love of one's neighbor—a love called not infrequently to assume forms which reach the point of real heroism. We must not be surprised, therefore, by the solemn admonition of Holy Scripture: "Honor the physician with the honor due him, for the Lord created him; for healing comes from the Most High" (Sir. 38:1-2).

YOUR ASSOCIATION'S AIMS

Your association came into being to promote the attainment of the high aims of the profession and to enrich them with the specific contribution of Christian values. To measure the importance of the contribution it intends to make to your activity as Christian doctors, it is enough to recall the terms of article 2 of the statutes. The latter indicates as purposes of the association the. qualification of the moral, scientific and professional formation of members; the promotion of medico-moral studies in the light of the principles of Catholic doctrine; the animation of the spirit of real human and Christian service in the relationship of doctors with their patient; action to ensure the most dignified exercise of the profession and for protection of the just interests of the medical class; and education of members to rightful ecclesial co-responsibility and to generous availability for every charitable activity connected with the exercise of the profession.

These are not resolutions which have remained only on paper. I am glad to acknowledge the action of sensitization and orientation carried out by the association in these years among the Italian medical class, both through varied and specialized publishing productions, and through the appreciated periodical *Orizzonte Medico*, and in the *Study Courses* (the proceedings of the recent one on "The Man of the Holy Shroud" were kindly presented to me) which have seen, in the space of eleven years, eminent specialists of the different sciences deal with anthropological subjects of fundamental interest, in search of an answer that will satisfy man and the Christian. I cannot but express appreciation and praise: the formative purpose, which is pursued by means of these instruments, deserves to be cordially approved, and efforts made in this direction must be warmly encouraged.

That applies particularly today, when powerful movements of opinion, effectively supported by the great media of mass communication, are trying to influence the consciences of doctors in every way, to induce them to lend their services in practices contrary not only to Christian, but also to natural morality, in open contradiction with professional ethics, expressed in the famous oath of the ancient pagan doctor.

PROPHETIC APPEAL

In the message for the World Day of Peace on last January 1st, my great Predecessor Paul VI of revered memory, addressing a special word to doctors who were pointed out as "wise and generous defenders of human life," expressed his confidence that alongside the "religious ministry" *there could be the "therapeutic min-*

istry" of doctors in affirming and defending human life in all "those particular contingencies in which life itself can be compromised through the positive and wicked intention of human will." I am certain that this heartfelt and prophetic appeal has met, and still meets, with wide support not only among Catholic doctors, but also among those who, though not sustained by faith, are, however, deeply aware of the higher requirements of their profession.

As minister of that God who is presented in Scripture as the "Lord who loves the living" (Wis. 11:26), I, too, wish to express my sincere admiration for all medical practitioners who, following the dictates of sound conscience, are able to resist daily enticements, pressure, threats and sometimes even physical violence, in order not to stain themselves with behavior that is harmful in any way to *that sacred good, which is human life.* Their courageous and consistent testimony is a very important contribution to the construction of a society which, in order to be fully human, cannot but be based *on respect and protection of the prime premise of every other human right, that is, the right to live.*

FREEDOM OF CONSCIENCE

The Pope willingly unites his voice to that of all doctors with a sound conscience, and adopts their fundamental requests: the request, in the first place, for recognition of the deeper nature of their noble profession which wishes them to be ministers of life and never instruments of death. *And then the request for full and complete respect, in the legislation and in facts, of freedom of conscience, understood as the fundamental right*

*of the person not to be forced to act contrary to his con-
science or prevented from behaving in accordance with
it.* Finally, as well as the request for *an indispensable
and firm juridical protection of human life at all its
stages, also the request for adequate operational structures, which will encourage the joyful acceptance of life
about to be born, its effective promotion during development and maturity, its careful and delicate protection
when its decline begins and up to its natural extinction.*

Catholic doctors in particular should be committed
to the service of life with generous enthusiasm. These, in
their faith in God the Creator, whose image man is, and
in the mystery of the eternal Word who descended from
heaven in the frail flesh of a helpless child, find a new
and higher reason for industrious dedication to loving
care and the disinterested safeguarding of every brother,
especially if he is little, poor, defenseless, threatened. It
consoles me to know that these convictions are deeply
rooted in your hearts: they inspire and direct your daily
professional activity and are able to suggest to you,
when it is necessary, even public, clear, and unmistakable stands.

EXEMPLARY WITNESS

How could I fail to mention, in this connection, the
exemplary witness you bore, with timely and compact
adherence to the indications of the episcopate, in the
recent and distressing matter of the legislation in favor
of abortion. It was a witness in which—I proudly stress
it in my capacity as Bishop of Rome—this city distinguished itself particularly, offering non-Catholic doctors also a reminder and a stimulus of providential
efficacy. *This responsible gesture will reach more*

effectively its aim of asserting the right of the medical and ancillary personnel to freedom of conscience, a right sanctioned by a special clause in the law; to personal consistency; to defense of the right to life and to social denunciation of a legal situation prejudicial to justice, a right adopted with authenticity of motivations and confirmed by disinterested generosity open to all the commitments and initiatives in the service of the human person.

I make no secret of the fact that consistency with Christian principles may mean for you the necessity of exposing yourselves to the risk of incomprehension, misunderstanding and even serious discrimination. In this sad case may you be assisted by the programmatic words by which a great colleague of yours, Blessed Giuseppe Moscati, was constantly inspired: "Love truth," he wrote in a personal note on October 17, 1922. "Show yourself as you are, without pretense, fearlessly and bluntly. And if truth costs you persecution, accept it; if torture, bear it. And if you had to sacrifice yourself and your life for truth, be strong in sacrifice" (cf. *Positio super virtutibus*, Romae, 1972). Is it not natural, moreover, that Christ's prophecy: "If they persecuted me, they will persecute you" (Jn. 15:20), should come true in the Christian's life? It will be the case, then, to recall that the Divine Master reserved a special beatitude for those who are reviled and persecuted "on His account" (cf. Mt. 5:11-12).

HELP FROM MARY

Confirming to you, therefore, together with my esteem, my cordial encouragement to continue along the way of courageous testimony and exemplary service in favor of human life, I implore upon your good resolutions the help of the Blessed Virgin, whom you love to invoke as *"Salus Infirmorum et Mater Scientiae."* I implore the protection of St. Luke, "the beloved physician" (Col. 4:14), whom you honor as your patron saint. And thinking with fatherly affection of your colleagues of the association scattered all over Italy, of their respective families, as well as of so many sick persons to whom your daily concern goes, I raise my hands over you and them to impart warmly a special apostolic blessing, petitioning all desired heavenly consolation.

YOU ARE THE GUARDIANS
OF HUMAN LIVES

On January 26, 1980, John Paul II received in audience participants in the specialized meeting for midwives, organized by the Catholic Medical Operators Association. The meeting, attended by over two hundred midwives, was dedicated to the subject "In Defense of Life and the Family." The Holy Father delivered the following address.

Beloved sisters!

1. I willingly granted the desire, expressed by you, for a special meeting, in which you could bear witness to the devotion that unites you with the Pope, and receive from him a word of comfort and guidance in carrying out the delicate tasks connected with your profession.

I know the high purposes by which your association is inspired and I am acquainted, too, with the courageous choices it has made in these years, to remain faithful to the dictates of conscience illuminated by faith. I am glad, therefore, to be able to express to you personally my cordial appreciation and to bring you, at the same time, my fatherly exhortation to persevere in the resolution of consistent adherence to the ethical norms of your profession, which is not infrequently subjected to strong pressure on the part of those who would like to force it to carry out acts which are in direct contrast with the purposes for which it was created and operates.

"Service for life and the family" was and is, in fact, the essential *raison d'être* of this profession, as you opportunely stressed in the very subject of your meeting; and it is precisely in this noble service that the secret of its greatness must be sought. It is up to you to watch solicitously over the marvelous and mysterious process of generation, which takes place in the mother's womb, in order to follow its normal development and to facilitate its happy outcome with the birth of the new creature. You are, therefore, the guardians of human life, which is renewed in the world, bringing to it, with the infant's fresh smile, the joy (cf. Jn. 16:21) and the hope of a better future.

THE VERY HIGH VALUE OF HUMAN LIFE

2. *It is necessary, therefore, that you should each cultivate within yourself a clear awareness of the very high value of human life: it is a unique value in the whole of visible creation. The Lord, in fact, created everything on earth for man; man, on the other hand*—as the Second Vatican Council stressed—is "the only creature that God wanted for his own sake" (GS 24).

This means that, *as regards his being and his essence, man cannot be ordained to any creature, but only to God.* This is the deep content of the well-known passage in the Bible according to which "God created man in his own image...male and female He created them" (Gn. 1:27); and this is also what it is desired to recall when it is affirmed that *human life is sacred. Man, as a being supplied with intelligence and free will, takes his right to life directly from God, whose image he is, not from his parents, or from any society or human authority.* Only God, therefore, can "dispose" of this extraordinary gift of His: "I, even I, am he, and there is no God beside me; I kill and I make alive; I wound and I heal; and there is none that can deliver out of my hand" (Dt. 32:39).

Man, therefore, *possesses life as a gift*, of which he cannot consider himself the owner, however; for this reason, he cannot feel he is the arbiter of life, whether his own or that of others. The Old Testament formulates this conclusion in one of the ten commandments: "You shall not kill" (Ex. 20:13), with the clarification that follows immediately afterwards: "Do not slay the innocent and righteous, for I will not acquit the wicked" (Ex. 23:7). Christ, in the New Testament, confirms this commandment as the condition to "enter life" (cf. Mt. 19:18); but—significantly—He follows it with the mention of the commandment that sums up every aspect of moral law, bringing it to completion, that is, the commandment of love (cf. Mt. 19:19). Only he who loves can accept completely the requirements that spring from respect for the life of one's neighbor.

In this connection, you certainly remember the words of Christ in the Sermon on the Mount: on this occasion Jesus refers almost polemically to the "You shall not kill" of the Old Testament, seeing in it an expression of the "insufficient" justice of the scribes and Pharisees (cf. Mt. 5:20) and inviting people to look more deeply into themselves, to detect the wicked roots, from which all violence against life springs; not only he who kills is guilty, but also he who harbors malevolent sentiments and speaks offensive words to his neighbor (cf. Mt. 5:21ff.). *There is a verbal violence which prepares the ground and helps to produce the psychological conditions that trigger off physical violence.*

He who wishes to respect life and, in fact, puts himself generously in its service, must cultivate in himself, feelings of understanding for the other, participation in his affairs, human solidarity, in a word, feelings of sincere love. *The believer can do so more easily, because he recognizes in every man a brother (cf. Mt. 23:8), in whom Christ identifies Himself to the extent of considering what is done to him as done to Himself* (cf. Mt. 25:40, 45).

BEARING WITNESS FOR YOUR ESTEEM OF LIFE

3. *Also the unborn child is a man; and in fact, if a very special title of identification with Christ is being among "the least" of His brethren (cf. Mt. 25:40), how can we fail to see a particular presence of Christ in the human being in gestation who, among other human beings, is really the most little and helpless, deprived as he is of all means of defense, even of a voice to protest against the blows struck at his most elementary rights?*

It is your task to bear witness, before everyone, of the esteem and respect you cherish in your hearts for human life; to take up its defense boldly, when necessary; to refuse to cooperate in its direct suppression. *There is no human regulation that can make legitimate an action that is intrinsically wicked, far less oblige anyone to consent to it.* The law, in fact, takes its binding value from the function it carries out—in faithfulness to divine law—in the service of the common good; and this, in its turn, is such to the extent to which it promotes the well-being of the person. So before a law that puts itself in direct conflict with the good of the person, which, in fact, denies the person in himself, suppressing his right to life, the Christian, mindful of the words of the Apostle Peter before the Sanhedrin: "We must obey God rather than men" (Acts 5:29), cannot but refuse, politely but firmly.

Your commitment, however, is not limited to this, so to speak, negative function. It extends to a whole set of positive tasks of great importance. It is up to you to strengthen in the hearts of parents, desire and joy in the new life which has sprung from their love; it is up to you to suggest the Christian view of it, showing with your attitude that you recognize in the child, formed in the mother's womb, a gift and a blessing of God (cf. Ps. 127:3ff.); it is up to you, further, to be close to the mother, to make her aware of the nobility of her mission and to strengthen her resistance to the promptings of human faintheartedness; it is up to you, finally, to do everything in your power to ensure the baby a healthy and happy birth.

And how could I fail to recall also, in a broader view of your service for life, the important contribution of advice and practical guidance you can offer to individual married couples, who wish to carry out responsible procreation, in respect of the order established by God? To you, too, are addressed the words of my Predecessor Paul VI, exhorting members of the medical personnel to persevere "in promoting on every occasion solutions inspired by faith and upright reason" and to endeavor to "bring forth conviction and respect for them in their environment" (HV 27).

It is obvious that, to carry out all these complex and delicate tasks properly, you must seek to acquire a professional competence beyond criticism, continually updated in the light of the most recent progress of science. It will be this proved competence which, in addition to enabling you to carry out timely and adequate interventions at the strictly professional level, will win for you among those who have recourse to you the consideration and the credit which will make them ready to accept your advice in the moral questions connected with your office.

SOME GUIDELINES

4. Here, then, are some guidelines, by which you are exhorted to direct your civil and Christian commitment. It is a commitment which presupposes a deep sense of duty and generous adherence to moral values, human understanding and tireless patience, courageous firmness and motherly tenderness. *Gifts that are not easy*, as experience teaches you. Gifts, however, that are demanded by a profession which, by its nature, is placed at the level of the mission. Gifts, however, which are normally rewarded by the testimonies of esteem and affectionate gratitude which reach you from those who have benefited from your assistance.

In the light of Mary I invoke on you and your activity the copious gifts of divine goodness, while, as a token of special benevolence, I grant you all the propitiating apostolic blessing.

ART MUST NOT VIOLATE
THE RIGHT OF PRIVACY

Thousands gathered in St. Peter's Square on April 29, 1981, for the weekly general audience. Continuing his treatment of the theology of the human body, the Holy Father delivered the following address.

Before his main address the Holy Father spoke on St. Catherine of Siena whose feast occurs on this day.

Dear brothers and sisters,

Today's audience falls on the feast of St. Catherine of Siena, the patron saint of Italy together with St. Francis of Assisi. The memory of the humble and wise Dominican virgin fills the hearts of us all with spiritual exultation and makes us thrill with joy in the Holy Spirit, because the Lord of heaven and earth has revealed His secrets to the simple (cf. Lk. 10:21). Catherine's message, animated by pure faith, fervent love and tireless dedication to the Church, concerns each of us and sweeps us along sweetly to generous imitation. I am glad, therefore, to address a special greeting to the Italians present at this meeting and to the whole dear Italian people.

Listen, dear faithful, to these words of St. Catherine: "In the light of faith I acquire wisdom; in the light of faith I am strong, constant and persevering; in the light of faith I hope: I do not let myself stop along the road. This light teaches me the way" *(Dialogue,* chap. CLXVII).

Let us implore through her intercession an ever deeper and more ardent faith, so that Christ may be the light of our way, of that of our families and of the whole of society, thus ensuring beloved Italy true peace, founded on justice and above all on respect of divine law, for which the great Saint of Siena yearned.

1. We have already dedicated a series of reflections to the meaning of the words spoken by Christ in the Sermon on the Mount, in which He exhorts to purity of heart, calling attention even to the "lustful look." We cannot forget these words of Christ even when it is a question of the vast sphere of artistic culture, particularly that of a visual and spectacular character, as also when it is a question of the sphere of "mass" culture—so significant for our times—connected with the use of the audiovisual communications media. We said recently that the above-mentioned sphere of man's activity is sometimes accused of "porno-vision," just as the accusation of "pornography" is made with regard to literature. Both facts take place by going beyond the limit of shame, that is, of personal sensitivity with regard to what is connected with the human body, with its nakedness, when in the artistic work by means of the media of audiovisual production *the right of the privacy of the body in its masculinity or femininity is violated*, and— in the last analysis—*when that intimate and constant destination to the gift and to mutual donation, which is inscribed in that femininity and masculinity through the whole structure of the being-man, is violated*. That deep inscription, or rather incision, decides the nuptial meaning of the body, that is, the fundamental call it receives to form a "communion of persons" and to participate in it.

THE HUMAN BODY
AS MODEL OR SUBJECT

2. It is obvious that in works of art, or in the products of audiovisual artistic reproduction, the above-mentioned *constant destination to the gift, that is, that deep inscription of the meaning of the human body, can be violated only in the intentional order of the reproduction and the representation;* it is a question, in fact—as has already been previously said—of the human body as model or subject. However, if the sense of shame and personal sensitivity are offended in these cases, that happens because of their transfer to the dimension of "social communication," therefore owing to the fact that what, in man's rightful feeling, belongs and must belong strictly to the interpersonal relationship—which is linked, as has already been pointed out, with the "communion of persons itself," and in its sphere corresponds to the interior truth of man, and so also to the complete truth about man—becomes, so to speak, public property.

At this point it is not possible to agree with the representatives of so-called naturalism, who demand the right to "everything that is human" in works of art and in the products of artistic reproduction, affirming that they act in this way in the name of the realistic truth about man. *It is precisely this truth about man—the whole truth about man—that makes it necessary to take into consideration both the sense of the privacy of the body and the consistence of the gift connected with the masculinity and femininity of the body itself, in which the mystery of man, peculiar to the interior structure of the person, is reflected.* This truth about man must be taken into consideration also in the artistic order, if we want to speak of a full realism.

VALUE OF THE BODY
IN INTERPERSONAL COMMUNION

3. In this case, therefore, it is evident that the deep governing rule related to the "communion of persons" is in profound agreement with the vast and differentiated area of "communication." *The human body in its nakedness*—as we stated in the preceding analyses (in which we referred to Gn. 2:25)—*understood as a manifestation of the person and as his gift, that is, a sign of trust and donation to the other person who is conscious of the gift, and who is chosen and resolved to respond to it in an equally personal way, becomes the source of a particular interpersonal "communication."*

As has already been said, this is a particular communication in humanity itself. That interpersonal communication penetrates deeply into the system of communion *(communio personarum)*, and at the same time grows from it and develops correctly within it. Precisely because of the great value of the body in this system of interpersonal "communion," to make of the body in its nakedness—which expresses precisely "the element" of the gift—the object-subject of the work of art or of the audiovisual reproduction, is a problem which is not only aesthetic, but at the same time also ethical. In fact, that "element of the gift" is, so to speak, suspended in the dimension of an unknown reception and an unforeseen response, and thereby it is in a way "threatened" in the order of intention, in the sense that it may become an anonymous object of "appropriation," an object of abuse. Precisely for this reason *the integral truth about man constitutes, in this case, the foundation of the norm according to which the good or evil of determined actions, of behavior, of morals and situations, is modeled.* The truth about man, about what is particularly personal and interior in him—precisely because of his body and his sex (femininity-masculinity)—creates here precise limits which it is unlawful to exceed.

RECOGNIZING LIMITS

4. These limits must be recognized and observed by the artist who makes the human body the object, model or subject of the work of art or of the audiovisual reproduction. Neither he nor others who are responsible in this field have the right to demand, propose or bring it about that other men, invited, exhorted or admitted to see, to contemplate the image, should violate those limits together with them, or because of them. It is a question of the image, in which that which in itself constitutes the content and the deeply personal value, that which belongs to the order of the gift and of the mutual donation of person to person, is, as a subject, uprooted from its own authentic substratum, to become, through "social communication," an object and what is more, in a way, an anonymous object.

5. The whole problem of "porno-vision" and "pornography," as can be seen from what is said above, is not the effect of a puritanical mentality or of a narrow moralism, just as it is not the product of a thought imbued with Manichaeism. It is a question of an

extremely important, fundamental sphere of values, before which man cannot remain indifferent because of the dignity of humanity, the personal character and the eloquence of the human body. All those contents and values, by means of works of art and the activity of the audiovisual media, can be modeled and studied, but also can be distorted and destroyed "in the heart" of man. As can be seen, we find ourselves continually within the orbit of the words spoken by Christ in the Sermon on the Mount. Also the problems which we are dealing with here must be examined in the light of those words, which consider a look that springs from lust as "adultery committed in the heart."

It seems, therefore, that reflection on these problems, which are important to "create a climate favorable to education to chastity," constitutes an indispensable appendage to all the preceding analyses which we have dedicated to this subject in the course of the numerous Wednesday meetings.

VII. Reaffirmations of the Church's Basic Teachings on Scientific Research and the Reasons for Rejecting Contraception, Abortion...

a) "Testifying to the Fullness of Truth," Ad Limina *Visit of Some Indonesian Bishops, June 7, 1980.*

b) "May the Gospel Be the Leaven of Family Relations," *to Council of "Equipes Notre-Dame," September 17, 1979.*

c) "Memorial, Actualization, Prophecy of the History of the Covenant," *to Two International Groups of Researchers, November 3, 1979.*

TESTIFYING TO THE FULLNESS OF TRUTH

Pope John Paul II's English-language address June 7, 1980, to the third group of Indonesian bishops making their ad limina *(official five-year) visits to Rome to report on their dioceses.*

Venerable and dear brothers in our Lord Jesus Christ,

I am very grateful for your visit today, grateful for the greetings you bring me from your local churches, grateful for your own fraternal love in Christ Jesus, grateful for the ecclesial communion we celebrate together in Catholic unity. This ecclesial communion—this Catholic unity—was the theme of my address to your brother bishops from Indonesia who were here less than two weeks ago. It is likewise the basis for this *ad limina* visit and for every *ad limina* visit to Rome.

Precisely because of this ecclesial communion, I personally, as Successor of Peter, experience deeply the need to make every effort to understand as fully as possible the problems of your local churches and to assist in solving these problems in accordance with the will of Christ for His Church. The issues you have presented to me affect the well-being of your people. Some of them raise questions that touch the Catholic Faith and Catholic life in general. *All of them represent pastoral concerns that in differing ways are the object of your responsibility and mine, matters to be examined with the assistance of the Holy Spirit in the light of the perennial value of God's Word, upheld by the Magisterium of the Church, and in the context of ecclesial communion....*

In moral questions as in doctrinal issues we must continue to proclaim the Church's teaching "in season and out of season" (2 Tm. 4:2). Hence we urge our people to admit only one measure of Christian love: to love one another as Christ has loved us (cf. Jn. 13:34). We charge them to bear constant witness to Christ's justice and His truth.

In our ministry at the service of life, we are called to testify to the fullness of the truth we hold so that all may know the stand of the Catholic Church on the utter inviolability of human life from the moment of conception. Hence, we proclaim with deep conviction that any *willful destruction of human life by procured abortion for any reason whatsoever is not in accord with God's commandment, that it is entirely outside the competence of any individual or group and that it cannot redound to true human progress.*

In the question of *the Church's teaching on the regulation of birth we are called to profess in union with the whole Church the exigent but uplifting teaching recorded in the Encyclical,* Humanae vitae, *which my Predecessor Paul VI put forth "by virtue of the mandate entrusted to us by Christ" (AAS 60,* 1968, *p. 485).* Particularly in this regard we must be conscious of the fact that *God's wisdom supersedes human calculations and His grace is powerful in people's lives.* It is important for us to realize the direct influence of Christ on the members of His Body in all realms of moral challenges. On the occasion of the *ad limina* visit of another group of bishops I made reference to this principle, which has many applications, saying, "Let us never fear that the challenge is too great for our people. They were redeemed by the precious blood of Christ. They are His people. Through the Holy Spirit Jesus Christ reserves to Himself the final responsibility for the acceptance of

His Word and for the growth of His Church. It is He, Jesus Christ, who will continue to give the grace to His people to meet the requirements of His Word, despite all difficulties, despite all weaknesses. And it is up to us to continue to proclaim the message of salvation in its entirety and purity with patience, compassion and the conviction that what is impossible with man is possible with God. We ourselves are only part of one generation in salvation history, but 'Jesus Christ is the same yesterday, today, and for ever' (Heb. 13:8). He is indeed able to sustain us as we recognize the strength of His grace, the power of His Word and the efficacy of His merits" (*AAS* 71, 1979, pp. 1423f.).

Christ's grace does not eliminate the need for compassionate understanding and increased pastoral effort on our part, but it does point to the fact that in the last analysis everything depends on Christ. It is Christ's Word we preach. It is His Church we construct day after day, according to His criterion. Jesus Christ has built His Church on the foundation of the Apostles and prophets (cf. Eph. 2:20), and in a special way on Peter (cf. Mt. 16:18). But it remains His Church, the Church of Christ: "...and on this rock I will build my church." Our people are ours only because they are, above all, His. Jesus Christ is the Good Shepherd, the Author of our Faith, the Hope of the world.

It is important for us to reflect on the mystery of the headship of Christ over His Church. Through His Holy Spirit Jesus Christ gives grace and strength to His people and He invites all of them to follow Him. At times, beginning with Peter, Christ calls His people to be led, as He Himself explains, where they do not wish to go (cf. Jn. 21:18).

Venerable brothers, my recent pastoral visits confirm something that we have all experienced. *Our people are constantly turning to us with the expectation and the plea: Proclaim to us the Word of God; speak to us about Christ.* Their request is an echo of the request spoken of by St. John and made to the Apostle Philip, "We wish to see Jesus" (Jn. 12:21). Truly the world entreats us to speak about Christ. It is He who will shape the new heavens and the new earth. It is He who by His word of truth fashions and controls the destinies of our people.

With renewed pastoral love and zeal let us proclaim His saving Word to the world. Relying on the assistance of Mary, Mother of the Incarnate Word, let us together commend our people and our ministry to Him who alone has "the words of eternal life" (Jn. 6:68).

With these sentiments I send my greetings back to all the members of your local churches and especially to all the Christian families. I offer my encouragement and gratitude to the priests and religious and to all who collaborate with you in the cause of the Gospel. To the sick and suffering goes my special blessing and to everyone the expression of my love in our Lord and Savior Jesus Christ.

MAY THE GOSPEL BE
THE LEAVEN
OF FAMILY RELATIONS

On September 17, 1979, the Holy Father received in audience the International Council of the Movement Equipes Notre-Dame *and delivered the following address.*

Dear brothers and sisters,

I am happy to meet the regional (or "super-regional") leaders of the *Equipes Notre-Dame.* Through this first contact, however brief it may be, kindly understand the esteem, the encouragement, the trust that I would like to express in regard to your movement, in line with everything that my venerated Predecessor Paul VI already said to you. I rejoice at the vitality of the *Equipes,* and their extension to various countries, in particular among young couples.

You wish to live married love and parental love in the light of the Gospel and the teachings of the Church, in an atmosphere which highly values prayer, the sharing between married couples, and deep exchanges between spouses on all human and spiritual problems. The leaven of the Gospel must penetrate in the first place the everyday and fundamental realities of family relations. It is necessary to renew in this way, at the base, the cells of the Church and society. The Pope relies on the contribution of marriage spirituality made by your movement.

THE PERFECTION
OF CHRISTIAN LIVING

I encourage, therefore, the members of the *Equipes Notre-Dame* to seek more and more the perfection of *their Christian life in and through the Sacrament of Marriage,* and I hope that many other Christian spouses will do likewise. What riches, what exigencies, what dynamism spring forth, if this sacrament is lived from day to day, in faith, in the image of the reciprocal gift of Christ and His Church! *What strength when spouses have the simplicity to help each other, under the eyes of the Lord, to progress in their faith, in their mutual love, if need be in their forgiveness, in their common commitment in service of their family, the Church community and social milieu!* What an example for the children, who then have, with their parents, their first experience of the mystery of the Church!

You yourselves have already experienced—especially couples that have long been members of the movement—that all this is at once very demanding and very comforting. Oh! I know you, too, are not sheltered from the temptations, the trials that other families know, from the contradictions that the ideal of the family meets with in modern society. But you humbly take the means to overcome them. Take it to heart to nourish your convictions, your meditations, your action, at the real sources: the Word of God read in Church, Christian doctrine and ethics recalled by the Magisterium, the true spirituality of marriage and the other sacraments, with the help of the priests whom the Church places at your disposal.

I hope that you will let the family apostolate of the Church, in your respective countries, benefit from your convictions and your experience, by joining, according to possibilities, in the immense efforts that are being carried out or that should be carried out in this field. It is necessary, indeed, to let *God's marvelous plan on mar-*

ried love, procreation and family education shine forth before the eyes of the young generations, and that will be credible only through the witness of those who put it into practice in their lives, with all the resources of faith.

NEED OF THEOLOGY

The whole Church, in fact, must commit herself to this effort. Personally, I am taking advantage at present of the opportunity of the general audiences on Wednesdays to offer elements of reflection on the family. The next Synod of Bishops will tackle "the role of the Christian family." You are called, not only to be interested and to give your attention to it, but to make your contribution to preparing it, by making known, within your diocesan communities, your reflections on the different points of the program published by the Synod Secretariat. *For the tasks of the family can be taken up in a Christian way only by studying the theology of marriage, with its riches of graces and its ecclesial dimension, and by living this spirituality in practice within the home.*

It is with these sentiments that I express my confidence to you, as well as to all men and women of *Equipes Notre-Dame*, and to their chaplains, encouraging you to continue to make your efforts within the framework of the Church, according to the doctrine of the Church, in liaison with the pastors of the Church and other movements whose action is complementary to yours. I willingly bless you, and all those who are dear to you, particularly your children.

MEMORIAL, ACTUALIZATION, PROPHECY OF THE HISTORY OF THE COVENANT

On November 3, 1979, the Holy Father received in audience the delegates of the "Centre de Liaison des Equipes de Recherche" (Research Teams' Liaison Center) and the members of the Board of Directors of the Federation of Organizations for Research and Promotion of Natural Methods of Family Planning.

John Paul II delivered the following address.

Dear friends,

1. I am particularly happy to meet here members of the Research Teams' Liaison Center (CLER). In the apostolate of married couples, on which the conciliar decree *Apostolicam actuositatem* (no. 11) laid such stress, you have played a pioneering role, long before the Second Vatican Council. And at present your teams —in which doctors, psychologists, marriage counselors and educators pool their skills and their convictions as Christians—play a very appreciable part, not only *to study questions connected with the regulation of births and the fertility of the couple, but also to provide practical help for married couples in all the problems of their conjugal and family life, and to contribute in the best sense to the sexual education of the young.* You have kept your trust in the Church and in her Magisterium, certain that, working in this way, you were not mistaken. Your pilgrimage is an opportunity to thank the Lord, to reflect on the work carried out in order to continue it with more and more courage and faithfulness, and to draw closer your bonds with the Church that you wish to serve, at the moment when the Synod of Bish-

ops is preparing for its meeting on the role of the Christian family. I express to you, with the thanks of the Church, my congratulations and deep encouragement.

THOROUGHNESS OF YOUR ORGANIZATION'S WORK

2. Allow me to greet, at the same time, the members of the Board of Directors of the International Federation of Family Action (FIDAP or IFFLP), which is going to hold its meeting in Rome, with the members and consultants of our Committee for the Family. This federation carries out, even in the great international organizations, similar work, from which CLER continues to benefit: research and promotion of natural methods of family planning and education to family life. I rejoice at the thoroughness and extension of your activity, and its convergence with the pastoral action of the Catholic Church in these fields.

With all of you, there is no need for the Pope to dwell on these considerations about which you are already firmly convinced. Moreover, I have also had the opportunity very often recently to speak of family problems, for example, to lay people gathered at Limerick in Ireland, to the American bishops, and to families gathered for Mass at the Capitol Mall, Washington. I will stress, however, some important aspects.

THE NEED TO DISCUSS THEOLOGICAL ASPECTS

3. In the first place, for Christians it is essential to open the discussion by considering right away the theological aspect of the family, and meditating, conse-

quently, on the sacramental reality of marriage. Sacramentality cannot be understood except in the light of the history of salvation. Now this history of salvation is qualified as a history of covenant and communion between Yahweh and Israel first of all, then between Jesus Christ and the Church, in this age of the Church, while waiting for the eschatological covenant. Likewise, the Council states: "Our Savior, the Spouse of the Church, now encounters Christian spouses through the Sacrament of Marriage (GS 48).

This marriage is, therefore, at once a memorial, an actualization and a prophecy of the history of the covenant. "This mystery is a great one," St. Paul says. *When they marry, Christian spouses do not just begin their adventure, even understood in the sense of sanctification and mission; they begin an adventure which integrates them responsibly in the great adventure of the universal history of salvation.* A memorial, the sacrament gives them the grace and the duty to commemorate God's great works and bear witness to them before their children. An actualization, it gives them the grace and the duty to put into practice in the present, with regard to each other and to their children, the exigencies of *a love that forgives and redeems.* A prophecy, it gives them the grace and the duty of living and bearing witness to the hope of the future meeting with Christ.

CONJUGAL LOVE INVOLVES TOTALITY

4. Certainly, every sacrament involves participation in Christ's nuptial love for His Church. But, in marriage, the method and the content of this participation are specific. The spouses participate in it as spouses,

together, as a couple, so that the first and immediate effect of marriage *(res et sacramentum)* is not supernatural grace itself, but the Christian conjugal bond, a typically Christian communion of two persons because it represents the mystery of Christ's incarnation and the mystery of His covenant. The content of participation in Christ's life is also specific: *conjugal love involves a totality, in which all the elements of the person enter—* appeal of the body and instinct, power of feeling and affectivity, aspiration of the spirit and of will. *It aims at a deeply personal unity, the unity that, beyond union in one flesh, leads to forming one heart and one soul; it demands indissolubility and faithfulness in definitive mutual giving; and it is open to fertility* (cf. HV 9). In a word, it is certainly a question of the normal characteristics of all natural conjugal love, but with a new significance which not only purifies and strengthens them, but raises them to the extent of making them the expression of specifically Christian values. That is the perspective to which Christian spouses must rise: that is their grandeur, their strength, their exigency, and also their joy.

LOVE AND CONTINENCE

5. Responsible parenthood must also be envisaged in this perspective. On this plane, *the spouses, the parents, may meet with a certain number of problems which cannot be solved without deep love, a love which comprises also an effort of continence.* These two virtues, love and continence, appeal to a common decision of the spouses and to their will to submit to the doctrine of faith, to the teaching of the Church. On this vast subject, I will limit myself to three observations.

CHURCH'S DOCTRINE CLEAR

6. In the first place, *there must be no deception regarding the doctrine of the Church, such as it has been clearly set forth by the Magisterium, the Council, and my Predecessors. I am thinking especially of Paul VI's Encyclical Humanae vitae,* of his address to the Notre-Dame Teams on May 4, 1970, and of his numerous other interventions. It is necessary to set one's course constantly by this standard of perfection for imitation in conjugal relations, governed by and respectful of the nature and finalities of the conjugal act, *and not according to a more or less wide, more or less avowed, concession to the principle and practice of contraceptive morals.* God calls spouses to the holiness of marriage, for their own good and for the quality of their witness.

TO ASSIST OTHERS

7. This point being firmly established, out of obedience to the Church—and it is to your honor that you abide by it, come what may—it is no less important to help Christian couples, and others, to strengthen their own convictions, *by seeking with them the deeply human reasons for acting in this way. It is good that they should catch a glimpse of how this natural morality corresponds to anthropology, rightly understood, so as to avoid the traps of permissive public opinion or laws, and even to contribute, as far as possible, to correcting this public opinion.*

Many elements of reflection can contribute to forging healthy convictions which help the obedience of the Christian or the attitude of the man of good will. And I know that it is also an important part of your educative task. For example, *at a time when so many ecological movements call for respect for nature, what are we to think of an invasion of artificial procedures and substances in this eminently personal field?* To resort to technical measures in place of self-control, self-renunciation for the sake of the other, and the common effort of husband and wife, does not this mark a regression from that which constitutes man's nobility? Do we not see that man's nature is subject to morality? Have we measured the whole significance of a continually accentuated rejection of the child on the psychology of parents, bearing as they do the desire for a child inscribed in their nature, and on the future of society? And what are we to think of an education of the young in regard to sexuality which would not put them on their guard against pursuit of immediate and selfish pleasure, dissociated from the responsibilities of conjugal love and procreation? Yes, it is necessary to educate to true love in many ways, in order to prevent the moral and spiritual fabric of the human community from deteriorating, on this essential point, as a result of hazy or false ideas.

ADHERING TO CONVICTIONS

8. Respect for human life already conceived is, of course, part, in a special way, of the convictions to be enlightened and strengthened. It is a point at which the responsibility of the man and the woman must lead them to accept and protect the human being that they have procreated and that they never have the right to eliminate. It is a field in which friends and relations, society, doctors, marriage counselors, and legislators have the duty to permit this responsibility to be exercised, always in the sense of respect for human life,

in spite of difficulties and to provide help in cases of persons in distress. *The Church has spoken out unanimously in every country on this point, so that there is no need to stress it.*

The legislation on abortion may inevitably lead many people not to feel any longer this respect and this responsibility for human life, considering a serious fault a trivial one. *It must even be added that the generalization of contraception by artificial methods also leads to abortion, for both are, at different levels, certainly, in the same line of fear of the child, rejection of life, lack of respect for the act or the fruit of union such as it is willed between man and woman by the Creator of nature. Those who study these problems thoroughly know this well, contrary to what certain lines of reasoning or certain movements of opinion might seek to make one believe.* Congratulations on what you are doing and will do to instruct consciences on this point of respect for life.

TO LIVE RESPONSIBLE PARENTHOOD

9. Finally, it is necessary to use every possible means *to provide practical help for couples to live this responsible parenthood, and here your contribution is irreplaceable. The scientific researches that you carry out and pool in order to acquire more precise knowledge of the female cycle and permit more serene utilization of natural methods of regulating births, deserve to be better known, encouraged and effectively proposed for application.* I am happy to know that a growing number of persons and organizations, on the international plane, appreciate these efforts for natural regulation. To these men of science, doctors and specialists, I

address all my good wishes and encouragement, *for what is at stake is the good of families and societies in their legitimate concern to harmonize human fertility with their possibilities, and, provided that an appeal is always made to the virtues of love and continence, it is a question of the progress of human self-mastery in conformity with the Creator's plan.*

I encourage likewise all qualified lay people, all the married couples who, as counselors, teachers or educators, give their assistance to help couples to live their conjugal love and their responsibility as parents in a worthy way, helping the young at the same time to prepare to do so.

I assure each of you, your collaborators, families and dear children, of my prayer for your magnificent apostolate and impart to you my fatherly apostolic blessing.

VIII. Selected Documents of Offices of the Holy See and Various Bishops on Human Life in All Its Sanctity

a) Document of the Synod of Bishops, "A Message to Christian Families in the Modern World," November, 1980.

b) Pastoral Instruction of the Permanent Council of the Italian Episcopate on "The Christian Community and the Welcoming of Unborn Human Life," December 8, 1978.

c) Joint Pastoral Letter of the Bishops of Kenya on "The Family and Responsible Parenthood," August, 1979.

d) Document of Lucas Moreira Neves, Vice-President of the Pontifical Council for the Laity, on "Humanae Vitae—Ten Years Afterward: Towards a More Human Civilization," January 15, 1979.

e) Document of the Holy See for the International Year of the Disabled Persons, March 4, 1981.

f) Declaration on Euthanasia of the Sacred Congregation for the Doctrine of the Faith, May 5, 1980.

g) Address of Archbishop Dermot Ryan, of Dublin, Ireland, on "Abortion, Euthanasia, and the Pluralist Society," January 26, 1981.

A MESSAGE
TO CHRISTIAN FAMILIES
IN THE MODERN WORLD

Document of the Synod of Bishops: November, 1980.

I. INTRODUCTION

1. We have come to the end of the Synod. For the past month we bishops from all over the world have met here in Rome in union with the Holy Father and under his leadership. Before returning to our own countries, we wish to address these few words to you. It is not our intention to give answers to all the complex questions raised in our day about marriage and the family. We only want to share with you the love, confidence, and hope which we feel. As your bishops and pastors, who are also your brothers in the Faith, we have been united with you during these weeks; nor have we forgotten that we, too, grew up in families with all their joys and sorrows. To you and to our own families we are deeply grateful.

II. THE SITUATION
OF FAMILIES TODAY

2. In our discussions of family life today we have found joys and consolations, sorrows and difficulties. We must look first for the good things and seek to build on them and make them perfect, confident always that God is present everywhere in His creatures, and that we can discern His will in the signs of our times. We are

encouraged by the many good and positive things that we see. We rejoice that so many families, even in the face of great pressure to do otherwise, gladly fulfill the God-given mission entrusted to them. Their goodness and fidelity in responding to God's grace and shaping their lives by His teaching give us a great hope.

The number of families who consciously want to live the life of the Gospel, giving witness to the fruits of the Spirit, continues to grow in all our lands.

3. During this past month we have learned much about the many and varied cultural conditions in which Christian families live. The Church must accept and foster this rich diversity, while at the same time encouraging Christian families to give effective witness to God's plan within their own cultures. But all cultural elements must be evaluated in light of the Gospel, to insure that they are consistent with the divine plan for marriage and the family. This duty—of acceptance and evaluation—is part of the same task of discernment.

4. A more serious problem than that of culture is the condition of those families who live in need in a world of such great wealth. In many parts of the globe, as well as within individual countries, poverty is increasing as a result of social, economic, and political structures which foster injustice, oppression and dependence. Conditions in many places are such as to prevent many young men and women from exercising their right to marry and lead decent lives. *In the more developed countries, on the other hand, one finds another kind of deprivation: a spiritual emptiness in the midst of abundance, a misery of mind and spirit which makes it difficult for people to understand God's will for human life, and causes them to be anxious about the present and*

fearful of the future. Many find it difficult to enter into and live up to the permanent commitment of marriage. Their hands are full, but their wounded hearts are waiting for a Good Samaritan who will bind up their wounds, pouring on them the wine and oil of health and gladness.

5. Often certain governments and some international organizations do violence to families. The integrity of the home is violated. *Family rights in regard to religious liberty, responsible parenthood, and education are not respected.* Families regard themselves as wards and victims, rather than as human beings responsible for their own affairs. Families are compelled—and this we oppose vehemently—to use such immoral means as contraception or, even worse, sterilization, abortion, and euthanasia for the solution of social, economic, and demographic problems. The Synod therefore strongly urges a charter of family rights to safeguard these rights everywhere.

6. *Underlying many of the problems confronting families, and indeed the world at large, is the fact that many people seem to reject their fundamental vocation to participate in God's life and love.* They are obsessed with the desire to possess, the will for power, the quest for pleasure. Instead of looking upon their fellow human beings as brothers and sisters, members of the human family, they regard them as obstacles and adversaries. *Where people lose their sense of God, the heavenly Father, they also lose their sense of the human family.* How can human beings see one another as brothers and sisters if they have lost their consciousness of having a common Father? *The Fatherhood of God is the only basis for the unity of the human family.*

III. GOD'S PLAN FOR MARRIAGE AND THE FAMILY

7. *God's eternal plan* (cf. Eph. 1:3ff.) *is that all men and women should participate and share in the divine life and being* (cf. 1 Jn. 1:3; 2 Pt. 1:4). The Father summons people to realize this plan in union with their fellow human beings, thus forming the People of God (cf. LG 9).

8. In a special way, the family is called to carry out this divine plan. It is, as it were, the first cell of the Church, *helping its members to become agents of the history of salvation and living signs of God's loving plan for the world.*

God created us in His own image (cf. Gn. 1:26), and He gave us the mission to increase and multiply, to fill the earth and subdue it (cf. Gn. 1:28). To carry out this plan man and woman are joined in an intimate union of love for the service of life. *God calls spouses to participate in His creative power by handing on the gift of life.*

In the fullness of time, the Son of Man born of a woman (Gal. 4:4) enriched marriage with His saving grace, elevating it to the level of a sacrament and causing it to share in the covenant of His redemptive love sealed with His blood. Christ's love and gift to the Church and those of the Church to Christ become the model of the mutual love and self-giving of man and woman (cf. Eph. 5:22-32). *The sacramental grace of matrimony is a source of joy and strength to the spouses.* As ministers of this sacrament, they truly act in the person of Christ Himself and bring about their mutual sanctification. Spouses must be conscious of this grace and of the presence of the Holy Spirit. Each day, dear brothers and sisters, you must hear Christ saying to you: "If only you recognized God's gift" (cf. Jn. 4:10).

9. *This divine plan shows us why the Church believes and teaches that the covenant of love and self-giving between two people joined in sacramental marriage must be both permanent and indissoluble.* It is a covenant of love and life. *The transmission of life is inseparable from the conjugal union.* The conjugal act itself, as the Encyclical *Humanae vitae* tells us, must be fully human, total, exclusive, and open to new life (HV 9 and 11).

10. God's plan for marriage and the family can only be fully understood, accepted, and lived by persons who have experienced conversion of heart, that radical turning of the self to God by which one puts off the "old" self and puts on the "new." All are called to conversion and sanctity. We must all come to the knowledge and love of the Lord and experience Him in our lives, rejoicing in His love and mercy, His patience, compassion, and forgiveness, and loving one another as He loves us. *Husbands and wives, parents and children, are instruments and ministers of Christ's fidelity and love in their mutual relationships.* It is this which makes Christian marriage and family life authentic signs of God's love for us and of Christ's love for the Church.

11. But the pain of the cross, as well as the joy of the resurrection, is part of the life of one who seeks as a pilgrim to follow Christ. Only those who are fully open to the Paschal Mystery can accept the difficult but loving demands which Jesus Christ makes of us. If because of human weakness one does not live up to these demands, there is no reason for discouragement. "Let

them not be discouraged, but rather have recourse with humble perseverance to the mercy of God" (HV 25).

IV. THE FAMILY'S RESPONSE TO GOD'S LOVE

12. Just as we are doing, you also are seeking to learn what your duties are in today's world. In looking at the world, we see facing you certain important tasks of education. *You have the tasks of forming free persons with a keen moral sense and a discerning conscience, together with a perception of their duty to work for the betterment of the human condition and the sanctification of the world.* Another task for the family is to form persons in love and also to practice love in all its relationships, so that it does not live closed in on itself, but remains open to the community, moved by a sense of justice and concern for others, as well as by a consciousness of its responsibility toward the whole of society. It is your duty to form persons in the Faith—that is, in knowledge and love of God and eagerness to do His will in all things. It is also your task to hand on sound human and Christian values and to form persons in such a way that they can integrate new values into their lives. *The more Christian the family becomes, the more human it becomes.*

13. In fulfilling these tasks, the family will be, as it were, a "domestic Church," a community of faith living in hope and love, serving God and the entire human family. Shared prayer and the liturgy are sources of grace for families. In fulfilling its tasks the family must nourish itself on God's Word and participate in the life of the sacraments, especially reconciliation and the

Eucharist. Traditional and contemporary devotions, particularly those associated with the Blessed Virgin, are rich sources of growth in piety and grace.

14. Evangelization and catechesis begin in the family. Formation in faith, chastity, and the other Christian virtues, as well as education in human sexuality, must start in the home. Yet, the outlook of the Christian family should not be narrow and confined only to the parish; it should embrace the whole human family. Within the larger community it has a duty to give witness to Christian values. It should foster social justice and relief of the poor and oppressed. Family organizations should be encouraged to protect their rights by opposing unjust social structures and public and private policies which harm the family. Such organizations should also exercise a healthy influence on the communications media and build up social solidarity. Special praise is due to those family organizations whose purpose is to help other married couples and families appreciate God's plan and live by it. This like-to-like ministry should be encouraged as part of comprehensive family ministry.

15. Out of a sense of fidelity to the Gospel, the family should be prepared to welcome new life, to share its goods and resources with the poor, to be open and hospitable to others. *Today the family is sometimes obliged to choose a way of life that goes contrary to modern culture in such matters as sexuality, individual autonomy, and material wealth.*

In the face of sin and failure, it gives witness to an authentically Christian spirit, sensitive in its life, and in the lives of others there, to the values of penance and forgiveness, reconciliation and hope. It gives evidence of the fruits of the Holy Spirit and the beatitudes. It practices a simple style of life and pursues a truly evangelical apostolate toward others.

V. THE CHURCH AND THE FAMILY

16. During the Synod we have grown in awareness of the Church's duty to encourage and support couples and families. We have deepened our commitment in this regard.

17. Family ministry is of very special interest to the Church. By this we mean efforts made by the whole People of God through local communities, especially through the help of pastors and lay people devoted to pastoral work for families. They work with individuals, couples, and families to help them live out their conjugal vocation as fully as possible. This ministry includes preparation for marriage; help given to married couples at all stages of married life; catechetical and liturgical programs directed to the family; help given to childless couples, single-parent families, the widowed, the separated and divorced, and, in particular, to families and couples laboring under burdens like poverty, emotional and psychological tensions, physical and mental handicaps, alcohol and drug abuse, and the problems associated with migration and other circumstances which strain family stability.

18. The priest has a special place in family ministry. *It is his duty to bring the nourishment and consolation of the Word of God, the sacraments, and other spiritual aids to the family, encouraging it and in a human and patient way, strengthening it in charity so that families which are truly outstanding can be formed* (cf. GS 52).

One precious fruit of this ministry, along with others, ought to be the flourishing of priestly and religious vocations.

19. In speaking of God's plan the Church has many things to say to men and women about the essential equality and complementarity of the sexes, as well as about the different charisms and duties of spouses within marriage. Husband and wife are certainly different, but they are also equal. The difference should be respected but never used to justify the domination of one by the other. In collaboration with society, the Church must effectively affirm and defend the dignity and rights of women.

VI. CONCLUSION

20. As we reach the end of our message, we wish to say to you, brothers and sisters, that *we are fully aware of the frailty of our common human condition.* In no way do we ignore the very difficult and trying situation of the many Christian couples who, although they sincerely want to observe the moral norms taught by the Church, find themselves unequal to the task because of weakness in the face of difficulties. All of us need to grow in appreciation of the importance of Christ's teachings and His grace, and to live by them. Accompanied and assisted by the whole Church, those couples continue along the difficult way toward a more complete fidelity to the commands of the Lord. "The journey of married couples, like the whole journey of human life, meets with delays and difficult and burdensome times. But it must be clearly stated that anxiety or fear should never be found in the souls of people of good will. For is not the Gospel also good news for

family life? For all the demands it makes, is it not a profoundly liberating message? The awareness that one has not achieved his full interior liberty and is still at the mercy of his tendencies, and finds himself unable to obey the moral law in an area so basic, causes deep distress. But this is the moment in which the Christian, rather than giving way to sterile and destructive panic, humbly opens up his soul before God as a sinner before the saving love of Christ" (Pope Paul VI, Address to the *Equipes de Notre-Dame*, May 4, 1970).

21. Everything we have said about marriage and the family can be summed up in two words: love and life. As we come to the end of this Synod, we pray that you, our brothers and sisters, may grow in the love and life of God. In turn we humbly and gratefully beg your prayers that we may do the same. We make St. Paul's words to the Colossians our final words to you: "Over all these virtues put on love, which binds the rest together and makes them perfect. Christ's peace must reign in your hearts, since as members of the one body you have been called to that peace. Dedicate yourselves to thankfulness" (Col. 3:14-15).

THE CHRISTIAN COMMUNITY AND THE WELCOMING OF UNBORN HUMAN LIFE

Pastoral instruction of the Permanent Council of the Italian Episcopal Conference, December 8, 1978.

INTRODUCTION

1. Faithfulness to the mission received from the Lord and the task of discerning in the light of the Gospel, the concrete situations of human existence, urge the Church to state precisely, once more, her position with regard to the social phenomenon of abortion and to the answer that the civil law has given to it.

With the introduction of the law in favor of abortion, in Italy also, the situation, in fact, has recently become worse.

2. *The Christian community cannot close its eyes to the distressing reality of abortion, its shocking expansion and the indications—social, economic, family, psychological welfare, and even real and proper selfishness—with which people claim to motivate the interruption of pregnancy.*

Before such serious problems Christians cannot take refuge in attitudes of resigned fatalism or vain alarmism, nor can they exhaust their commitment in condemning in words the injustice of this law. They are called, rather, to assume wider and positive responsibilities in welcoming and serving unborn human life.

That is possible if awareness of the mission that the Lord has entrusted to His Church, is renewed. It is the mission of proclaiming the Gospel and communicating to man the new life of grace. Thus the Church defends and advances man himself, protecting him in all his rights, first among which is the fundamental right to life.

3. After its many, repeated interventions—in particular the documents "The right to be born" (1972) and "Abortion and law on abortion" (1975)—the Italian Episcopal Conference now offers the whole ecclesial community the fundamental points of a catechesis on responsibility with regard to welcoming unborn life.

First Part
THE DOCTRINE OF THE CHURCH ON ABORTION AND ON ITS CIVIL REGULATION

I. Abortion in Itself: A Moral Disorder

4. The Church, in the light of the Word of God and of sound reason, has always judged induced abortion, that is, the deliberate and direct interruption of the generative process of human life, a serious moral crime.

5. The Church believes that God is the provident Creator of all human life. "It is he that made us and we are his" (Ps. 100:3); we are thus a gift of the living God.

Life was given to us not in absolute ownership, but as a treasure to be administered and for which we will have to account to the Lord (cf. Mt. 25:14-30; Lk. 19:12-27).

God watches over human life with His love (cf. Gn. 9:5-6) and defends it with His commandment: "You shall not kill" (Ex. 20:13; Mt. 5:21).

For this reason man's life is sacred and inviolable in its whole span of development, from the origin to the end.

Jesus Christ, the Son and Image of the Father, perfecting the ancient law and summing it up in the commandment of love of one's neighbor, obliges us to respect the life of others, to aid it and advance it. Therefore the suppression of a brother's life is a radical contradiction of the commandment of love, which love drives the disciple of Christ to the point of giving his own life for the sake of brothers.

6. The Church, at all times and in every country, has always accepted and reproposed God's Word and commandment about the absolute inviolability of innocent human life, even if only conceived. *Tradition presents itself, as regards moral judgment on abortion, with a unanimity that knows no divergences and with a firmness that does not admit of exceptions.*

Right from its origins, the Christian community, accepting the word and example of Christ in His love for children, courageously opposed the pagan world by defending the value of unborn human life. We read, for example, in the Didaché. "You shall not kill,...you shall not cause the child to perish with abortion or kill him after birth.... The way of death is the following: ...they do not recognize their Creator, they kill their children and cause God's creatures to perish with abortion."[1]

To denounce the moral seriousness of abortion and to discourage believers from having recourse to it, the Church did not fail to intervene in various Councils, often inflicting very severe penalties too.[2]

7. Confirming the sense of faith of the Christian community, the Magisterium has authoritatively and

repeatedly declared the serious moral unlawfulness of abortion: Pontiffs, episcopal conferences, individual bishops, all are in agreement and firm on this moral judgment.[3]

The Second Vatican Council affirms: "God, the Lord of life, has entrusted to men the noble mission of safeguarding life, and men must carry it out in a manner worthy of themselves. Life must be protected with the utmost care from the moment of conception: abortion and infanticide are abominable crimes..." (GS 51).

On the subject of abortion, Paul VI declared that *the teaching of the Church "has not changed and is immutable"* (Address on December 9, 1972).

The Pontiff himself, at the close of the fifteenth year of his pontificate, was able to state: "And we, who consider absolute faithfulness to the teachings of the Council our precise care, have taken as the program of our pontificate the defense of life, in all the forms in which it can be threatened, disturbed or even suppressed. But the defense of life must begin from the very sources of human existence.... Hence the repeated affirmations of the doctrine of the Catholic Church, on the painful reality and distressing effects of divorce and abortion, contained in our ordinary Magisterium as well as in particular documents of the competent Congregation. We were moved to express them solely by our supreme responsibility as teacher and universal Pastor, and for the good of mankind!" (Homily on June 29, 1978)

8. Not only Christian faith but also sound reason condemns abortion morally, since it is a violent suppression of a helpless innocent human being, in need of everything and everyone.

Abortion is certainly one of the most radical injustices that can be perpetrated with regard to man: far from being recognized in his uniqueness as a person, he is oppressed in his right to existence; the first right, on which all the others are based, and which cannot be recuperated once it is lost.

The injustice of abortion is furthermore aggravated by the fact that *the conceived creature is an innocent being without any possibility of defending itself,* and by the fact that it is suppressed by those who called it into existence and by those who should protect and defend life, such as doctors.

The sound conscience of every man finds within itself, as an indisputable and sacred principle, respect for every human life right from its conception; and the world of medicine, from the most ancient times, has made this principle the luminous center of its toil and its art.[4]

9. *There are some people who claim to justify abortion on the basis of the fact that the unborn child is not yet a human being. This position is completely unacceptable, because from conception there can emerge only a concrete human being.*

This is plain to reflection itself and rational analysis, which evaluates the conceived creature as a human being on the basis of its origin and structure and its typically and exclusively human purpose.

It is recognized by law, which declares it is in the service of one and all and protects juridically also unborn children: "The child, owing to his physical and intellectual immaturity, needs particular protection and special care, including adequate juridical protection, both before and after birth."[5]

It is confirmed by modern science, according to which in the whole process of generation, from the fecundated cell to the birth of the child, *there is no qualitative change of species from a stage of generic animality to humanity real and proper, but a sole and continuous individual development of maturing of the person.*

It should be recalled, finally, that "from the moral point of view the following is certain: even if there were a doubt concerning the fact that the fruit of conception is already a human person, it is objectively a serious sin to dare to assume the risk of a murder. He who will be a man is already one" (Tertullian).[6]

II. Abortion and Those Who Carry It Out: The Offense and the Censure

10. For reasons now shown, the persons who knowingly and freely ask for abortion, carry it out or collaborate in carrying it out, stain themselves with a very serious sin.

As for every other sin, the moral judgment on those who have recourse to abortion or collaborate in it, will have to be formulated in reference both to the value of human life, and to the different situation of persons. The latter will have to be carefully evaluated in realistic terms, without falling *a priori* either into condemnation or into absolutions, and reserving a more delicate consideration for all those persons who are distraught with anguish and drama.

11. On the Christian who stains himself seriously with abortion, the Church inflicts the penalty of excommunication: "Those who induce abortion, not

excluding the mother, if the effect is attained, incur excommunication *latae sententiae* reserved to the Ordinary" (C.J.C., can. 2350, par. 1).

Owing to excommunication, the Christian is deprived of the sacraments, in particular of the Eucharist (C.J.C., can. 2260, par. 1; can. 855, par. 1).

To avoid distorted interpretations, and even more to grasp positively the content and deep spirit of the "penal" intervention of the Church, we point out the following:

a) with excommunication, the Christian sinner remains excluded from the fullness of ecclesial communion, and therefore cannot participate in the Sacrament of the Eucharist.

The seriousness of this penalty is the result of the seriousness of exclusion from the Eucharist, as the impossibility of participating in the supreme moment of Christian life, that is, in the moment in which the Covenant is renewed and the Church is built up by the Spirit of Christ in a religious and brotherly community, reconciled with God and in its members.

b) Like every penalty in the Church, excommunication because of abortion has above all a preventive and "medicinal," or pedagogical aim.

Actually, with it the Church denounces abortion as an action that is absolutely incompatible with the demands of the Gospel, and intends to help on his way to conversion the person who has had recourse to abortion. Noting that the Christian who is guilty of abortion excludes himself from the fullness of her communion, the Church makes a particularly strong appeal to him to repent of his sin, revise his position, and return to the new life of grace.

At the same time, the excommunication becomes a "reminder" to believers in order that they may be held back before the temptation of asking for and carrying out abortion.

The true meaning of the excommunication can be understood only in the light of the ecclesial dimension of the Christian's sin and of his reconciliation. The Christian, who is a member of the Body of Christ, not only offends God with his sin, but also and at the same time "wounds" the holy Church of God (cf. LG 11).

Furthermore anyone who is guilty of abortion seriously contradicts an aspect of the Church's mission such as that of putting herself in the service of unborn life, and therefore makes its concrete implementation less credible and effective.

In this way the excommunication characterizes, openly and strongly, as a serious anti-ecclesial act, the abortion carried out by the Christian.

c) It is understandable, therefore, why the release from this excommunication is reserved to the Ordinary, that is, the bishop of the local Church, or to a priest authorized by him.

d) Excommunication is incurred under certain conditions. The penalty of the Church presupposes both the real seriousness of the personal sin of one who has had recourse to abortion and has carried it out, and knowledge of the existence of this same penalty.

The excommunication for induced abortion is *latae sententiae*. This means that it does not need to be pronounced for every single case of abortion, but exists as a general norm, so that anyone who induces abortion incurs it merely by deliberately doing so.

e) In a social and cultural framework which is very insensitive to the positive significance of the penalty, there are some people who ask themselves whether or not it is opportune that the Church should keep this excommunication, and there are others who reject it as outdated historically and contrary to the genuine spirit of the Gospel.

Actually, it is not difficult to solve the question and the objection, if one grasps the real significance of the excommunication in the framework of the mission and the life of the Church. *Owing to the seriousness of the crime and the current mentality which is disinclined to admit it, the Church, by means of the excommunication, keeps alive and active the sense of the value of life and acts in defense of the weakest and most innocent.*

f) Others again wonder why the Church keeps the excommunication for induced abortion and does not inflict it in the case of crimes of another nature, no less serious than abortion itself.

On reflection the fact is obvious that abortion is a qualified murder, because the unborn child is completely incapable of personal defense; the penal intervention of the Church acts in defense of the unborn child, all the more so in that the state, at least in some cases, as in Italy, no longer considers abortion as an offense, while it continues to regard murder as an offense.

III. Abortion in Civil Law: the Moral Judgment

12. The discussion on abortion cannot be restricted to its moral dimension in relation to the individual person who asks for it or carries it out: it must be considered also in a social perspective.

Actually, abortion is a social phenomenon for many reasons: it involves in depth the relationship between two human beings, the woman and her child; it has repercussions on the couple and on the family and, in an even wider sense, on the social environment in which they are integrated. For this reason abortion cannot fail to arouse the interest and intervention of the whole political community.

13. In its intervention with regard to unborn life, the political community cannot restrict itself to the issuing of a law, necessary though it is, which forbids abortion as a crime—to be punished, however, with justice and fairness, taking into account the concrete situations in which it was committed. This law, in fact, would not by itself solve the whole complex and difficult social phenomenon of abortion.

The state must rather aim primarily at an educative intervention, working out and spreading a culture that respects and promotes the value of life and the sense of responsibility towards it.

It must also aim at a social intervention, stimulating and offering a series of initiatives, aids, and possibilities of prevention and support of unwanted and difficult pregnancies.

14. Often, however, also because of its inadequate cultural and social commitment, the political community has to cope with the distressing phenomenon of clandestine abortions, with the negative results of the dangers for the woman's health and life, the economic speculation of a certain medical and ancillary personnel, discrimination between the social classes, etc.

Thus a legislative intervention also becomes necessary: it is the problem of a "legal regulation," that is, the position of the civil law before this social phenomenon.

15. For this problem the principle of civil tolerance is often invoked, in virtue of which the state can, or even must, tolerate some evil to avoid more serious evils.[7]

But the principle of civil tolerance, in its concrete application, does not at all justify the positive authorization to suppress directly an innocent being, as if the state could grant some the "right" to ask for, and others to carry out, abortion: "Human law may renounce punishing, but it cannot make honest what is contrary to natural law, because this opposition is sufficient to cause a law no longer to be a law."[8]

The application of the principle of civil tolerance to legalized abortion is illegitimate and unacceptable because the state is not the original source of the inborn and inalienable rights of the person. Neither is it the creator and absolute arbiter of these same rights, but must put itself in the service of the person and of the community by means of the recognition, protection and promotion of human rights.

Thus when it authorizes abortion, the state radically contradicts the very meaning of its presence and seriously compromises the whole juridical system, *because it introduces into it the principle which justifies violence against a helpless innocent being.*

16. The moral judgment on the civil law that authorizes abortion emerges clearly from what precedes: it is a law that is intrinsically and seriously immoral.

This law, unlike just and honest ones, is not binding on the conscience: therefore it cannot, in the slightest, undermine the principle of the inviolability of every innocent human life, which remains unchanged and immutable. Man feels bound only by the law written by God in his heart, a law which, commanding him not to kill, authoritatively judges and absolutely rejects a similar human law.

17. The negative moral judgment on the Italian law in favor of abortion can also be seen from the following elements:

a) its contradiction with the values and the fundamental principles of the natural-divine moral law, owing to the lack or in any case the inadequacy of juridical protection of the "right to life" that belongs to every human being;

b) the aberrant faculty attributed to the woman's freedom to decide in purely individualistic terms, outside and contrary to all responsibility as regards the "right" of the unborn child;

c) the serious distortion of some fundamental roles in society: *the rights of the father of the conceived child are, in fact, violated, as also are the rights and duties of parents with regard to their daughter who is a minor; then, too, the medical profession of service to life is violently forced not only to performances that are completely alien to it, but also and more seriously to a task which is directly opposed to the protection and advancement of human life;*

d) the exaggerated individualism which inspires the law in favor of abortion is even more serious owing to the fact that it is recognized by the state, which in its turn compels all citizens, even those who are declaredly against abortion, to make some contribution;

e) the danger, which is not at all a hypothetical one, in spite of explicit assertions to the contrary, of making legalized abortion a means of regulating births;

f) the limits and ambiguities of the recognized right of the medical and ancillary personnel to object;

g) the contradiction of the law as regards professional ethics, because it obliges those who do not officially formulate conscientious objection to carry out the interruption of pregnancy in every case, even if in a single case their conscience forbids them to do it.

Second Part
THE PASTORAL ACTION OF THE CHRISTIAN COMMUNITY IN FAVOR OF UNBORN LIFE

I. The Responsibility of the Ecclesial Community

18. Before the phenomenon of abortion, the *first responsibility of the Church is to proclaim forcefully the novelty and originality of the Christian message.* This message proclaims the greatness of every man, even if only conceived, as the image of the living God in Jesus, and instills in everyone a new love, bestowed by Jesus Christ, which is capable of coping positively with even the most difficult situations.

19. The present seriousness of the phenomenon of abortion urges the Church to assume fully her community and individual responsibility. All her members, excluding no one, are involved in the task of protecting

and fostering human life, and—in this field too—each one is entrusted with an unrepeatable and irreplaceable task.

In this context an appeal must be made to the commitment of the local Church and of particular Christian communities as such; respect, love and welcoming of unborn life must be expressed with specific community and ecclesial acts.

20. Going on now to the contents and operators, we will indicate the tasks common to all, and the specific ones of some categories of persons.

With regard to the common tasks, we point out the operational goals and propose some instruments to reach them; with regard to the specific ones, we take into consideration the tasks of Christian couples and families, tasks of the expectant mother, of the medical and ancillary personnel, of religious personnel, of medical directors and members of boards of directors, of tutelary judges and of priests.

II. Operational Goals

21. The effective rejection of abortion passes through a lucid and energetic struggle against the causes that encourage it.

It must be recognized that *the most determinant general cause is found again in contempt for, and rejection of, the absolute inviolability of human life not-yet-born. That is the fruit of a culture which considers man an absolute value, freed of all bonds with God and with a universal and immutable moral norm, engaged only in pursuing his own welfare, materialistically and hedonistically understood, even with the instrumentalization of others, to the extent of refusing to acknowledge the most sacred and inviolable rights.*

Today culture presents itself, moreover, as largely dominated by the ironic and inhuman "logic of violence"; of this, abortion represents one of the most conspicuous and disquieting symptoms, especially *when it is demanded as a "right" of woman and of society.*

Speaking in this way, it is not our intention to forget the sad presence in our society of social causes, economic and legislative difficulties, psychological sufferings, etc., which often encourage the tragedy of abortion. In the paragraphs that follow we will also speak at length of these causes and of the commitments derived from them for a true and wise family policy.

22. In such a cultural and social context, the Church must, above all, teach herself and others the value of human life and the duty of loving it and welcoming it; drawing inspiration in all her daily choices from the beatitude of non-violence, "Blessed are the peacemakers, for they shall be called sons of God" (Mt. 5:9), and from the evangelical law of love and service for the poorest and the smallest.

23. Here also takes its place the effort to overcome some widespread but unacceptable mentalities, which lead to finding in abortion the solution to the distressing problem of unwanted and difficult pregnancies.

We are referring, in general, to the sexual culture which aims at separating and opposing to each other the exercise of sexuality and the procreation of a new life. This culture springs from a private and pleasure-seeking concept of sexuality itself. The latter can hardly appear as in the service of fruitful love when it puts itself in the service of the individual withdrawn in himself or open only to his partner, and when it is lived as a source of pleasure that is an end in itself. *Even when the value of*

the opening of sexuality to life is recognized, it is neces-
sary to consider the widespread presence of a certain
lack of esteem for large families.

We refer next, in particular, to the persistence of an
unenlightened and pharisaical mentality in judging the
various irregular forms of motherhood outside marriage, as in the case of unmarried mothers and of
women who are separated or divorced.

24. A fundamental stage in this educative work
concerns the prevention of unwanted pregnancy.

The essential aim is that of a timely, thorough, and
ongoing education to sexuality as a value and as the
commitment of the whole person in his physical and
spiritual dimension, and to the physical and spiritual
generation of human life as the goal of a love that is
responsible on the ethical plane.

A similar education must be given with particular
urgency to couples, in order that they may be helped
concretely in knowledge and choice of those methods of
regulating fertility which are lawful from the moral
point of view.

This educative work, even if it will not always yield
immediate fruits and will often have to develop in an
environment in which it is not easily understood and
shared, is, in the long run, the real human path for fully
responsible parenthood.

25. Finally, in the light of the impact, sometimes a
very considerable one, which living and working conditions themselves, and conditions of cultural growth and
of economic situations generate on the interruption of
pregnancy, a more courageous family policy is necessary, without delay.

That is, there will have to be developed a whole series of legislative, economic, welfare, health and social insurances, of trade union and cultural initiatives, capable of making "possible, always and everywhere, for every child that comes into this world, a welcome worthy of man."[9]

III. Operational Instruments

26. The instruments that the ecclesial community can and must use to reach the operational aims indicated, are many and varied: from catechesis on the value of life to the formation of conscience with regard to the duty of protecting it and advancing it, to initiatives of justice and charity, on the part both of the individual and of the community.

All Christians are called to use, with that freedom and "imagination" in intervention which springs from Christian love of life, the various gifts and ministries received from the Spirit in answer to the various and concrete requirements of the environment in which they are placed.

In this extremely varied context of possibilities, we press for two urgent initiatives: the family advisory bureaus and the centers for welcoming life.

1) Family advisory bureaus

27. As regards the family advisory bureaus, we repropose with renewed forcefulness what we recommended at the Twelfth General Assembly: "Sustained by the local Churches and connected with the other organisms of the family apostolate, let family advisory bureaus that are professionally well qualified and of reliable Catholic inspiration, be set up at the diocesan, or at least interdiocesan, or regional level. At the same

time, the contributions offered, also to Christians themselves, by the advisory bureaus already existing, should be put to good use, in a spirit of openness and discernment."[10]

28. The first pastoral commitment is for an adequate exploitation of advisory bureaus of Christian inspiration.

That means, among other things, the commitment to:

a) create them where they do not exist and are seen to be necessary, and qualify them more and more where they already exist;

b) ensure in them the clear and effective inspiration of Christian morality for the various problems concerning sexuality, marriage and the family;

c) spread, with scientific thoroughness and appealing to the joint responsibility of the couple as such, the "natural" methods for regulating fertility, bringing forth in this field the irreplaceable apostolate from couple to couple;

d) reject recourse to male and female sterilization when it is aimed solely and directly at making generative fertility incapable of procreation[11];

e) become more critical before the over-simple and erroneous opinion which considers that the only effective form of reducing and eliminating abortion is artificial contraception;

f) prepare carefully the personnel of the advisory bureaus to tackle the psychological problems of those who intend to have recourse to abortion or have already done so, offering realistic alternatives to the former, and renewed reasons for hope and life to the latter;

g) develop in the Christian community a favorable attitude to the advisory bureaus and effective solidarity as regards aid for their operational necessities.

29. Another pastoral commitment concerns the presence of Christians in public and free advisory bureaus.

Before some laws which aim at greatly reducing the operational space of Christians, the latter are called to defend as much as possible the real significance of the advisory bureau. This is, that it is a service, particularly a psychological and social one, for the couple and the family, in the line of positive assistance for married love and for life.

With the weight of their professional capacity and their dedication, Christians will be able to dedicate themselves consistently to the tasks proposed by the law itself (cf. articles 2 and 5), of information and aid for women to remove the causes which might induce them to interrupt pregnancy.

At the same time they will have the democratic courage to denounce those violations of the law which take place when people go beyond the limits fixed by it.

Furthermore, they will be able to demand respect for their right to be exonerated—by virtue of conscientious objection—from contributing to the legislative process aimed at the interruption of pregnancy.

2) The centers for welcoming life

30. A second instrument which needs to be planned and made operative in the local Churches are the centers for welcoming life. Such centers:

a) must be supported by the interest and the contribution, also financial, of all members of the community;

b) they must meet the needs of pregnant women in difficulty by means of:

—the moral assistance of understanding, dialogue, and support;

—medical, psychological, legal and moral consultation;

—social work in terms of material and economic aid, by means of looking for jobs or houses, financial support, etc.;

—a real welcoming of the child about to be born, by offering the mother all possible help to keep the child, bring it up and educate it;

c) they must also be places of possible adoption to propose to women who decide not to keep their child.

IV. The Specific Duties of Some Categories of Persons

31. If the responsibility of welcoming unborn life involves the whole ecclesial community, it concerns some categories of persons, however, in a more direct and urgent way, in relation to their conditions and profession.

1) The expectant mother

32. The woman called to have to accept an unwanted and difficult pregnancy, often finds herself in a difficult and painful climate of solitude, if not even of rejection. This situation commits Christians to a real and proper "solidarity" with the expectant mother.

It is not enough to abstain from all judgment of condemnation and to ensure sincere understanding. It is necessary, rather, to open the woman up to hope by means of the timely offer of that concrete assistance which the situation reveals as necessary.

It is clear that the first solidarity must be realized within the couple and the family: the close affection and readiness to help and share in every way, on the part of the husband, parents, relatives and friends, can keep alive an atmosphere of serene expectation and confidence, which makes the period of pregnancy less difficult.

33. In the present rediscovery of the wider and more significant roles of woman in the field of her personal perfection and of her contribution to the good of society and the Church, it is necessary to rethink positively the educative and social value of "motherhood."

This is not limited to the mere biological fact of reproduction, nor does it confine woman to domestic life and work, but is a fundamental form of married love, which brings about at the same time the maturity of the couple and its service for the human and ecclesial community.

34. With admiring gratitude, we recall the testimony of so many mothers who, though finding themselves in difficult and painful situations, succeed in going through with their pregnancy with a fortitude which only faith and love of life can inspire and sustain.

Their testimony, while it denounces the moral misery of a society often shaken by impulses of death, selfishness, and love of comfort, offers reliable motives for hope in a future society that will be able to find its renewal in the energies of life, love, and generosity which are present and operating in it, even if hidden and passed over in silence.

2) Couples and Christian families

35. Married couples are called to offer the Church and society the testimony of that "ministry of life" which springs from their participation in love of God, the Creator and Father, and, through the sacrament of marriage, love of Christ the Redeemer and of the Church, the bride and mother.

The ministry of life of the couple is not carried out merely in the work of generating and bringing up their children; it is also expressed in the most varied forms of "spiritual fruitfulness." Among them let us recall:

—the readiness to welcome and help also the children of others, in the awareness that they are all children of God, the one universal Father;

—disinterested generosity in restoring, to children who are abandoned and alone, the affectionate warmth of a family by means of adoption;

—solicitous participation in the various initiatives in defense of human life.

Parents have a special responsibility in educating their children to the real meaning of human life, to the value it possesses and the tasks it entrusts: the daily choices of respect, love and active solicitude for the smallest and the weakest constitute the most concrete and determinant atmosphere for an education to welcoming unborn life.

3) Priests

36. The priest, the guide and inspirer of Christian communities, has precise and special responsibilities also in the field of unborn life.

In proclaiming the Word of God, he will preach the commandment of "You shall not kill" and of love for brothers, illustrating the inviolable personal dignity of the human being, even if only conceived, and the special injustice of the violation of this dignity.

In the work of formation to Christian life, he will educate the faithful to welcome and serve every human life in a responsible way, also through the family advisory bureaus and the centers for welcoming life, and, for the persons concerned, through the declaration of conscientious objection as well.

He will not fail, furthermore, to enlighten the faithful regarding the distinction—and sometimes the opposition—between what is authorized and prescribed by civil law and what meets the deepest and indelible exigencies of moral law. That is made necessary particularly by the growing gap between legality and morality, and by the more and more widespread mentality that what the civil law prescribes or permits is morally acceptable. Thanks to this necessary enlightenment, the faithful will combat the false conviction that abortion, which can now be practiced legally in some cases, is therefore a less blameworthy action.

37. In the Sacrament of Reconciliation, the priest is called to relive the spirit and attitude of Jesus Christ towards evil and towards the sinner: "To diminish in no way the saving teaching of Christ constitutes an eminent form of charity for souls. But this must ever be accompanied by patience and goodness, such as the Lord Himself gave example of in dealing with men. Having come not to condemn but to save (cf. Jn. 3:17), He was indeed intransigent with evil, but merciful towards individuals."[12]

He will therefore receive in a deep and living spirit of brotherhood even those who are guilty of abortion, understanding—though without justifying—the immediate and deep motivations which induced them to carry out this action.

Furthermore he will always maintain great respect for the person who has had an abortion, though having to tackle, in a delicate and clear way, the problem of the moral significance of the act.

The same spirit of brotherhood will guide the priest in the confession of doctors and medical assistants who have failed, although in different ways, in their mission of defending human life. This brotherhood must be accompanied by the pastoral commitment to clarify any responsibilities involving excommunication and to demand observance of the duties of Christian life for the future.

38. The whole action of the confessor is geared to reconciling the penitent with God and with the Church. He will accompany him along the way of conversion, helping him to repent sincerely of his sin, and to ask the God of life for forgiveness, with humble confidence and with resolve not to relapse.

The minister of reconciliation will also lead the penitent to understand, accept and carry out an adequate "penance" or sacramental satisfaction.

In this connection keep in mind what the *Ordo Paenitentiae* recalls: "The type and the extent of the satisfaction must be proportioned to every individual penitent, in such a way that everyone may atone in the area in which he has sinned, and treat his ill with an effective medicine...and transform his life in some way" (no. 6 c).

39. The confessor is also called to bring to the knowledge of the penitent the penalty of excommunica-

tion for induced abortion, to verify if the penitent has incurred it, and, if so, explain the ecclesial significance of the penal intervention.

For absolution of the censure, the confessor will send the penitent to the bishop or to the priest authorized by the bishop, or "in an urgent case" he will absolve according to the indications and the spirit of the discipline in force in the Church. He will not want, on the contrary, to nullify the opportunity of grace, offered by the sacramental meeting, by hasty or undeserved absolutions in cases of doubtful necessity, but will put the situation to good use for a real process of catechesis and conversion.

4) Medical and ancillary personnel

40. Among the categories most directly concerned in the problem of pregnancy is that of physicians and all those dedicated to health and life.

Their professional task, which, for believers, takes the form of a "real and excellent ministry of charity,"[13] makes them collaborators of God in defense and development of creation in the delicate and decisive field of human life.

In this light, the radical contradiction of those who directly induce abortion and those who cooperate in it, is evident. *No excuse can be put forward by invoking the state law which authorizes abortion: the injustice of such a law cannot serve as a basis either of rights or of duties for conscience.*

41. Conscience has the right to raise objection in face of the law in favor of abortion.

This right is based on the dignity and freedom of the person, who cannot be forced to act against his conscience or prevented from behaving in conformity with it.

It is a native and inalienable right, which the civil regulations of society must recognize, sanction, and protect: otherwise man's personal dignity is denied and the state becomes the original source and the final arbiter of the rights and duties of persons.

42. The duty of raising conscientious objection arises whenever the request of the civil law conflicts with the priority and inviolable exigencies of conscience, as happens in the case of legalized abortion.

The very great value of human life, which is at stake here, makes this duty a serious moral obligation, rooted in the law written in every man's heart. The Church reproposes it in her legislation, striking with excommunication Christians who induce abortion or collaborate in it (cf. C.J.C., can. 2350, par. 1).

We recall here some of the moral principles set forth in our "notification" of July 1, 1978:

"a) direct abortive action is never lawful;

"b) close cooperation in direct abortive action, such as takes place with the services required of the operating theater team and with the issue of certificates which, by their content and their legal value, are a real and proper authorization for abortion, is not lawful;

"c) the danger of scandal, also because of the position of some persons such as women religious, may make unlawful other forms of cooperation which are not close." [14]

43. Conscientious objection to induced abortion is recognized also, though with limitations, by the recent

Italian law which exonerates the objector from carrying out the procedures and activities specifically and necessarily aimed at causing the interruption of pregnancy.

In this way, conscientious objection is seen to be of two kinds, even if they are connected: the "natural" or moral one, based on the human dignity of the person, and the "legal" one, recognized and determined by the civil law.

As regards conscientious objection, mention should be made of some uncertainties and ambiguities present in the civil law. Without prejudice to the unacceptability of the law itself, these make desirable and urgent either an interpretation or even an amendment regarding the conscientious objector's possibility of participating in the procedures. Thus beyond the serious moral obligation of the "natural" objection, which is always present, it is opportune that not only the obstetric-gynecological personnel, but also the medical and ancillary personnel, should continue to express themselves in favor of legally recognized objection.

44. Above all, the physician who is a conscientious objector remains committed to saving and promoting life, taking advantage also of the possibilities offered by the civil law itself.

Every family doctor or practitioner in surgeries or advisory bureaus—informing in advance that he is a conscientious objector and cannot issue the written certificate at the end—can and should carry out the interview and make the examinations and tests even if the woman should formulate the hypothesis of interrupting pregnancy.

In this perspective the following are lawful and necessary:

—prior assistance, if it is not specifically and necessarily aimed at abortion;

—the administration of all the treatments requested and necessary for the safety and health of the woman, as a result of complications that have arisen;

—assistance after the intervention, as a testimony of loving concern for the difficulties that the interruption of pregnancy itself does not eliminate, when it does not make them worse.

45. The dangers of discrimination and damage that conscientious objectors meet with, call for a more lively and active spirit of solidarity, both within the medical and ancillary personnel, and within the Christian and civil community. Social, trade union, and political forces should take particular interest in ensuring the democratic exercise of the rights of all.

46. The defense of conscientious objection, and its high significance as personal consistency and social denunciation of an unjust legal situation, will find easier implementation and will be more credible if the medical and ancillary personnel raises objection with authentic motivations and opens up with disinterested generosity to the wider and complex field of commitments and initiatives in favor of life.

5) The religious personnel

47. Men and women religious, by virtue of their evangelical profession are called to be privileged models of Christian charity also in the field of the protection and promotion of life.

For this reason the work of religious personnel is seriously unacceptable in private clinics in which abortion is practiced. Their presence may be useful, on the other hand, in public hospitals, in which, however, they will have to avoid not only any occasion or appearance of scandal, but above all courageously to promote all initiatives in defense of life.

6) Medical directors and members of the boards of directors of hospitals and nursing homes

48. Medical directors, who are also doctors, are, as doctors, in the moral situation already indicated and evaluated for medical personnel.

If, on the other hand, they are not doctors, while they are not recognized by the civil law in their right to conscientious objection, they are called by the same law to ensure that in hospitals and authorized nursing homes the procedures for, and the interventions of, abortion should be carried out. In this way their specific function is distorted. Respect for their freedom of conscience, on the contrary, demands that they, too, should be recognized as having the right to objection.

The position of members of the boards of directors of hospitals and nursing homes is a similar one. The specific functions of their presence in the delicate areas of hospital organization are placed in the service of the life and health of sick persons, and not of the suppression of human beings.

The action of these persons will have to take advantage of all forms that are democratically possible to safeguard unborn life, and it can be called morally lawful only when, having evaluated all the elements and all the circumstances, it does not become a cause of abortive effects.

7) Tutelary judges

49. The tutelary judge is involved in the application of the law in favor of abortion in cases of minors

without the consent of the one who exercises parental authority, and in cases of women debarred because of unsoundness of mind (cf. articles 12 and 13).

The tutelary judge, whom the law does not recognize as having the right to conscientious objection, but whose decision cannot be impugned, is morally obliged to refuse his consent, since this latter assumes the form of a real and proper authorization for abortion and is therefore cooperation in it.

V. The Political Commitment of Believers with Regard to the Law in Favor of Abortion

50. The life of faith commits Christians to building up an earthly city which will really be capable of loving and welcoming *the life of everyone, and in particular of the smallest and the weakest.*

Their competent and honest contribution, vivified by the Spirit of Christ, will be expressed with priority in original educative work in the schools and in the other cultural centers, and with a wide social, juridical and political action aimed at anticipating and supporting unwanted and difficult pregnancies.

51. It is part of the more specifically political commitment of Christians:

a) to recall, courageously and with democratic methods, the duty of respecting human life from its beginning, denouncing, consequently, the iniquity of the law in favor of abortion;

b) to carry out a critical reading of the present regulations on abortion: without neglecting the very limited positive elements, they will have to point out the deep contradictions it presents as regards the Constitution and within the articles themselves;

c) to demand strict observance of all the positive clauses of the law which defend the continuation of pregnancy, checking their implementation and denouncing any violations;

d) to support conscientious objectors from a human, trade union, and political standpoint, so that they will not be isolated and will not be subjected to injustice on the administrative and political plane;

e) to work for a replacement of the present law, which is morally unacceptable, with regulations that completely respect the right to life.

52. Of particular importance is the commitment of legislators inspired by Christian principles, both because they are more directly responsible for laws which have an impact on the morals of citizens, and because of the testimony of love of justice and disinterested concern for the true common good which they are called to offer.

Aware of their responsibility, legislators must not feel dispensed from the moral duty of working to limit as much as possible the negative effects of the law which is in force in favor of abortion, and, above all, to give an impetus towards replacing it. This is all the more urgent in that the law issued is clearly unjust.

CONCLUSION

"The glory of God is living man."

53. Today *the world expects of Christians a new commitment, in favor of unborn life, which will express, in the concrete work of individuals and of the*

*community, the evangelical proclamation of the invi-
olable value of the life of every man who comes into this
world.*

The efficacy of this commitment will depend on the
extent to which it is integrated in a work widened to the
defense and advancement of human life wherever and
however it is threatened and mortified, from inhuman
working and housing conditions to torture and the
death penalty, from the rejection of the physically and
psychically handicapped to physical and moral violence
and to kidnappings, etc. (cf. GS 27).

54. Carrying out its responsibilities, the ecclesial
community puts its trust in God, the author and lover of
every life,[15] and in man himself: created in the image
and likeness of God, man is moved by a secret and inex-
tinguishable thirst for life, justice, real love, honesty,
and moral renewal.

Our history, however, records also the wickedness
of the human heart, the permissiveness of social morals,
the iniquity of legislations in favor of abortion, the
distressing reality of innocent lives that will never see
the light of the sun and the smile of brothers, and will
not be reborn in water and the Spirit. But also this man,
in whom the divine image is seriously distorted, is called
to salvation, can accept from God the gift of conversion,
and can be recalled to the fundamental values of existence by the very disasters carried out with his hands.

With this trust in God and in man, the Christian
will renew his commitment of serving and welcoming
unborn human life, convinced that he is collaborating
with God and glorifying Him in the work of His hands,
because "the glory of God is living man."[16]

NOTES

1. Didaché II, 2; V, 2. Cf. also Athenagoras, *Libellus Pro Christianis*, 35; Tertullian, *Apologeticum* IX, 8; Basil, *Lettera 188, Ad Amphilochium*, can. 2; Ambrose, *Hexaemeron* 5, 18, 58; etc.

2. See the Council of Elvira, can. 63; the Council of Ancira, can. 21; the Council of Mainze, can. 21; etc.

3. See G. Caprile, *Non Uccidere. Il Magistero della Chiesa sull'aborto*, Rome 1973.

4. See the *Hippocratic Oath*, which says: "I will give no deadly drug to any, though it be asked of me, nor will I counsel such, and especially I will not aid a woman to procure abortion. I will keep my life and my profession pure and pious." See E. Nardo, *Procurato aborto nel mondo greco romano*, Milan 1971, pp. 58-66.

5. *Declaration of the Rights of the Child*, voted by the United Nations General Assembly, November 20, 1959. Note that also Italian civil legislation recognizes the rights of the unborn child (Civil Code, articles 1, 339, 462, 687, 715, 784).

6. Sacred Congregation for the Doctrine of the Faith, *Dichiarazione sull'aborto procurato*, no. 13.

7. The Sacred Congregation for the Doctrine of the Faith expresses itself as follows: "The civil law cannot embrace the whole sphere of morality, or punish all misdeeds: no one demands that of it. It must often tolerate what is, when all is said and done, a lesser evil, in order to avoid a greater one" *(ibid.,* no. 20).

8. *Ibid.,* no. 21.

9. *Ibid.,* no. 23.

10. C.E.I., *Evangelizazione e sacramento del matrimonio,* conclusive deliberations.

11. Cf. *Humanae vitae,* no. 14; furthermore, the Sacred Congregation for the Doctrine of the Faith, *La sterilizzazione negli ospedali cattolici,* March 13, 1975.

12. *Humanae vitae,* no. 29.

13. Pius XII, *to the Fourth International Congress of Catholic Doctors,* September 29, 1949.

14. See *Notificazione della Presidenza C.E.I.,* July 1, 1978, no. 4.

15. "For you love all things that exist, and have loathing for none of the things which you have made, for you would not have made anything if you had hated it. How would anything have endured if you had not willed it? Or how would anything not called forth by you have been preserved? You spare all things, for they are yours, O Lord who love the living" (Wis. 11:24-26).

16. Irenaeus, *Adv. haer.* IV, 20, 7.

JOINT PASTORAL LETTER OF THE BISHOPS OF KENYA ON THE FAMILY AND RESPONSIBLE PARENTHOOD

The General Assembly of the United Nations set aside the year 1979 as the "International Year of the Child." In doing this it wanted to focus the attention of the world on the special needs of children. It wanted to challenge all of us to do our utmost to protect their rights and ensure that the children of our time get the care and attention they require.

We, your bishops, are anxious to use this occasion to examine the situation in our country, and to make some practical proposals that would promote the welfare of the children in Kenya. Our aim is to encourage individuals and groups to have a deep and practical concern for the promotion of their good, and we are convinced that loyalty to the teaching of Christ and His Church is the surest and most effective means of fostering this great work. We feel it is our duty to God and to our people, therefore, to try to promote Christian values that are sometimes ignored, and to oppose ideas and trends that are contrary to the teaching of the Gospel and hence to the welfare of our people.

In promoting the welfare of children there are many elements in our traditions that can be of great assistance to us. These are part of our cultural heritage that should not be lost. *For our people, children are seen as a gift from God. They are a sign of God's blessing, a blessing that is received with gratitude and treasured with love.* They are a joy to their parents and a welcome gift to the community in which they are born. Even from an early age they are integrated into the life of the community, and assume roles in accordance with their sex, age and ability.

This attitude of the past is in accordance with the teaching of the Gospel where Christ said: "Let the little children come to me..." (Mt. 19:14). We recommend that these traditional values be maintained and treasured, and that they be passed on to future generations. We find that these values contrast sharply with some recent trends and ideologies that have gained favor in many parts of the world, and are becoming more and more prevalent among our own people.

The character of a society can be judged by its attitude to its children. If we uphold and develop the traditions we have inherited, traditions vindicated by the teaching of Christ, then we lay a solid foundation for future generations and for the true development of our people.

FAMILY

We cannot be serious about promoting the interests and the rights of children unless we are fully committed to promoting the interests of the family. It is impossible to promote the good of children without promoting the good of the family. Already the bishops of East Africa, and the representatives from episcopal conferences of all Africa, have stressed the importance of this subject, and it is not our intention here to cover the same ground again. What is aimed at is to review some of the areas of major importance in our society, and to make some practical suggestions. It is for individuals, for families, and for communities to adopt some practical and concrete means to help in the building up of strong united families. In this way the children will be provided with the atmosphere and the facilities they need for their growth and development.

a) Socio-economic factors: A family is not an isolated unit in society; it is part of a larger unit. The general health of the larger society affects the family. It is encouraging to find in Kenya that there has been such wonderful progress in the socio-economic development of the country, in an atmosphere of peace, brotherliness and political maturity. The peace and stability that we experience is a major asset to the well-being of families. Efforts must be intensified to maintain peace and prosperity, and to ensure that the development of the country is in the interests of all.

b) Employment: Employment is necessary so that a family is self-sufficient, and can maintain its dignity and self-respect. It is especially important that the breadwinner of the family be able to get suitable employment near home. In particular, it is highly desirable that rural workers, and especially those in the agricultural sector, get just wages, so that the menfolk are not obliged to go to the towns and cities in search of employment. This often causes the family to break up. For rural families, it is highly desirable that they own some land. Thus the just distribution of land is a major social concern. The consequences of carrying out a proper program here could be of very considerable benefit to the families of today, and ensure the stability and progress of the community of the future.

c) Absentee fathers: The growing tendency for the father of the family to be absent from the home most of the year should be looked on as a social evil that needs to be corrected. *No economic planning that promotes such a system can be in the real interests of the people.*

d) Housing: Families living in towns are often under severe strain because of the lack of housing, or the conditions of the housing. It is obviously not easy to provide sufficient and suitable housing for all who are now flocking to the towns. However, every effort should be made to try to accommodate families properly. They should not be at the mercy of unscrupulous landlords who charge exorbitant rents, and evict at will. The high rents and the difficulties families find in acquiring their own houses are the cause of a lot of suffering and conflict in families.

e) Working mothers: It is often regarded as the norm in our present-day society, that both father and mother be employed outside the home. Such an attitude needs to be carefully reconsidered. It should be understood that the most important work a mother has to do is to provide for the proper rearing and upbringing of her children. A woman who is devoted to her home and her family is, in fact, working in a very real sense and making a very real contribution to the development of the country. Let it not be thought that the process of nation building takes place only outside the home. *The woman who gives her time and talents to her home and family is not depriving her family by not earning a salary.* On the contrary, she is making a very significant contribution to her children in a way that no money can supply.

When both parents are working away from home, the children are often left in the care of other children. This is a twofold injustice: it is unfair to those in charge and to those who have to be tended. Even when competent persons are entrusted with the care of the children, they are not an adequate substitute for the parents. The structure of employment in our towns in particular needs to be reconsidered, so that the children get the care they need. *The thinking here should be towards providing the fathers of families with wages sufficient to support the family, so that it is not necessary for the mother to be a wage earner too.* Perhaps, as an intermediate measure, the part-time employment of mothers of families ought to be considered and promoted.

f) Alcoholism: The problem of excessive drinking and of alcoholism has reached almost epidemic proportions in some sections of our society. Its effects on the family are usually of a very serious nature, and the vast propaganda that encourages the sale of alcohol is really propaganda against the family. Moves to curtail the distribution and sale of alcohol are welcome, but a lot more needs to be done.

Excessive use of alcohol is often a symptom of a deeper evil. It is an escape from the obligations of the family: it can be a protest against the conditions of work, or against the conditions of the home. It can be an indication of the lack of social and leisure amenities in a community. More often it is a result of conflict within the family circle rather than a cause of conflict. Therefore, what is of vital importance here is for everyone to be aware of the evil, the very grave evil, of the abuse of alcohol in our society, and for all to be concerned with correcting it. To promote good communications within the family is often the most effective means of reducing the problem. It is strongly recommended that Church communities throughout the country get involved in promoting more and more the good of the families by organizing workshops, seminars, retreats, and such like, to build up family relationships and bring happiness to the home. It is heartening to see that such work has already begun in some places. This should be encouraged and further developed.

At the same time it is the concern of the whole community, and of public authorities in particular, to do everything possible to alleviate the evil brought about by the abuse of alcohol. The Church is willing to support efforts made in this regard.

g) Single-parent family: The basic need of any child is a family where both parents cooperate harmoniously in its upbringing. Both parents have the right and the duty to devote themselves to the rearing and the education of the children they are responsible for having brought into the world. Where either parent neglects this duty, a serious wrong is done to the other parent and the child. The tendency for girls to have children outside marriage is, therefore, one that should be opposed by all. It is not in the interests of the unmarried mothers themselves, and the consequences for the children are very serious. *It is true that motherhood has a value: but this is within the context of the family.* It is not enough that the mother provides food, shelter and education for her child; the child needs also the care of a father and, if this is missing, the child always suffers. In addition to this it must, of course, be clearly understood that the act of intercourse outside marriage is gravely sinful.

RESPONSIBLE PARENTHOOD

What has been said so far indicates the concern of the bishops, and the whole Church in Kenya, for the welfare of the families of this country. The Catholic

Church is totally committed to promoting whatever will lead to the good of the people and communities here. Now an important issue has to be dealt with, the question of responsible parenthood.

The teaching of the Catholic Church was outlined in 1968 by the late Pope Paul VI in the Encyclical *Humanae vitae. On this point there is no hesitation. The developments of the past ten years have helped to strengthen the conviction of many people regarding the position of the Pope. There is therefore no change in the doctrine as outlined by Pope Paul VI.* It is unfortunate that this teaching has not been widely understood. And here there is a lot of work to be done, for unless the Church's teaching is understood and accepted, there is a lot of doubt and confusion. The teaching of the Church is very necessary for our people, so that they may be guided in what is the right path for them to follow.

Obviously it is a good thing that couples and communities should have a responsible attitude towards the bringing of children into the world, and the rearing and educating of these children once they are born. But not every method that assists in the control of fertility is acceptable; and in our own society today many solutions are being proposed that are unacceptable to the Church. It is not in the interest of couples, nor in the interest of our society, to promote these methods, though this is being widely done.

ABORTION

The most radical method of birth prevention, and one which deserves the most serious and forthright condemnation, is the termination of pregnancy by abortion. Whatever the terms used and whatever the motivation proposed, *abortion is the killing of unborn human beings.* The Church, and society at large, must insist on the *right of all humans to life. This is the most fundamental human right, and it applies to all humans equally, even those who are not yet born.* Direct abortion is direct killing, and this may never be tolerated. The damage caused to the mother is of a very serious nature, and this should not be underestimated. It is important for our people not to be led astray by false theories about abortion. They should be brought to realize that *from the time of conception one is dealing with human life, and this may not be destroyed. That the woman has control over the child conceived in her womb in such a way that she can decide to have it destroyed is totally false.*

STERILIZATION

Direct sterilization of the man or woman, whether temporary or permanent, is not a lawful method of birth control or prevention. By direct sterilization we mean every sterilization which of itself, that is, of its own nature and condition, has immediately the sole effect of rendering a person infertile, so that children cannot be conceived. This, an unwarranted interference with the integrity of the human person, is always immoral and absolutely forbidden, notwithstanding any subjectively right intention or any other reason.

Indirect sterilization, on the other hand, may sometimes be lawful. In this case the sterilization, although foreseen, is not caused with the direct intention of making conception impossible, but in order to cure a disease that may be present in a particular organ of the body. For instance a cancerous womb may be removed to protect the life of a woman, although it is foreseen that the operation will certainly make it impossible for her to bear children. Those responsible for the teaching of religion and morality should be conversant with the teaching of the Church in this regard, and be prepared to give assistance to medical practitioners and to all who are interested.

CONTRACEPTIVES

The use of artificial contraceptives is immoral. *The teaching of the Church in this regard is clear, and our people should be taught the meaning and the consequences of this teaching.* This is not an unthinking restriction on the findings of modern science. It is a positive protection of the dignity of the person, and of the couple joined in a bond of love in marriage.

The use of contraceptives in no way enhances the freedom and the dignity of the woman; quite the contrary. Such use does not improve the quality of the marital relationship. There is evidence from societies where the use of contraceptives is widespread, that the rate of marriage breakdowns is reaching alarming proportions. What will be the effects of the widespread use of contraceptives on the generations now growing up? The indications are that they will be very serious indeed. However, as in the case of sterilization, so here too, it is lawful to use medicine to cure some illnesses even though this medicine may have an indirect contraceptive effect.

Some contraceptive devices being used, in reality lead to abortion, that is, they produce an abortion: This is the effect of most of the intrauterine devices (I.U.D's), and also of some of the pills and injections that are given. Also, some drugs used have very serious side effects, and so are banned in many countries.

Medical science is more and more alarmed at the side effects of many of the contraceptives in use today. But other disciplines likewise are beginning to show concern at the effects on society, on individuals, and especially on the young, of the interference with the normal processes of the human body. In Kenya we have the United Nations Secretariat for the Environment— the body that is interested in the preservation of the natural habitat.

It would be ironic if more attention were given to the natural habitat of man than to his natural physiology and psychology which need to be preserved and not tampered with.

POSITIVE PROPOSALS— OUR PASTORAL CONCERN

a) The Church in Kenya, as everywhere, is committed to fidelity to the teaching of Christ—*to Tradition and to the Magisterium (teaching authority).* It knows that such fidelity is in the interests of the people of our country. *It does not consider the people of Kenya incapable of responding to the demands of the Christian-Catholic doctrine.* We, your bishops, would do a disservice to the people if we did not expect of them the goodness and the fidelity that they are capable of by the grace of God.

We, shepherds of your souls, are aware of the problems of the people, and are vitally interested in their solution. In the past, as is generally recognized, the

Church has played a major part in the development of education and medicine in the country. Always with deep respect for the dignity of the human person, the Church will continue to develop medical services so that these do not become a kind of inhuman administration of drugs or mechanical application of remedies, but rather the expression of genuine care, for the true well-being of our people in their distress and suffering.

b) Lawful methods of responsible parenthood. *In the area of responsible parenthood, there is need for education and medical care. Pope Paul VI called for the development of methods that could be used by parents, so that they could plan their families in a mature and responsible way, without prejudice to their natures, or to the nature of their families.* There has been very considerable progress in this field during the last ten years. *And now, with confidence, people are proposing methods that are reliable, safe, readily available, and morally and culturally acceptable to our people.* It is hoped that these methods will become better known and more widely used in the future. In recent years the Church has encouraged the adoption of methods of Natural Family Planning, and already a number of initiatives have been taken. Now with the experience gained, a more intensive and more effective program can be undertaken for the benefit of our people.

These methods require that husband and wife enter into a special relationship with each other, that they cooperate and communicate freely, and come to joint decisions. So, their mutual love and understanding is greatly strengthened, and their married life takes on a new and deeper meaning because it comes to be based on a relationship that is in harmony with their human personality and with the nature of marriage as God wishes it to be.

These natural methods of family planning require careful and competent teaching, and it is important that those who wish to instruct others in their use should be well-trained in them, and clear in the way they present them. Here lies a fruitful apostolate for many of our married people. By learning these methods and teaching them to others they can provide a wonderful service to their fellow men. As Pope Paul VI wrote: "Among the fruits which ripen forth from a generous effort of fidelity to the divine law, one of the most precious is that married couples themselves frequently feel the desire to communicate their experience to others...." It is married couples themselves who become apostles and guides to other married couples. This is surely, among so many forms of apostolate, one which seems so opportune today.

c) **Program of the Kenya Episcopal Conference.** For some years the Church has been active in promoting the education of parents in the use of the natural method of family planning. The Kenya Episcopal Conference now plans to implement, through the Kenya Catholic Secretariat, a nationwide program which will encourage and support Christian family life.

This program will seek to promote a better understanding *of the meaning of human life, the dignity of the person, and the sacredness of Christian marriage.* One component of this will be training in child-spacing according to the natural method of family planning.

In this program, the K.C.S. will collaborate with the Family Life Counseling Association of Kenya

(FLCAK), a voluntary organization, formed in 1977, devoted to promoting family life and spreading information on Natural Family Planning.

A training program is being worked out for teachers of Natural Family Planning in Kenya. It is hoped that many couples will cooperate in this program.

MEDICAL ETHICS
IN CATHOLIC HOSPITALS

In line with what has been said, it is important that Catholic hospitals, clinics and dispensaries give practical as well as theoretical witness to the sanctity of human life, both at its beginning in conception, and at every stage in its existence. *As institutions dedicated to this ideal, they cannot, without being false to the principles for which they stand, be associated in any way with practices or programs they believe to be wrong.*

For this reason they should do everything they can to have on their staff, doctors, nurses, and health-care workers who are committed to these principles and are opposed to abortion, sterilization, and the various contraceptive procedures that are condemned by the Church. They should also make their policies known to all patients and to those who attend these patients in the hospitals. In this way they uphold God's plan and exercise a very important pastoral mission in the world today.

Catholic medical personnel in non-Catholic institutions may sometimes be faced with problems of conscience in these matters, e.g., if they are asked to cooperate in providing services or treatments that they believe to be wrong. It is important, therefore, that they be as well informed as possible so that they will be able to make a responsible judgment. While the circumstances in individual cases may vary considerably, the following general principles should be kept in mind.

Any cooperation with others in an immoral action that is accompanied by personal approval of the decision to perform such an action is always sinful, since it involves a deliberate identification of oneself with the sinful intention.

The same is true even when one does not approve of the decision, but agrees to cooperate immediately and directly in the evil action itself. For instance, one may disagree with another's decision to procure an abortion. But if, in spite of this, one helps directly in the action that causes the abortion, one commits the same sin as if one approved. Provided one does not agree with the evil intention, and does not help directly in an action that is intrinsically evil, there are times when cooperation is lawful. These occur when the following three conditions are simultaneously verified:

a) When the act by which one cooperates is good in itself, or at least morally indifferent, e.g., the preliminary preparation of a theater for an immoral operation, the preparation and aftercare of the patient, etc.

b) When there is a sufficiently grave reason for cooperating in a particular case. For medical personnel this means that the more immoral an operation or a particular form of treatment is, and the more essential one's help is in undertaking it, the more serious one's reason must be for cooperating in it.

c) When every effort is made to avoid the danger of giving scandal or bad example to others, e.g., by explaining the circumstances which make one's cooperation lawful.

In coming to a decision as to whether cooperation is lawful or not in their circumstances, Catholic medical personnel should give careful consideration to these general principles and be guided by them. Where they find it difficult to apply them to a particular case, they should consult the local pastor or chaplain for his advice, and try to reach a balanced judgment in the light of all the factors involved.

Sometimes this judgment may indicate that cooperation would not be lawful. In these cases, while Catholic medical workers should refrain from judging the motives of their colleagues or patients who do not agree with them, they should make their conscientious objections clearly known and refuse to participate. This may be very difficult at times, as they may be condemned or unfairly treated for their stand. But the Gospels leave no doubt that a courageous witness to their convictions is the right course to follow: "Blessed are those who suffer persecution for justice' sake, for theirs is the kingdom of heaven" (Mt. 5:10). Where undue pressures are brought to bear on them—like threats of dismissal or loss of privileges, etc.—they should have recourse to the Church authorities in their area, who will do all in their power to protect and support them.

CONCLUSION

The late founder of our nation, Mzee Jono Kenyatta, told the bishops of Eastern Africa (AMECEA) in July, 1976: *"The Church is the conscience of society, and today a society needs a conscience. Do not be afraid to speak. If we go wrong and you keep quiet, one day you may have to answer for our mistakes."* It is the duty of Catholics to witness to their convictions, otherwise they will not be loyal to the Church as the conscience of society.

We, the shepherds of your souls, wish to remind you that the Christian religion is supernatural. To be faithful to it we need divine help. "Without me," Christ said, "you can do nothing" (Jn. 15:5). It is by our own personal effort and by prayer through Christ our Savior, that God gives us the grace we need to have faith in Him, and to be obedient to His commands. Therefore, let us pray with humility, that all families, following the example of the Holy Family of Nazareth, where Jesus grew in grace and wisdom before God and man, may be guided by the same Spirit, and help to make our Kenya pleasing to God and to all men.

> We bless you, and remain,
> Yours devotedly in Christ,

Maurice Cardinal OTUNGA, *Archbishop of Nairobi;* Caesar M. GATIMU, *Bishop of Nyeri;* Tiberius MUGENDI, *Bishop of Kisii;* Silas NJIRU, *Bishop of Meru;* Zacchaeus OKOTH, *Bishop of Kisumu;* John NJENGA, *Bishop of Eldoret;* William DUNNE, *Bishop of Kitui;* Philip SULUMETI, *Bishop of Kakamega;* Colin DAVIES, *Bishop of Ngong;* Nicodemus KIRIMA, *Bishop of Mombasa;* Charles CAVALLERA, *Bishop of Marsabit;* Raphael NDINGI, *Bishop of Nakuru;* Urbanus KIOKO, *Bishop of Machakos;* John MAHON, *Bishop of Lodwar;* Mons. Leo WHITE, *Prefect Apostolic of Garissa.*

"HUMANAE VITAE"—
TEN YEARS AFTERWARDS
TOWARDS A MORE HUMAN
CIVILIZATION

Some documents receive at the very moment in which they appear an almost spontaneous welcome and produce in public opinion or in social conscience the result that was expected of them. Perhaps there will be little talk of them subsequently, but that is of little importance: their destiny is fulfilled, and so is their mission.

Other documents, on the contrary, as soon as they are published cause such strong contradiction and such acute rejections (often more emotional than rational in origin), that their essential message is, as it were, dimmed, and at least apparently they do not reach the effect estimated. It could be said that they carry out their mission in the long-term period.

This is the history of some texts of profane literature, but it can also be the history of some documents of the Magisterium of the Church at all levels. I recall this phenomenon on rereading *Humanae vitae* ten years after its publication. It seems to me, in fact, that not a few aspects of the evolution of society in the course of these ten years have driven home better the significance of the main themes of the encyclical. If it has not yet become a popular text, received with enthusiasm by public opinion, it is recognized more easily today than ten years ago that *it is right in the great principles it invokes and in the stands that constitute its substance.*

POLES OF
HUMANAE VITAE

It is therefore easier to see, ten years afterwards, what are the principal poles of this important document of the Magisterium of Paul VI.... Let us say at once that they do not contradict each other, but on the contrary complete and enrich each other.

The first is what I would willingly call its humanistic dimension. I give this adjective the very deep and rich meaning understood by *Gaudium et spes* when it hopes for a "new humanism" (no. 7) "where man is defined before all else by his responsibility to his brothers and at the court of history" (no. 55): a humanism which, to be more and more rich (cf. no. 52), must not be exclusively earthly (no. 56). *Humanae vitae is humanistic to the extent to which, by means of each of its sections and above all with the thread that connects and unifies them all, it contains an invitation, and even more an impetus, towards what is most authentic and most noble in man, contrary to what has been called "the inhuman trends" of man himself.*

The second pole is the pastoral dimension of the document. I see this pastoral dimension particularly in the determination, which is present everywhere in the encyclical, to point out a high, demanding, difficult ideal—without which true humanism does not exist, far less evangelical and Christian humanism. I see it also in another determination: always to go towards the man and woman eager to embrace the ideal, in order to understand their varying difficulties, to offer them effective help, to show them the way and encourage them in their progress along it.

TRUE HUMANISM

The proposal and pursuit of true humanism are the vital nerve of the whole encyclical. They are at the center of the doctrinal principles (nos. 11-13 and 18) like a source of light. But they are also on the horizon of the pastoral directives (nos. 19-30) and therefore of the practical indications, that is, the program of life proposed by the document. The very refusal of artificial methods of contraception, far from being based—as has often been repeated—on abstract moral postulates, sets out from the requirements of the dignity of the human person, and therefore from a concrete humanistic perspective: *these methods diminish or take away man's full responsibility and put him at the mercy of technique;* they are too often used in the service of moral degradation; too often, too, they are used to instrumentalize woman, etc. (cf. no. 17).

In what does this true humanism consist? The encyclical bases it on an "integral vision of man and of his vocation" (no. 7), *a vocation which is not exhausted in a natural and earthly dimension but is prolonged in a supernatural and eternal dimension.*

Furthermore, if it were desired to seek in the encyclical the elements of what it calls "a human civilization" (no. 18), the following, which are only some among the most important ones, could be indicated.

In the first place *an effort of man not to give himself up as a slave to technical means, but to assume more and more fully the responsibilities of his own actions, paying their price.*

It is, therefore, certainly, the dominion of nature, in obedience to the Bible commandment; but above all in the awareness that to dominate nature means in the first place achieving self-mastery through control of one's instincts.

Another element, at the level of marriage, is *deep and mutual respect of the personal dignity of each of the partners*, a dignity which is complete only if the spiritual values (evangelical values, for a Christian, which integrate and at the same time go far beyond mere biophysiological and even psychological values) are considered.

FROM EROS TO AGAPÉ

There is, moreover, knowledge of what real love is: *eros*, yes, but *eros* which extends to *agapé:* love, therefore, which goes beyond the mere thrill of sensuality, which goes beyond the carnal gift of oneself, which goes beyond the mere pursuit of self-fulfillment and, therefore, all danger of selfishness, in order to be— as the encyclical describes—deeply human ("an act of the free will, intended to endure and to grow by means of the joys and sorrows of daily life"—no. 9), faithful, exclusive and fruitful (a fruitfulness which is also biological and which expresses and gives concrete form to spiritual fruitfulness).

There is finally in the encyclical the call to respect of man's law—natural law and positive law. It is thanks to this that man presents his human aspect; to such an extent that man is betrayed, and can even be destroyed, if, out of ignorance, laziness or such and such a prejudice, this respect disappears.

The Pope wishes to promote this humanism above all on the level of each person and, since here it is a question of marriage, on the level of each couple. Everyone is, in this sense, invited to self-mastery; to the ascesis that it involves; to the carrying out, with one's own "companion for eternity," of a personal choice, in the field of fertility, which sets the two on a path of conscious and free commitment, not a mechanical and exterior one. *If the use of natural methods has a deep human significance, this happens, precisely, according to the testimony of those who use them, because these methods lead the spouses to a self-mastery which is a cause of inexpressible enrichment of their love, both individually and as a couple.*

The encyclical wishes to promote this humanism also on the social plane. It wishes to open the way towards a more human civilization. It is in this sense that the Pope appeals to men of science to help to humanize the whole question of fertility and procreation. It is also in this sense that he denounces the inhuman aspect of the interference of public authorities in the sanctuary of the conscience of each person and each couple. *It is, in fact, immoral for a government to pursue in its own country a population policy which fails to recognize or even contradicts moral principles.* It is even more immoral for a foreign government to interfere in this way in another country either directly by means of moral pressure, or indirectly, for example, by conditioning the financial aid that this country urgently needs to a certain population policy.

The Pope asks public authorities for a farsighted and courageous social policy to help the peoples that wish or need to increase their population. In this sense, the Pope of *Humanae vitae* is exactly the one of *Populorum progressio* and of the address to the UN (October 5, 1965); and it would be inconsistent to set the two in opposition or dissociate them. And it is in this sense that *Humanae vitae* was a prophetic cry in favor of the poor peoples, which are often tricked in what would be vital for their development: certain population growth.

RESPONSIBLE PARENTHOOD

The humanistic dimension of *Humanae vitae* could be summed up in the expression used several times in the encyclical itself: "responsible parenthood." This expression must be understood not in a minimalistic and restrictive sense but in its strongest sense. *It means that each couple must assume, as something essential, not only the responsibility of having or not having a child, but also the responsibility of the means to use, not taking recourse to the easy way out through determinism by external methods, which are unnatural and for that very reason inhuman.* When it is known that too many children in the Third World—but also in the other two worlds—are born from relations lacking all responsibility, because they are based only on instinct, it can well be said that the central message of *Humanae vitae*, which is that of responsible parenthood, is full of positive consequences for the whole of contemporary civilization.

The greatness of *Humanae vitae* lies in the fact that the Pope did not conceal from himself for a single moment, nor did he want to hide from others, how difficult and exacting is the ideal which he proposes to Christian couples. But it is with great resoluteness that the encyclical also proposes concrete and global pastoral aid for the couples of today, as well as those of tomorrow, in order to make their efforts as effective as possible.

These are the two indispensable and complementary aspects of what we call a pastoral operation.

PASTORAL CHARITY

In the first place, therefore, to hide nothing of a high but exacting ideal, the Pope will go so far as to write that "to diminish in no way the saving teaching of Christ constitutes an eminent form of charity for souls" (no. 29): in other words, it is a form of pastoral charity. And the Pope gives an example, speaking clearly of discipline, of "serious engagement and much effort" (no. 20), of "imprescriptible demands" (no. 25), of difficulties, sometimes serious ones, which make one think of the little door and the narrow way foreseen by the Gospel. Even the word "heroism" is not absent from the perspectives of the encyclical.

But alongside this, it is necessary to be always ready to offer effective pastoral aid. The message which the Pope addresses in *Humanae vitae* to the bishops and priests as pastors, to Christian couples and to family movements, aims precisely at giving concrete shape to this valid help.

Not without reason the Pope, in the context of this pastoral support for married couples, calls priests to patience and to spiritual kindness following the example of the Lord, "intransigent with evil, but merciful towards individuals" (no. 29).

It is above all in intense sacramental life that a family can find, in the midst of great difficulties, the necessary support. It is a very significant fact that the Pope encourages married couples, even those who have the painful experience of their own weakness (nos. 17

and 19), to have recourse tirelessly to the sacraments: Penance, the Eucharist (nos. 25 and 29) and marriage "lived in its entire human and Christian fullness" (no. 30; cf. also no. 25). Penance is, moreover, conceived in the encyclical not just as the sacrament of forgiveness and reconciliation, but as a source of mercy, grace and strength, from which one drinks deep because one knows that one is weak, one knows that the aim to be attained is a hard one and that there are difficult moments.

Then, aware that the law of God in this field "would not be practicable without the help of God" (no. 20), the Pope stresses repeatedly the necessity of prayer (nos. 25 and 29).

A pastoral aid that bishops and priests will give their faithful is that of clinging from the depths of their being to the teaching of the encyclical (no. 28) and of transmitting to the faithful consistent, clear and well-grounded teaching. The faithful who, at the cost of so many struggles and faced with so many obstacles, endeavor to live according to this difficult ideal have the right to find in their pastors firm adherence to the Magisterium, unshakable unity of thought and of word (cf. no. 28).

But even scientists, the public authorities, all those who have some influence on the mass media—to the extent to which they collaborate to create a less polluted atmosphere from the moral point of view, to reveal the full significance of chastity, and to train in self-discipline—offer pastoral support indirectly. This "concerted pastoral action" (no. 30), this global operation capable of embracing all aspects of man's life, is of great value in the Pope's eyes, because it alone offers a considerable number of Christians the help they need (nos. 22, 23 and 24).

Finally, let us point out briefly what Paul VI considered an eminent form of apostolate in this matter: *the word and the testimony of married couples "who become apostles and guides to other married couples"* (no. 26).

Understood in this way, this particular help is seen to be beneficial not only from the strictly religious point of view but also from other standpoints which are important for the regulation of births according to natural methods: the education of the young to firm and courageous chastity, a joint effort for the creation of an atmosphere that is morally healthier, a more refined sense of woman's dignity, a higher price given to life from its beginnings, a clearer view of the family as the cell of society.

TEN YEARS AFTERWARDS

Is it necessary to insist? Ten years after the publication of *Humanae vitae* it is clear that these two dimensions keep all their relevance today.

Observers free of prejudices, and unbiased, affirm unceasingly that Paul VI spoke prophetically in favor not so much of abstract values as of very concrete elements of mankind's heritage: elements that would have been destroyed if an authoritative voice had not defended them. Scientists of repute admit, in their own ways, that the pontifical teaching is right when they state that we are still far from gauging all the serious disadvantages (biological, physiological and psychological) of certain artificial contraceptive methods, and that, in any case, these disadvantages are undeniable and more harmful than people admit. Then, too, in silence and discretion, a good number of couples are trying to live the ideal proposed by the encyclical and bear a humble but convinced witness to the spiritual maturity they have succeeded in reaching. Would it perhaps be exaggerating to say that the time has come to read *Humanae vitae*—the encyclical that has been under the cross fire of countless disputes, the encyclical that was a "sign of contradiction" at the moment of its publication and for the span of some years—in a way less distorted by emotional attitudes, in a more serene and thorough way? I would not hesitate to assert, on my part, that in the years to come it will be able to yield increasingly abundant fruits in the framework of a richer and more authentic humanism. It will be the incomparable voice of this Church, "a sincere and disinterested friend of men," an "expert in humanity," always ready to contribute "towards the establishment of a truly human civilization" (no. 18).

LUCAS MOREIRA NEVES
Vice-President
of the Pontifical Council for the Laity

TO ALL WHO WORK FOR THE DISABLED

Document of the Holy See for the International Year of Disabled Persons, March 4, 1981.

From the very beginning the Holy See received favorably the United Nations' *initiative* of proclaiming 1981 "the International Year of Disabled Persons." These persons deserve the practical concern of the world community, both by reason of their numbers (it is calculated that they exceed four hundred million), and especially for their particular human and social condition. Therefore, in this noble enterprise, the Church could not fail to show her caring and watchful solicitude, for by her very nature, vocation and mission she has particularly at heart the lives of the weakest and most sorely tried brothers and sisters.

For this reason, the Church has followed with close attention everything that has been done up to the present time on behalf of the disabled on the legislative level, both national and international. Worthy of note in this regard are the United Nations' Declaration of the rights of the disabled, and the Declaration concerning the rights of the mentally retarded, as also the progress and future prospects of scientific and social research, plus the new proposals and initiatives of various sorts now being developed in this area. These initiatives show a renewed awareness of the duty of solidarity in this specific field of human suffering; also to be borne in mind is the fact that in the Third World countries the lot of the disabled is even more grave and calls for closer attention and more careful consideration.

The Church fully associates herself with the initiatives and praiseworthy efforts being made in order to improve the situation of the disabled, and she intends to make her own specific contribution thereto. She does so, in the first place, through fidelity to the example and teaching of her Founder. *For Jesus Christ showed special care for the suffering, in all the wide spectrum of human pain.* During His ministry He embraced them with His merciful love, and He showed forth in them *the saving power of the redemption that embraces man in his individuality and totality.* The neglected, the disadvantaged, the poor, the suffering and sick were the ones to whom He specially brought, in words and actions, the proclamation of the Good News of God's kingdom breaking into human history.

The community of Christ's disciples, following His example, has down the centuries caused to flourish works of extraordinary generosity, works that bear witness not only to faith and hope in God but also unshakable love and faith in the dignity of man, *in the unrepeatable value of each individual human life, and in the transcendent dignity of those who are called into existence.*

In their view of faith and in their concept of man, Christians know that *in the disabled person there is reflected in a mysterious way the image and likeness which God Himself impressed upon the lives of His sons and daughters.* And as they remember that Christ Himself mystically identified Himself with the suffering neighbor and took as done to Himself everything done for the least of His brethren (cf. Mt. 25:31-46), Christians feel a call to serve, in Him, those whom physical accidents have affected and disabled; and they are resolved not to omit any of the things that must be done, even at the cost of personal sacrifice, in order to alleviate their disadvantaged condition.

At this moment, one cannot fail to think, with lively gratitude, of all the communities and associations, all the men and women religious and all the lay volunteers who spend themselves in work for the disabled, thus manifesting the perennial vitality of that love that knows no barriers.

It is in this spirit that the Holy See—while expressing its gratitude and encouragement for what has been done by those responsible for the common good, by the international organizations and by all those who work for the handicapped—considers it useful to recall briefly a few principles that may be useful guides in dealing with the disabled, and also to suggest some practical points.

I. BASIC PRINCIPLES

1. The first principle, which is one that must be stated clearly and firmly, is that the *disabled person* (whether the disability be the result of a congenital handicap, chronic illness or accident, or from mental or physical deficiency, and whatever the severity of the disability) *is a fully human subject, with the corresponding innate, sacred and inviolable rights.* This statement is based upon the firm recognition of the fact that *a human being possesses a unique dignity and an independent value, from the moment of conception and in every stage of development, whatever his or her physical condition.* This principle, which stems from the *upright conscience* of humanity, must be made the inviolable basis of legislation and society.

Indeed, on reflection one may say that *a disabled person*, with the limitations and sufferings that he or she suffers in body and faculties, *emphasizes the mystery of the human being, with all its dignity and nobility*. When we are faced with a disabled person, we are shown the hidden frontiers of human existence, and we are impelled to approach this mystery with respect and love.

2. Since the person suffering from handicaps is a subject with full rights, he or she must be *helped to take his or her place in society in all aspects and at all levels, as far as is compatible with his or her capabilities*. The recognition of these rights and the duty of human solidarity are a commitment and task to be carried out, and they will create psychological, social, family, educational and legislative conditions and structures that will favor the proper acceptance and complete development of the disabled individual.

The Declaration of the Rights of the Disabled states, in Section 3, that "disabled persons have the right to respect for their human dignity. Disabled persons, whatever the origin, nature and seriousness of their handicaps and disabilities, have the same fundamental rights as their fellow citizens of the same age, which implies first and foremost the right to enjoy a decent life, as normal and full as possible."

3. *The quality of a society and a civilization is measured by the respect shown to the weakest of its members*. A perfect technological society which only allowed fully functional members and which neglected, institutionalized or, what is worse, eliminated those who did not measure up to this standard or who were unable to carry out a useful role, would have to be con-

sidered as radically unworthy of man, however economically successful it might be. Such a society would, in fact, be tainted by a sort of discrimination no less worthy of condemnation than racial discrimination; it would be discrimination by the strong and "healthy" against the weak and the sick. It must be clearly affirmed that *a disabled person is one of us, a sharer in the same humanity*. By recognizing and promoting that person's dignity and rights, we are recognizing and promoting our own dignity and our own rights.

4. The fundamental approach to the problems connected with the sharing by the disabled in the life of society must be inspired by the *principles of integration, normalization and personalization*. The principle of *integration* opposes the tendency to isolate, segregate and neglect the disabled, but it goes further than an attitude of mere tolerance. It includes a commitment to make the disabled person a subject in the fullest sense, in accordance with his or her capacities, in the spheres of family life, the school, employment, and, more generally, in the social, political and religious communities.

As a natural consequence there derives from this principle that of *normalization*, which signifies and involves an effort to ensure the complete rehabilitation of the disabled person, using all means and techniques now available, and, in cases where this proves impossible, the achievement of a living and working environment that resembles the normal one as much as possible.

Thirdly, the principle of *personalization* emphasizes the fact that in the various forms of treatment, as also in the various educational and social means employed to eliminate handicaps, it is always the dignity, welfare and total development of the handicapped person, in all his or her dimensions and physical, moral and spiritual faculties, that must be primarily considered, protected and promoted. This principle also signifies and involves the elimination of collectivized and anonymous institutions to which the disabled are sometimes relegated.

II. OPERATIVE LINES

1. One cannot but hope that such statements as those of the Declaration cited will be given full recognition in the international and national communities, avoiding limiting interpretations and arbitrary exceptions and perhaps even unethical applications which end by emptying the statements of meaning and import.

Developments in science and medicine have enabled us today to discover in the fetus some defect which can give rise to future malformations and deficiencies. *The impossibility at present of providing a remedy for them by medical means has led some to propose and even to practice the suppression of the fetus. This conduct springs from an attitude of pseudo-humanism which compromises the ethical order of objective values and must be rejected by upright consciences.* It is a form of behavior which, if it were applied at a different age, would be considered gravely anti-human. Furthermore, *the deliberate failure to provide assistance, or any act which leads to the suppression of the newborn disabled person, represents a breach not only of medical ethics but also of the fundamental and inalienable right to life.* One cannot, at whim, dispose of human life by claiming an arbitrary power over it. Medicine loses its title of nobility when, instead of attacking disease, it attacks life; in fact, prevention should be against the illness, not against life. *One can never claim that one wishes to bring comfort to a family by suppressing one of its members.* The respect, the dedication, the time and means required for the care of handicapped persons, even of those whose mental faculties are gravely affected, is the price that a society should generously pay in order to remain truly human.

2. A consequence of clear affirmation of this point is the duty to undertake more extensive and thorough research in order to overcome the causes of disabilities. Certainly much has been done in recent years in this field, but much more remains to be done. *Scientists have the noble task of placing their skill and their studies at the service of bettering the quality and defense of human life.* Present developments in the fields of genetics, fetology, perinatology, biochemistry and neurology, to mention only some disciplines, permit us to foster the hope of noticeable progress. A unified effort of research will not fail, it is hoped, to achieve encouraging results in the not too distant future.

These initiatives of fundamental research and of application of acquired knowledge deserve, therefore, more decisive encouragement and more concrete support. It is the hope of the Holy See that international institutions, the public powers in individual nations, research agencies, non-governmental organizations and private foundations will more and more foster research and allot the necessary funds for it.

3. The priority to be given to the prevention of disabilities should also make us reflect on the distressing phenomenon of the many persons that undergo a stress and shock that disturb their psychic and interior life.

Preventing these disabilities and fostering the health of the spirit signifies and implies unified and creative effort in favor of integral education, and an environment, human relations and means of communication in which *the person is not damaged in his more profound needs and aspirations—in the first place moral and spiritual ones—and in which the person is not submitted to violence which can end by compromising his interior balance and dynamism.* Spiritual ecology is needed as much as natural ecology.

4. When, notwithstanding the responsible and rigorous application of all the techniques and cures possible today, the disability cannot be remedied or reversed, it is necessary to seek and bring about all the remaining possibilities of human growth and of social integration which remain open for the person affected. Apart from the right to appropriate medical treatment, the United Nations' Declaration enumerates other rights which have as their objective the most complete possible integration or reintegration into society. Such rights have very wide repercussions on the whole of the services which exist at present or which must be developed, among which might be mentioned the organization of an adequate educational system, responsible professional training, counseling services and appropriate work.

5. One point seems to merit particular attention. The United Nations' Declaration on the Rights of Disabled Persons affirms: *"Disabled persons have the right to live with their families or with foster parents"* (no. 9). *It is extremely important that this right be put into effect.* It is in the home, surrounded by loved ones, that a handicapped person finds the surroundings which

are most natural and conducive to his development. Taking account of this primordial importance of the family for the development of the handicapped person and his integration into society, those responsible for socio-medical and orthopedagogical structures should make the family the starting point in planning their programs and make it the principal dynamic force in the process of social care and integration.

6. From this viewpoint, it is necessary to take into account the decisive importance which lies in the help to be offered at the moment that parents make the painful discovery that one of their children is handicapped. The trauma which derives from this can be so profound and can cause such a strong crisis that it shakes their whole system of values. The lack of early assistance or adequate support in this phase can have very unfortunate consequences for both the parents and the disabled person. For this reason one should not rest content with only making the diagnosis and then leaving the parents abandoned. Isolation and rejection by society could lead them to refuse to accept or, God forbid, to reject their disabled child. *It is necessary, therefore, for families to be given great understanding and sympathy by the community and to receive from associations and public powers adequate assistance from the beginning of the discovery of the disability of one of their members.*

The Holy See, conscious of the heroic strength of mind required of those families that have generously and courageously agreed to take care of and even adopt disabled children, wants to assure them of its appreciation and gratitude. The witness which these families render to the dignity, value and sacredness of the human person deserves to be openly recognized and supported by the whole community.

7. When particular circumstances and special requirements for the rehabilitation of the disabled person necessitate a temporary stay or even a permanent one away from the family, the homes and institutions which take the family's place should be planned and should function in a way as near to the family model as is possible and should avoid segregation and anonymity. It must be arranged that, during their stay in these centers, the bonds linking the disabled persons with their families and friends should be cultivated with frequency and spontaneity. Apart from their professional competence, loving care and dedication of the parents, relatives and educators have obtained, as many have testified, results of unexpected effectiveness for the human and professional development of disabled persons. Experience has demonstrated—and this is an important point for reflection—that in a favorable and human family setting, full of deep respect and sincere affection, disabled persons can develop in surprising ways their human, moral and spiritual qualities and even, in their turn, bring others peace and joy.

8. The affective life of the disabled will have to receive particular attention. Above all when their handicap prevents them from contracting marriage, it is important not only that they be adequately protected from promiscuity and exploitation, but that they also be able to find a community full of human warmth in which their need for friendship and love may be respected and satisfied in conformity with their inalienable moral dignity.

9. Handicapped children and young people obviously have the right to instruction. This will be

assured them to the extent possible either through an ordinary school or a specialized school for people with their handicap. Where home schooling is required, it is hoped that the competent authorities will supply the family with the necessary means. Access to higher learning and opportune post-school assistance ought to be made possible, and aid should be given for this purpose.

10. A particularly delicate moment in the life of the disabled person is the passage from school to placement in society or professional life. In this phase the person needs particular understanding and encouragement from various sectors of the community. Public authorities should guarantee and foster, with effective measures, the right of disabled persons to professional training and work, so that they can be inserted into a professional activity for which they are qualified. Much attention should be focused on working conditions, such as the assignment of jobs in accordance with the handicaps, just wages, and the possibility of promotion. Highly recommended is advance information for employers regarding the employment, the situation and the psychology of the disabled. These encounter various hindrances in the professional sector: for example, a sense of inferiority about their appearance or possible productiveness, worry about having accidents at work, etc.

11. Obviously, the disabled person possesses all the civil and political rights that other citizens have, and it should, as a general rule, be made possible for him or her to exercise them. However, certain forms of disability—for instance, the numerically important category of those who have mental handicaps—consti-

tute an obstacle to the responsible exercise of these rights. Even in these cases action should be taken not in an arbitrary manner or by applying repressive measures, but on the basis of rigorous and objective ethical and juridical criteria.

12. On the other hand, *the disabled person must be urged not to be content with being only the subject of rights, accustomed to receiving care and solidarity from others, with a merely passive attitude.* He is not only a receiver; he must be helped to be a giver to the full extent of his capabilities. An important and decisive moment in his formation will be reached when he becomes aware of his dignity and worth and recognizes that something is expected from him, and that he, too, can and should contribute to the progress and well-being of his family and community. The idea that he has of himself should, of course, be realistic, but also positive, allowing him to see himself as a person capable of responsibility, able to exercise his own will and to collaborate with others.

13. Many individuals, associations and institutions are today dedicated by profession, and often by a genuine humanitarian and religious calling, to helping the disabled. In many cases they have demonstrated a preference for "voluntary" personnel and educators, because they see in them a particular sense of unselfishness and solidarity. *This observation makes clear that, although technical and professional competence is certainly necessary and ought indeed to be cultivated and improved, by itself it is not sufficient.* A rich human sensitivity must be added to competence. Those who commendably dedicate themselves to the

service of the disabled should have scientific knowledge of their disabilities, but they should also comprehend with their hearts the person who bears the handicap. They should learn to become sensitive to the special signs with which the disabled express themselves and communicate. They should acquire the art of making the proper gesture and saying the right word. They should know how to accept with calmness possible reactions or forms of emotion and learn to dialogue with the parents and families of the disabled. This competence will not be fully human unless it is interiorly sustained by suitable moral and spiritual dispositions: attentiveness, sensitivity and particular respect for everything in the human person that is a source of weakness and dependence. Care and help for disabled persons then becomes a school of genuine humanity, a demanding school, a noble school, an uplifting school.

14. It is very important and even necessary that professional services receive material and moral support from the public authorities with a view to being organized in the most adequate way possible and to having the specialized interventions function effectively. Many countries have already provided, or are in the process of providing, exemplary legislation that defines and protects the legal status of the disabled person. Where such legislation does not yet exist it is the duty of the government to provide an effective guarantee and to promote the rights of the disabled. To this end, it would be advantageous for families and voluntary organizations to be associated in drawing up juridical and social norms in this matter.

15. *Even the best legislation, however, risks having no effect on the social context and not producing full*

results if it is not accepted into the personal conscience of the citizens and the collective consciousness of the community.

Handicapped persons, their families and relatives are part of the whole human family. However large their number may unfortunately be, they form a minority group within the whole community. This is enough to entail the danger that they may not be given sufficient general interest. Add to that the often spontaneous reaction of a community that rejects and psychologically represses that which does not fit into its habits. People do not want to be faced with forms of existence which visibly reflect the negative aspects of life. This gives rise to the phenomenon of exclusion and discrimination as a kind of mechanism of defense and rejection. Since, however, man and society are truly human when they enter into a conscious and willing process of accepting even weakness, of solidarity and of sharing in others' sufferings, the tendency referred to must be countered by education.

The celebration of the International Year of Disabled Persons, therefore, offers a favorable opportunity for a more precise overall reconsideration of the situation, of the problems and of the requirements of millions of those who make up the human family, particularly in the Third World. It is important that this occasion not be allowed to pass by in vain. With the contribution of science and of all levels of society, it should lead to a better understanding of the disabled person and of his dignity and rights; and, above all, it should foster sincere and active love for every human being in his or her uniqueness and concrete situation.

16. Christians have an irreplaceable mission to carry out in this regard.

Recalling their responsibility as witnesses to Christ, they must adopt as their own the Savior's sentiments towards the suffering and stimulate an attitude of charity and examples of it in the world, so that there is never any lack of interest in our brothers and sisters who are less endowed. The Second Vatican Council identified in that charitable presence the essential core of the apostolate of lay people. It recalled that Christ made love of one's neighbor His personal commandment "and enriched it with a new meaning when He identified Himself with His brothers as the object of charity.... For, in assuming human nature, He united all of humanity to Himself as His family, and He made charity the distinguishing mark of His disciples in the words: 'By this all men will know that you are my disciples, if you have love for one another' (Jn. 13:35). In the early days the Church linked the 'agape' to the Eucharistic supper and by so doing showed herself entirely united around Christ. So, too, at all times, she is recognized by the distinguishing sign of love and, while rejoicing at initiatives taken elsewhere, she claims charitable works as her own inalienable duty and right. That is why mercy to the poor and the sick, and works of charity and mutual aid for the alleviation of all kinds of human needs are held in special honor by the Church" (AA 8).

In this International Year of Disabled Persons, Christians will, therefore, stand side by side with their brothers and sisters of all organizations in order to foster, support and increase initiatives suitable for alleviating the situation of the suffering and for inserting them harmoniously into the context of normal civil life, to the extent that this is possible. Christians will make their contribution in personnel and resources, especially through the deserving institutions that—in the name of Christ and of His love and with the marvelous example of people wholly consecrated to the Lord—devote themselves especially to giving education, professional training and post-school assistance to young disabled persons and to caring generously for the worst cases. Parishes and youth groups of various kinds will give special care to families in which one of these children, marked by sorrow, is born and grows to maturity; they will also study, continually apply and, if necessary, revise suitable methods of catechesis to the disabled, and they will pay attention to their insertion into cultural and religious activities, so as to ensure that they will be full members of their Christian community, in accordance with their clear right to appropriate spiritual and moral education.

17. Celebrating the Day of Peace at the beginning of this year, the Holy Father mentioned publicly in the Vatican Basilica the initiatives of the International Year of Disabled Persons and called for special attention to solving their serious problems. He now renews his call to show concern for the lot of these brothers and sisters of ours. He repeats what he said then: "If only a minimum part of the budget for the arms race were assigned for this purpose, important successes could be achieved and the fate of many suffering persons alleviated" (Homily on January 1, 1981). His Holiness applauds the various initiatives that will be undertaken on the international level and also those that will be attempted in other fields; and he urges especially the

sons and daughters of the Catholic Church to give an example of total generosity. Entrusting the dear disabled persons throughout the world to the motherly protection of the Holy Virgin, as he did on that occasion, he repeats his hopeful trust that, "under Mary's maternal gaze, experiences of human and Christian solidarity will be multiplied, in a renewed brotherhood that *will unite the weak and the strong in the common path of the divine vocation of the human person" (ibidem)*.

From the Vatican, March 4, 1981.

DECLARATION ON EUTHANASIA

Prepared by the Sacred Congregation for the Doctrine of the Faith, May 5, 1980.

INTRODUCTION

The rights and values pertaining to the human person occupy an important place among the questions discussed today. In this regard, the Second Vatican Ecumenical Council solemnly reaffirmed the lofty dignity of the human person, and in a special way his or her right to life. The Council therefore condemned crimes against life "such as any type of murder, genocide, abortion, euthanasia, or willful suicide" (Pastoral Constitution *Gaudium et spes*, no. 27).

More recently, the Sacred Congregation for the Doctrine of the Faith has reminded all the faithful about Catholic teaching on procured abortion.[1] The Congregation now considers it opportune to set forth the Church's teaching on euthanasia.

It is indeed true that, in this sphere of teaching, the recent Popes have explained the principles, and these retain their full force[2]; but the progress of medical science in recent years has brought to the fore new aspects of the question of euthanasia, and these aspects call for further elucidation on the ethical level.

In modern society, in which even the fundamental values of human life are often called into question, cultural change exercises an influence upon the way of looking at suffering and death; moreover, medicine has increased its capacity to cure and to prolong life in particular circumstances, which sometimes give rise to moral problems. Thus people living in this situation experience no little anxiety about the meaning of advanced old age and death. They also begin to wonder whether they have the right to obtain for themselves or their fellowmen an "easy death," which would shorten suffering and which seems to them more in harmony with human dignity.

A number of Episcopal Conferences have raised questions on this subject with the Sacred Congregation for the Doctrine of the Faith. The Congregation, having sought the opinion of experts on the various aspects of euthanasia, now wishes to respond to the Bishops' questions with the present Declaration, in order to help them to give correct teaching to the faithful entrusted to their care, and to offer them elements for reflection that they can present to the civil authorities with regard to this very serious matter.

The considerations set forth in the present document *concern in the first place all those who place their faith and hope in Christ, who, through His life, death and resurrection, has given a new meaning to existence and especially to the death of the Christian, as St. Paul says: "If we live, we live to the Lord, and if we die, we die to the Lord"* (Rom. 14:8; cf. Phil. 1:20).

As for those who profess other religions, many will agree with us that faith in God the Creator, Provider and Lord of life—if they share this belief—confers a lofty dignity upon every human person and guarantees respect for him or her.

It is hoped that this Declaration will meet with the approval of many people of good will, who, philosophical or ideological differences notwithstanding, have nevertheless a lively awareness of the rights of the human person. These rights have often, in fact, been proclaimed in recent years through declarations issued by International Congresses[3]; and *since it is a question here of fundamental rights inherent in every human person, it is obviously wrong to have recourse to arguments from political pluralism or religious freedom in order to deny the universal value of those rights.*

I. THE VALUE OF HUMAN LIFE

Human life is the basis of all goods, and is the necessary source and condition of every human activity and of all society. Most people regard life as something sacred and hold that no one may dispose of it at will, but believers see in life something greater, namely, a gift of God's love, which they are called upon to preserve and make fruitful. And it is this latter consideration that gives rise to the following consequences:

1. No one can make an attempt on the life of an innocent person without opposing God's love for that person, without violating a fundamental right, and therefore without committing a crime of the utmost gravity.[4]

2. *Everyone has the duty to lead his or her life in accordance with God's plan.* That life is entrusted to the individual as a good that must bear fruit already here on earth, but that finds its full perfection only in eternal life.

3. *Intentionally causing one's own death, or suicide, is therefore equally as wrong as murder;* such an action on the part of a person is to be considered as a rejection of God's sovereignty and loving plan. Furthermore, suicide is also often a refusal of love for self, the denial of the natural instinct to live, a flight from

the duties of justice and charity owed to one's neighbor, to various communities or to the whole of society —although, as is generally recognized, at times there are psychological factors present that can diminish responsibility or even completely remove it.

However, *one must clearly distinguish suicide from that sacrifice of one's life whereby for a higher cause, such as God's glory, the salvation of souls or the service of one's brethren, a person offers his or her own life or puts it in danger* (cf. Jn. 15:14).

II. EUTHANASIA

In order that the question of euthanasia can be properly dealt with, it is first necessary to define the words used.

Etymologically speaking, in ancient times *euthanasia* meant an *easy death* without severe suffering. Today one no longer thinks of this original meaning of the word, but rather of some intervention of medicine whereby the suffering of sickness or of the final agony are reduced, sometimes also with the danger of suppressing life prematurely. *Ultimately, the word euthanasia is used in a more particular sense to mean "mercy killing," for the purpose of putting an end to extreme suffering, or saving abnormal babies, the mentally ill or the incurably sick from the prolongation, perhaps for many years, of a miserable life, which could impose too heavy a burden on their families or on society.*

It is, therefore, necessary to state clearly in what sense the word is used in the present document.

By euthanasia is understood an action or an omission which of itself or by intention causes death, in order that all suffering may in this way be eliminated.

Euthanasia's terms of reference, therefore, are to be found in the intention of the will and in the methods used.

It is necessary to state firmly once more that nothing and no one can in any way permit the killing of an innocent human being, whether a fetus or an embryo, an infant or an adult, an old person, or one suffering from an incurable disease, or a person who is dying. Furthermore, no one is permitted to ask for this act of killing, either for himself or herself or for another person entrusted to his or her care, nor can he or she consent to it, either explicitly or implicitly. Nor can any authority legitimately recommend or permit such an action. For it is a question of the violation of the divine law, an offense against the dignity of the human person, a crime against life, and an attack on humanity.

It may happen that, by reason of prolonged and barely tolerable pain, for deeply personal or other reasons, people may be led to believe that they can legitimately ask for death or obtain it for others. Although in these cases the guilt of the individual may be reduced or completely absent, nevertheless the error of judgment into which the conscience falls, perhaps in good faith, does not change the nature of this act of killing, which will always be in itself something to be rejected. The pleas of gravely ill people who sometimes ask for death are not to be understood as implying a true desire for euthanasia; in fact, it is almost always a case of an anguished plea for help and love. *What a sick person needs besides medical care, is love, the human and supernatural warmth with which the sick person can and ought to be surrounded by all those close to him or her, parents and children, doctors and nurses.*

III. THE MEANING OF SUFFERING FOR CHRISTIANS AND THE USE OF PAINKILLERS

Death does not always come in dramatic circumstances after barely tolerable sufferings. Nor do we have to think only of extreme cases. Numerous testimonies which confirm one another lead one to the conclusion that nature itself has made provision to render more bearable at the moment of death separations that would be terribly painful to a person in full health. Hence it is that a prolonged illness, advanced old age, or a state of loneliness or neglect can bring about psychological conditions that facilitate the acceptance of death.

Nevertheless the fact remains that death, often preceded or accompanied by severe and prolonged suffering, is something which naturally causes people anguish.

Physical suffering is certainly an unavoidable element of the human condition; on the biological level, it constitutes a warning of which no one denies the usefulness; but, since it affects the human psychological makeup, it often exceeds its own biological usefulness and so can become so severe as to cause the desire to remove it at any cost.

According to Christian teaching, however, suffering, especially suffering during the last moments of life, has a special place in God's saving plan; it is in fact a sharing in Christ's passion and a union with the redeeming sacrifice which He offered in obedience to the Father's will. Therefore, one must not be surprised if some Christians prefer to moderate their use of painkillers, in order to accept voluntarily at least a part of their sufferings and thus associate themselves in a conscious way with the sufferings of Christ crucified (cf. Mt. 27:34). Nevertheless it would be imprudent to impose a heroic way of acting as a general rule. On the contrary, human and Christian prudence suggest for the majority of sick people the use of medicines capable of alleviating or suppressing pain, even though these may cause as a secondary effect semiconsciousness and reduced lucidity. As for those who are not in a state to express themselves, one can reasonably presume that they wish to take these painkillers and have them administered according to the doctor's advice.

But the intensive use of painkillers is not without difficulties because the phenomenon of habituation generally makes it necessary to increase their dosage in order to maintain their efficacy. At this point it is fitting to recall a declaration by Pius XII, which retains its full force; in answer to a group of doctors who had put the question: "Is the suppression of pain and consciousness by the use of narcotics...permitted by religion and morality to the doctor and the patient (even at the approach of death and if one foresees that the use of narcotics will shorten life)?" the Pope said: "If no other means exist, and if, in the given circumstances, this does not prevent the carrying out of other religious and moral duties: Yes."[5] In this case, of course, death is in no way intended or sought, even if the risk of it is reasonably taken; the intention is simply to relieve pain effectively, using for this purpose painkillers available to medicine.

However, painkillers that cause unconsciousness need special consideration. For a person not only has to be able to satisfy his or her moral duties and family obligations; he or she also has to prepare himself or herself with full consciousness for meeting Christ. Thus Pius XII warns: "It is not right to deprive the dying person of consciousness without a serious reason."[6]

IV. DUE PROPORTION IN THE USE OF REMEDIES

Today it is very important to protect, at the moment of death, both the dignity of the human person and the Christian concept of life, against a technological attitude that threatens to become an abuse. Thus some people speak of a "right to die," which is an expression that does not mean the right to procure death either by one's own hand or by means of someone else, as one pleases, *but rather the right to die peacefully with human and Christian dignity.* From this point of view, the use of therapeutic means can sometimes pose problems.

In numerous cases, the complexity of the situation can be such as to cause doubts about the way ethical principles should be applied. In the final analysis, it pertains to the conscience either of the sick person, or of those qualified to speak in the sick person's name, or of the doctors, to decide, in the light of moral obligations and of the various aspects of the case.

Everyone has the duty to care for his or her own health or to seek such care from others. Those whose task it is to care for the sick must do so conscientiously and administer the remedies that seem necessary and useful.

However, is it necessary in all circumstances to have recourse to all possible remedies?

In the past, moralists replied that one is never obliged to use "extraordinary" means. This reply, which as a principle still holds good, is perhaps less clear today, by reason of the imprecision of the term and the rapid progress made in the treatment of sickness. Thus some people prefer to speak of "proportionate" and "disproportionate" means. In any case, it will be possible to make a correct judgment as to the means by studying the type of treatment to be used, its degree of complexity or risk, its cost and the possibilities of using it, and comparing these elements with the result that can be expected, taking into account the state of the sick person and his or her physical and moral resources.

In order to facilitate the application of these general principles, the following clarifications can be added:

—If there are no other sufficient remedies, it is permitted, with the patient's consent, to have recourse to the means provided by the most advanced medical techniques, even if these means are still at the experimental stage and are not without a certain risk. By accepting them, the patient can even show generosity in the service of humanity.

—It is also permitted, with the patient's consent, to interrupt these means, where the results fall short of expectations. But for such a decision to be made, account will have to be taken of the reasonable wishes of the patient and the patient's family, as also of the advice of the doctors who are specially competent in the matter. The latter may in particular judge that the investment in instruments and personnel is disproportionate to the results foreseen; they may also judge that the techniques applied impose on the patient strain or suffering out of proportion with the benefits which he or she may gain from such techniques.

—It is also permissible to make do with the normal means that medicine can offer. Therefore one cannot impose on anyone the obligation to have recourse to a technique which is already in use but which carries a risk or is burdensome. Such a refusal is not the equivalent of suicide; *on the contrary, it should be considered as an acceptance of the human condition, or a wish to avoid the application of a medical procedure disproportionate to the results that can be expected, or a desire not to impose excessive expense on the family or the community.*

—When inevitable death is imminent in spite of the means used, it is permitted in conscience to make the decision to refuse forms of treatment that would only secure a precarious and burdensome prolongation of life, so long as the normal care due to the sick person in similar cases is not interrupted. In such circumstances the doctor has no reason to reproach himself with failing to help the person in danger.

CONCLUSION

The norms contained in the present Declaration are inspired by a profound desire to serve people in accordance with the plan of the Creator. *Life is a gift of God, and on the other hand death is unavoidable; it is necessary, therefore, that we, without in any way hastening the hour of death, should be able to accept it with full responsibility and dignity.* It is true that death marks the end of our earthly existence, but at the same time it opens the door to immortal life. Therefore, all must prepare themselves for this event in the light of human values, and Christians even more so in the light of faith.

As for those who work in the medical profession, they ought to neglect no means of making all their skill available to the sick and the dying; but they should also remember how much more necessary it is to provide them with the comfort of boundless kindness and heartfelt charity. Such service to people is also service to Christ the Lord, who said: "As you did it to one of the least of these my brethren, you did it to me" (Mt. 25:40).

At the audience granted to the undersigned Prefect, His Holiness Pope John Paul II approved this Declaration, adopted at the ordinary meeting of the Sacred Congregation for the Doctrine of the Faith, and ordered its publication.

Rome, the Sacred Congregation for the Doctrine of the Faith, May 5, 1980.

✠ Franjo Cardinal Seper
Prefect

✠ Jerome Hamer, O.P.
Titular Archbishop of Lorium
Secretary

NOTES

1. *Declaration on Procured Abortion*, November 18, 1974: *AAS* 66 (1974), pp. 730-747.

2. Pius XII, *Address to those attending the Congress of the International Union of Catholic Women's Leagues*, September 11, 1947: *AAS* 39 (1947), p. 483; *Address to the Italian Catholic Union of Midwives*, October 29, 1951: *AAS* 43 (1951), pp. 835-854; *Speech to the members of the International Office of Military Medicine Documentation*, October 19, 1953: *AAS* 45 (1953), pp. 744-754; *Address to those taking part in the IXth Congress of the Italian Anaesthesiological*

Society, February 24, 1957: *AAS* 49 (1957), p. 146; cf. also *Address on "reanimation,"* November 24, 1957: *AAS* 49 (1957), pp. 1027-1033; Paul VI, *Address to the members of the United Nations Special Committee on Apartheid*, May 22, 1974: *AAS* 66 (1974), p. 346; John Paul II: *Address to the Bishops of the United States of America*, October 5, 1979: *AAS* 71 (1979), p. 1225.

3. One thinks especially of Recommendation 779 (1976) on the rights of the sick and dying, of the Parliamentary Assembly of the Council of Europe at its XXVIIth Ordinary Session; cf. Sipeca, no. 1, March 1977, pp. 14-15.

4. *We leave aside completely the problems of the death penalty and of war, which involve specific considerations that do not concern the present subject.*

5. Pius XII, *Address* of February 24, 1957: *AAS* 49 (1957), p. 147.

6. Pius XII, *ibid.*, p. 145; cf. *Address* of September 9, 1958: *AAS* 50 (1958), p. 694.

ABORTION, EUTHANASIA AND THE PLURALIST SOCIETY

The following is an edited version of an address by Archbishop Dermot Ryan of Dublin to the Rotary Club on January 26, 1981.

...There is, however, another aspect to human knowledge which would seem to raise questions concerning our capacity to attain truth under the form of the good. Can we know what is good? What is right? Instinctively, we would answer these questions with a confident "yes," just as we instinctively take the view that the human mind can attain truth....

One might also think of the progress which has been made in medical science. It has brought healing and relief to a wide variety of illnesses and handicaps. It has prolonged human existence in a way which could scarcely have been foreseen a century ago. *While many doctors continue to maintain the noblest ideals of their healing art, the medical profession in some countries has been so far corrupted that it readily lends its techniques and its technology to kill, especially through abortion and euthanasia.* Population growth patterns have been so affected in some countries that they are facing a crisis of existence. Births have so declined that the proportion of elderly people increases; *the rising generation is insufficient in number either to care for the elderly—their own relatives and friends—or to earn enough to enable others to care for them.* The inevitable outcome of such a process is the practice of euthanasia. It is already beginning to establish itself as an acceptable solution for medical and social problems among the handicapped and the elderly....

Many people confronted by such approaches are often unwilling or unable to do some serious thinking about these matters for themselves. Perhaps they lack courage to do what really needs to be done to prevent such developments. *Or they may defend their own compliance with such groups, their yielding to such pressures, by invoking the concept of pluralism. "After all," they say, "we do live in a pluralist society. The rights of minority groups must not only be acknowledged; they must be enshrined and protected in legislation." And among such rights we are expected to list, without regard for the unborn child, the right of a woman to abortion.* So far, in many countries of the Western world and in almost all European countries, legislation permitting abortion has been passed by democratic governments. Specious arguments of various kinds, including the concept of pluralism, have been advanced in support of such legislation.

But how far does pluralism permit one to go? If a highly organized pressure group now comes forward and makes use of well-recognized techniques to bring pressure to bear on society and its public representatives to ensure legislation in favor of the elimination of all grandparents and others over the age of 75, who is to stop them? On what grounds are they to be stopped? After all, if a young human being in the mother's womb can lawfully be eliminated, why not a considerably older human being who, in a sense, has considerably less vitality and less hope for a full life than an unborn human being?

Needless to say, those in favor of euthanasia would not put the matter so crudely. In effect, however, it would ultimately amount to that. And once society has not only tacitly accepted abortion, but effectively supported it through legislation and the voting of public funds for its performance, the logic of their argument can scarcely be faulted.

Our few moments of reflection on this topic will inevitably lead us to another question: "Why indeed should the killing of all grandparents at the age of 75 be wrong? Why should it be unacceptable?" And why, at the same time, should so many people in the world at the present time regard abortion as something which is entirely acceptable? Are there any limits to pluralism? Where are they to be found? On what principles are they to be based?

The Church, of course, is accustomed to preach and to teach the Christian moral law as the guide in choosing between conduct which is good or bad. It has long relied on the ten commandments. *In recent times, it has been sometimes handicapped by moral theologians who have questioned the validity of the ten commandments.* Their views have in turn provoked some writing on the topic: "Whatever happened to the ten commandments?"—again, an instinctive reaction, that in spite of the theologians referred to, the commandments are still an effective guide to human conduct.

We are not, however, always dealing with a purely Christian society. *But a mixed society need not be without its moral standards. Such standards should be derived from the very nature of humankind.* In other words, *there is within human nature and even individual human beings an inherent dignity, capacity and purpose which are the expression of the Creator's plan for humanity.* Humanity should be seen as instinctively reflecting the will of the Creator and as instinctively tending towards the good of humanity as a whole and of individual human beings in particular in accordance with the mind of the Creator.

This understanding of man and his place in creation used to provide the parameters for reasonable conduct of individual human beings and of human beings gathered together in society. *These parameters have been abandoned, and humanity seems to have embarked on a process, if not of self-destruction, then at least on a process of self-corruption.*

This situation has largely arisen through a decline in man's capacity to appreciate and to deal with spiritual values and through the activities of pressure groups of various kinds. Through the manipulation of public opinion, such groups can influence political parties to adopt their policies and programs as part of their own policy. If elected, the parties are subjected to further pressure to implement those proposals by legislation. *And so, by what is only seemingly a democratic process, the wishes of a small minority become incorporated in the law of the land and serve rather to destroy the moral fiber of the nation and perhaps even to destroy the nation itself.*

The way in which the democratic process is being used at the present time should alert us all to the need to think for ourselves in a responsible way, to ask ourselves frequently whether our thinking is being done for us. And if so, by whom? *If we belong to any organization which claims through its officials to represent our views, we need to make sure that they do, in fact, do so.* This requires a diligence in attending meetings and in studying literature circulated to members which is rarely found among the majority of members of any organization, whether professional association, trade union, or football club. Members of such groups can often be taken by surprise by what is decided and done in their name. When they make a late challenge, they are usually informed that due notice had been given on the agenda, the relevant information had been supplied in the accompanying documentation and the matter had been voted on democratically at a meeting and had been carried by a majority of those present. These may well be only ten percent of the membership entitled to be present and to vote. *People who live in a democratic society need to be watchful in safeguarding their liberty, lest their slackness be exploited by groups whose aims are not only not democratic, but are ultimately detrimental to the welfare of society.* When opportunities are provided for presenting views and for electing our representatives, we should exercise our personal responsibilities in an informed and serious way....

If then democracy is to survive, the individual members of a democratic society must learn to think more deeply about the important issues of the present time. Unfortunately, much of our thinking in our democratic institutions is almost totally dominated by considerations of an economic and empirical kind. We need, however, to broaden our horizons, to reflect more deeply on issues of truth and justice. *We need to remind ourselves of the dignity of human nature, of the value of an individual human person and of the spiritual and social realities which are a part of man's existence and ultimately set the pattern for the living of a full human life in contentment and peace....*

Certain forces at work in Western society may well be threatening our very existence, more subtly, how-

ever, than by the open aggression of all-out war. Unless each one of us learns to take an active interest in what is going on and seeks to promote justice and truth and charity, the welfare of family life, and a reverence for humanity in the individual person, we may find the society of which we are members disintegrating around us. Many look for freedom to do what they like. Their claim for unfettered freedom too often means a dispensation from the service of others and shows little regard for the common good. It can also be an abdication of personal responsibility, for themselves or for others. If the way they choose for themselves turns out to be a failure, not only do they blame others for their failure, but expect the rest of society to pay for the consequences of that failure....

What is therefore required if democracy is to remain healthy is an increased capacity on the part of individuals to meet their obligations as members of a democratic society in an understanding and responsible way with a concern for spiritual as well as material values. It is also required of leaders of society that they inspire the people of the country with a vision which will encourage them to make the effort which is necessary if all the people of the country are to enjoy the benefits of a well-ordered society. It is a sign of weakness in a democratic society if the role of the political parties is seen to involve simply the handing out of goodies and the success or otherwise of administrations is to be measured in purely economic terms....

BIBLIOGRAPHY

Karol Wojtyla (John Paul II), *Love and Responsibility*, New York, Farrar, 1981.

John Paul II, *Role of the Christian Family in the Modern World*.

Andrew Woznicki, *A Christian Humanism: Karol Wojtyla's Existentialist Personalism*, New Britain, CT., Mariel, 1980.

Collections of Homilies by John Paul II, published by St. Paul Editions: *"You Are the Future, You Are My Hope"*; and *I Believe in Youth, Christ Believes in Youth*, two collections of talks and homilies to youth. *Original Unity of Man and Woman; Blessed Are the Pure of Heart; The Family—Center of Love and Life; Old Age—Crown of the Steps of Life; Healing and Hope; The Whole Truth About Man: John Paul II to University Students and Faculties*, selected with an Introduction by James V. Schall, S.J., St. Paul Editions, 1981.

James V. Schall, S.J.: *Human Dignity and Human Numbers*, Staten Island, Alba House, 1971. *Welcome Number 4,000,000,000*, Canfield, Ohio, Alba Books, 1977. *Christianity and Life*, San Francisco, Ignatius Press, 1981.

"Redemptor Hominis: The Amazement of God," *Homiletic and Pastoral Review*, October, 1979. "On Neutralizing a Pope," *H & PR*, March, 1980. "On Inquisitors and Pontiffs: Criticizing John Paul II," *H & PR*, June, 1981.

Daughters of St. Paul

MASSACHUSETTS
50 St. Paul's Ave., Jamaica Plain, Boston, MA 02130; **617-522-8911.**
172 Tremont Street, Boston, MA 02111; **617-426-5464; 617-426-4230.**

NEW YORK
78 Fort Place, Staten Island, NY 10301; **212-447-5071; 212-447-5086.**
59 East 43rd Street, New York, NY 10017; **212-986-7580.**
625 East 187th Street, Bronx, NY 10458; **212-584-0440.**
525 Main Street, Buffalo, NY 14203; **716-847-6044.**

NEW JERSEY
Hudson Mall—Route 440 and Communipaw Ave.,
Jersey City, NJ 07304; **201-433-7740.**

CONNECTICUT
202 Fairfield Ave., Bridgeport, CT 06604; **203-335-9913.**

OHIO
2105 Ontario Street (at Prospect Ave.), Cleveland, OH 44115;
216-621-9427.
25 E. Eighth Street, Cincinnati, OH 45202; **513-721-4838; 513-421-5733.**

PENNSYLVANIA
1719 Chestnut Street, Philadelphia, PA 19103; **215-568-2638.**

VIRGINIA
1025 King Street, Alexandria, VA 22314; **703-683-1741; 703-549-3806.**

FLORIDA
2700 Biscayne Blvd., Miami, FL 33137; **305-573-1618.**

LOUISIANA
4403 Veterans Memorial Blvd., Metairie, LA 70002; **504-887-7631;
504-887-0113.**
1800 South Acadian Thruway, P.O. Box 2028, Baton Rouge, LA 70821;
504-343-4057; 504-381-9485.

MISSOURI
1001 Pine Street (at North 10th), St. Louis, MO 63101; **314-621-0346;
314-231-1034.**

ILLINOIS
172 North Michigan Ave., Chicago, IL 60601; **312-346-4228; 312-346-3240.**

TEXAS
114 Main Plaza, San Antonio, TX 78205; **512-224-8101; 512-224-0938.**

CALIFORNIA
1570 Fifth Ave., San Diego, CA 92101; **619-232-1442.**
46 Geary Street, San Francisco, CA 94108; **415-781-5180.**

WASHINGTON
2301 Second Ave., Seattle, WA 98121.

HAWAII
1143 Bishop Street, Honolulu, HI 96813; **808-521-2731.**

ALASKA
750 West 5th Ave., Anchorage, AK 99501; **907-272-8183.**

CANADA
3022 Dufferin Street, Toronto 395, Ontario, Canada.

ENGLAND
199 Kensington High Street, London W8 63A, England.
133 Corporation Street, Birmingham B4 6PH, England.
5A-7 Royal Exchange Square, Glasgow G1 3AH, England.
82 Bold Street, Liverpool L1 4HR, England.

AUSTRALIA
58 Abbotsford Rd., Homebush, N.S.W. 2140, Australia.